WITHDRAWN

21,0

THE LIBERALS
AND IRELAND

THE LIBERALS
AND IRELAND

*The Ulster Question
in British Politics to 1914*

PATRICIA JALLAND

*Lecturer in History,
Western Australian Institute of Technology*

ST. MARTIN'S PRESS   NEW YORK

ISBN 0-312-48347-3

Library of Congress Cataloging in Publication Data

Jalland, Patricia.
    The Liberals and Ireland.

    Bibliography: p.
    Includes index.
    1. Great Britain – Politics and government – 1910–1936.
2. Irish question. 3. Liberal Party (Gt. Brit.)–
History.   I. Title.
DA576.J34   1980   941.081   79-26719
ISBN 0-312-48347-3

CONTENTS

List of Illustrations

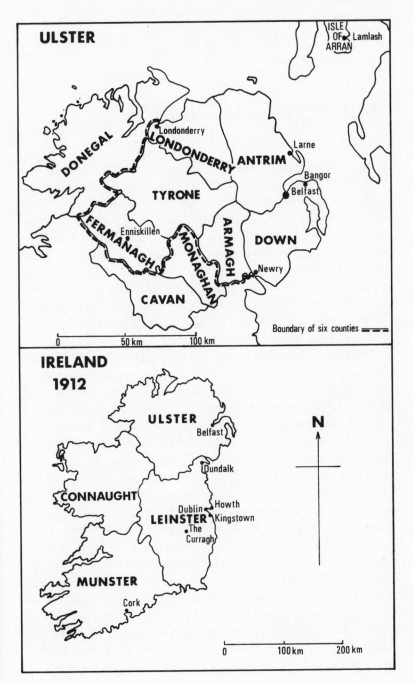

ULSTER

ISLE
OF
ARRAN
Lamlash

DONEGAL

LONDONDERRY
Londonderry

ANTRIM
Larne

TYRONE

Bangor
Belfast

FERMANAGH
Enniskillen

ARMAGH

DOWN

MONAGHAN

Newry

CAVAN

Boundary of six counties ═══

0   50 km   100 km

IRELAND
1912

ULSTER
Belfast

N

CONNAUGHT

Dundalk

Dublin   Howth
LEINSTER   Kingstown
•The
Curragh

MUNSTER

Cork

0   100 km   200 km

9

ACKNOWLEDGEMENTS

I have been extraordinarily fortunate in my friends and colleagues, who have generously contributed their time and talents to assist in the research and writing of this book. My greatest debt is to Dr. John Hooper and Dr. John Stubbs. John Hooper shared many of the burdens associated with this project. His constant support, confidence in the book, and practical assistance at every stage have been of inestimable value. John Stubbs contributed his expert knowledge of the Unionist Party, and made thoughtful and extensive suggestions on all drafts. Their friendship and enthusiasm throughout have been deeply appreciated.

Dr. Peter Clarke has particularly stimulated my ideas on the decline of the Liberal Party, both through his writings and in discussion. He also made valuable comments on the final drafts and supported the project at vital stages. Professor Trevor Lloyd gave very freely of his time and understanding of the period, making helpful draft criticisms and many suggestions. Dr. Cameron Hazlehurst gave unfailing encouragement and advice in the crucial first year of research, sharing his extensive knowledge of the manuscript sources, and kindly allowing me to consult his transcripts. I also wish to express my gratitude to those others who contributed to the creation of this book, especially Professor J.B. Conacher and Professor Stephen Koss, whose detailed comments on an earlier and longer draft greatly assisted the final revisions. Ms. Dee Jennings checked the final proofs, patiently traced copyright owners, and compiled the index with professional skill. Mrs. Jill Mabbitt typed the manuscript with notable efficiency. My friends Professor Albert Tucker and Mrs. Pauline Purcell made special contributions to the project.

Several funds and institutions gave generous awards which made the research and writing of this book possible: Canada Council Fellowship, 1970-3; Queen Elizabeth II Ontario Scholarship, 1973-74; Calouste Gulbenkian Research Fellowship at Lucy Cavendish College, Cambridge, 1973-76; and a Western Australian Institute of Technology Staff Development Research Award, 1979.

I am grateful to all those who allowed me access to their family archives. I also owe a special debt to all the librarians and archivists who assisted so willingly in the research for this book, particularly Mr. Porter and Dr. Philip Bull at the Bodleian Library, Oxford; Mrs. Christine Woodland, formerly archivist at Nuffield College, Oxford; and Mr. Alistair Elliot at Newcastle upon Tyne University Library. Mr. A.J.P. Taylor, formerly Honorary Director of the Beaverbrook Library, and Mr. W. Igoe created an ideal research base at the Beaverbrook Library until its regrettable closure in 1975.

The gracious permission of Her Majesty the Queen has been given for quotations from letters of King George V and other Crown copyright documents. Quotations from Crown copyright records in the Public Record Office appear by permission of the Controller of H.M. Stationery Office. Copyright permissions for manuscripts have also been kindly provided by the Earl of Birkenhead; Mr. Mark Bonham Carter (Asquith); the British Library Board (Balfour and Burns); C. and T. Publications Ltd. (Churchill); the Rt. Hon. Lord Gainford; the Marquess of Lansdowne; the Rt. Hon. Viscount Long of Wraxall; Mr. J.C. Medley (Birrell); the Trustees of the National Library of Scotland (Haldane); Lord Ponsonby of Shulbrede; the Hon. Godfrey Samuel; Mr. A.J.P. Taylor and the Trustees of the First Beaverbrook Foundation (Bonar Law and Lloyd George); and the Trevelyan family. Extracts from the papers of Lloyd George, Bonar Law, Sir Courtenay Ilbert and Lord Samuel are reproduced by courtesy of the Clerk of the Records of the House of Lords.

The following publishers have kindly granted copyright

permissions for printed sources: Cassell Ltd. (Austen Chamberlain, *Politics from Inside*, 1936); Wm. Collins Sons and Co. Ltd. (Roy Jenkins, *Asquith*, 1964); the Hamlyn Publishing Group Ltd. (Lord Riddell, *More Pages from my Diary 1908-14*, 1934); Hutchinson Publishing Group Ltd. (Christopher Addison, *Four and a Half Years*, 1934, and *Politics from Within 1911-1918*, 1924; L.S. Amery, *My Political Life*, 1953; Sir Almeric Fitzroy, *Memoirs*, 1925; General Sir Nevil Macready, *Annals of an Active Life*, 1924); John Murray (Publishers) Ltd. (*Inside Asquith's Cabinet*, edited by Edward David, 1977). I offer my apologies to any copyright holders I have been unable to locate.

This book is dedicated to my parents.

INTRODUCTION

This book explores the nature and role of the Irish question as a dominant force testing and weakening the British Liberal Party in the years preceding the First World War. The part played by the Irish question in the transformation of the Gladstonian Liberal Party in the 1880s and 1890s has received considerable attention from historians. In many respects, however, it is far more important to examine the relationship between the Irish question and the Liberal Party in the years 1911-14. This period is crucial in the development of Anglo-Irish relations, yet it has previously been almost entirely neglected. The Irish Home Rule Bills of 1886 and 1893 were essentially 'dry runs', due to the veto power of the House of Lords. The Parliament Act of 1911 at last made Home Rule a practical possibility. A unique opportunity existed in 1912 for the Liberal Party to settle the Irish question, before the Irish republican movement gained widespread support, and before violence and bloodshed made a peaceful solution almost impossible.

Irish historians have preferred to concentrate on the specifically Irish aspects of the period, minimising Irish involvement in British affairs. Thus, the more dramatic events in Ulster and at the Curragh from 1912-14 have been analysed in depth, as have the problems of the southern Unionists, the growth of Sinn Fein, and the 1916 Easter Rising. The failure of John Redmond's Nationalist Party, aiming for a limited form of Irish Home Rule by constitutional and peaceful methods, has attracted less attention, despite the excellent biographies of Redmond and Dillon by Denis Gwynn and F.S.L. Lyons.[1]

Historians have largely overlooked the vital role of the Irish question in the decline of the Liberal Party in the early twentieth century. The collapse of the Liberal Party has long been the subject of heated controversy among British historians, but discussion has largely revolved around issues other than Ireland. George Dangerfield opened the debate with his brilliant and impressionistic *Strange Death of Liberal England* in 1935. He argued that Liberalism was already moribund by 1909, unable to accommodate the new working class electorate. Liberalism finally collapsed between 1910-14, under the combined assault from the infant Labour Party, industrial agitation, the militant suffragettes, the constitutional crisis over the Lords, and impending civil war in Ireland.[2]

Dangerfield's thesis has been thoroughly re-assessed in recent scholarly research, in almost every aspect except Ireland. Peter Clarke has argued persuasively that by 1910 the Liberal Party had proved its ability to adapt to face the social and economic issues which were increasingly important to the growing working class electorate. He demonstrated that 'New Liberalism' was attracting strong support from the industrial working class in counties such as Lancashire in the elections of 1906 and 1910. Trevor Wilson has attacked Dangerfield's position from a different perspective, with his powerful thesis that the First World War was chiefly responsible for the death of a Liberal Party which had been healthy when the war broke out. He argued that the war undermined the Liberal philosophy and caused disastrous divisions among both the leadership and the rank and file of the party.[3] The arguments of both Clarke and Wilson have in turn been questioned by Henry Pelling, Ross McKibbin and Paul Thompson, who sympathise with Dangerfield at least in his emphasis on the crucial role of the infant Labour Party. They see the decline of the Liberal Party as an inevitable result of the expansion of the electorate, the rising power of the trade unions, and the growth of working class consciousness.[4]

The years 1911-14 are most important in the historical controversy over the Liberal decline, especially as they are not examined in the two major studies which approach the subject from a specifically Liberal perspective. Trevor Wilson's thesis assumed that the Liberal Party was healthy in 1914, but Peter Clarke's work only substantiates this hypothesis to 1911. Historians like Henry Pelling and Ross McKibbin have naturally been mainly concerned with issues integrally related to the rise of the Labour Party in their work on the pre-war period. To understand the decline of the Liberal Party more thoroughly, the party's development in the four years immediately preceding the war requires intensive scrutiny.

Since the years 1911–14 were dominated by the Home Rule issue, it is remarkable that the role of the Irish question in the decline of the Liberal Party has received so little attention up to now. Most British biographies and text books have given the subject only cursory treatment, with the notable exception of the biographies of Asquith and Bonar Law by Roy Jenkins and Robert Blake. They have provided valuable studies of the Irish policies of the two leaders, but these have understandably been limited and rather one-sided in their treatment.[5] Jenkins' masterly life of Asquith has included a powerful defence of Asquith's Irish policy, which raises new issues about the Liberal Party's treatment of the Ulster question. Cameron Hazlehurst suggested in 1970 that:

. . . the record of a prime minister under whom the nation goes to the brink of civil war must be subjected to the severest scrutiny. And, after fifty years, with almost all the relevant evidence now available, a new generation of scholars can attempt the searching examination of Asquith's career which has long been overdue.[6]

My book contributes to this reassessment by providing a detailed, analytical study of the Liberal Government's response to the growing crisis over Ulster from 1911–14. The main emphasis is placed on the activities of the Liberal Cabinet at the centre of power in Westminster. The influential roles of Asquith, Augustine Birrell, Lloyd George and Winston Churchill are examined particularly closely, showing how Lloyd George gradually replaced Birrell as the Prime Minister's second-in-command on Irish policy. The Prime Minister's contacts with his own backbenchers were limited, and he left the party whips to control the rank and file, whose influence on the Cabinet was almost negligible. This was partly a consequence of Asquith's style of politics, since his concept of government was fundamentally paternalistic and élitist. His Cabinet operated in a highly departmentalised manner, so that Irish policy was dominated by a few prominent ministers. This was illustrated most strikingly by the secrecy surrounding the Irish negotiations of 1913–14. The majority of the Cabinet were kept in the dark as much as the British public, the press and the members of parliament.

The Liberal Party had more to lose than gain from introducing a Home Rule Bill in 1912, more so than in 1886 and 1893. One Liberal minister, Lord Wolverhampton, believed that Home Rule was more unpopular than ever in March 1910, and gloomily predicted that it would be 'more bitterly fought than it was in Mr. Gladstone's time and I am afraid will break up the Liberal Party'.[7] Home Rule was obviously an electoral liability. It was also viewed by many of the younger radicals within the parliamentary party as an impediment to the growth of the social reforming impulses of New Liberalism, which were essential for the party's survival. If it was indeed true, as D.A. Hamer has suggested, that Home Rule in the 1890s provided a unifying crusade which helped to obscure the factional feuds in other policy areas,[8] this was certainly not the case in 1910-14. The Liberal Party was likely to gain in strength, unity and ideological coherence, by pushing ahead with the socio-economic reforms started in the years 1906-10, which reached their climax with the 1911 Insurance Act. Further reforms were under discussion in areas such as housing, education, and especially the land, and these were likely to win popular support whereas Home Rule would be a liability.

It was possible to fulfil the Home Rule pledge without completely alienating the progressive wing of the party, but only by resolving the Irish question permanently and rapidly. Unfortunately for the Liberals, the Ulster problem made a speedy and clean solution impossible. My central theme, therefore, is the inability of Asquith's Government to find an acceptable answer to the Ulster question. The book traces the development of the Ulster dilemma from 1886, and argues that the last Liberal Government missed one of the best opportunities for a peaceful British solution of this intractable problem.

In view of the vast scope of the topic and the demands of space, it is necessary to define the limits, as well as the aims of the book. This is not a study of public opinion and the press. The private papers of politicians on both sides strongly suggest that the impact of public opinion on the Government's

Irish policy was far less important for this earlier period than it became after 1918. Politicians generally believed that British voters, from 1910 to the early months of 1914, were apathetic and ignorant about Irish affairs. They were convinced that the electorate cared more for social and economic advantage than for constitutional questions like Home Rule, which had been traditionally more important electoral issues in the nineteenth century. Hostility to the Insurance Act was undoubtedly a powerful issue in by-election campaigns from 1911-13, whereas feelings about Home Rule appeared to play little part. Liberal voters only began to concern themselves with Home Rule in 1914 – and even then, their interest took the form of criticism of the Government's mismanagement and apparent weakness.

This study is primarily concerned with the Liberals and only examines other parties to throw light on my major themes. The Labour Party is scarcely mentioned, as Labour members fairly consistently supported the Government on Home Rule until spring 1914. The Irish Nationalists will be considered only in terms of their influence on individual ministers and specific policy decisions, especially as the part played by Redmond and Dillon has already been thoroughly examined by Denis Gwynn and F.S.L. Lyons. The Nationalist leaders were obliged to play the role of generally passive allies of the Liberal Government, acquiescing in a series of concessions they disliked in order to reach their goal of Home Rule. Though the book does not attempt to provide an in-depth analysis of the part played by the Unionist Party and its leaders, the Unionists do receive considerable attention. Unionist reactions to ministerial policies, and Opposition assessment of Liberal aims, motives and potential weaknesses, are analysed to provide a more complete picture.

Historical misconceptions about the Irish question in British politics have too easily arisen in the past because too few primary sources have been consulted, or else they have been examined for only one side in the controversy. Historical ignorance and political prejudice have combined to obscure the actual Liberal approaches and policies towards Ireland and the significance of the Irish question for the history of the Liberal Party. This book aims to provide a detailed analysis free from the familiar emotional rhetoric about British policy in Ireland. The historical facts must be established first, before reasonable judgments about the success or failure of policies can be made. In an age of élitist politics, those facts were created by the ideas and behaviour of a small but immensely influential group of men at Westminster. The personal papers of as many of these men as possible have accordingly been consulted. The Liberal treatment of the Irish question is a dramatic example of the importance of individuals in early twentieth century British politics. The repercussions of the failure of the last Liberal Government's Ulster policies are still felt in the continuing existence of the 'Irish question' today.

I
THE GLADSTONIAN LEGACY, 1885–1912

1 The Home Rule Commitment

From the twelfth century until the end of the eighteenth century Britain treated Ireland as a conquered nation, sending in troops and settlers to dominate and subjugate. In 1801 Britain attempted instead to control Ireland by political integration within the United Kingdom. This Act of Union was only successful in the Protestant dominated north-east province of Ulster, yet it became a fundamental issue in Ireland's subsequent struggle for independence. For the Irish Unionists, the Act of Union guaranteed the Protestants political and social ascendancy within Ireland, and they acquired valued privileges as an integral economic unit of the United Kingdom. For the British Conservative Party, the Act of Union gradually became an almost mystical part of their political creed, representing the symbolic vanguard of the inevitable forward march of Empire. Any threat to the Union with Ireland was interpreted as a challenge to the integrity of the British Empire. This belief so dominated the Conservative Party after 1886 that the term 'Unionist' was incorporated into the party's title and was commonly used when the Home Rule danger was most acute. Even the limited goal of Home Rule in Irish internal affairs, sought by the Irish Nationalist Parliamentary Party, involved altering an Act of Union which rapidly became sacrosanct. Such a repeal was practically impossible until the 1911 Parliament Act removed the permanent veto power of the Unionist dominated House of Lords.

Up to 1885, the Liberal Party tried to settle the endemic unrest in Ireland through a policy of coercion combined with economic, social and religious concessions, intended to secure Ireland's loyalty to Britain. The Liberal Party under Gladstone overcame fierce Conservative resistance, to grant reforms relating especially to land and religion, only to discover that such reforms did not dispel disaffection. By 1885, Gladstone finally became convinced that Britain could only pacify Ireland by coming to terms with the demands of Irish nationalism. These demands had been presented to the British Parliament far more forcefully since 1880, when Parnell seized control of the Irish Parliamentary Party and rapidly transformed it into a formidable, highly-disciplined machine. The power of the Irish Nationalist Party to disrupt parliamentary proceedings was increased by the effects of the 1884–5 Reform Acts. At the 1885 elections, Ireland for the first time was able to return an overwhelming majority of Nationalist members to the Westminster Parliament.

Gladstone's recognition of the need to give Home Rule to Ireland changed the fortunes of his party. He was converted to Home Rule in 1885, and his fanatical zeal for the Irish cause dominated and wrecked his last two ministries, in 1886 and 1893–4. In a practical sense, Gladstone's two Home Rule Bills of 1886 and 1893 could be no more than dry runs, since the House of Lords would inevitably block their passage. Yet they succeeded in establishing Home Rule as a major plank in the party's platform, despite immense initial opposition, and the Bills formed the basis for Asquith's Irish Bill in 1912.

The 1886 Home Rule Bill was drafted under great pressure in the short period between late January 1886, when Gladstone formed his third ministry, and the introduction of the measure on 8 April 1886. Consequently, the Bill was only twenty-two pages long, and somewhat clumsy in style. It established a single 'Legislative Body' in Ireland, composed of two 'Orders' generally sitting together and each possessing a suspensory veto to protect the interests of Irish minorities. The scope of the Irish assembly was strictly limited by enumerating those powers specifically reserved to the Imperial Parliament, including defence, police, trade and foreign policy. A further list of restrictions, relating chiefly to religion, was designed to safeguard the rights of the Irish Protestant minority. Gladstone's first Bill included a controversial provision excluding Irish representatives from the Westminster Parliament, to avoid Irish interference in the internal affairs of Great Britain, once the Irish had their own parliament. However, since the Imperial Exchequer retained control over Irish customs and excise, this decision raised the ancient cry of 'no taxation without representation'.

The defection of Joseph Chamberlain and the Whigs precipitated the defeat of the First Home Rule Bill on Second Reading, and helped the Conservatives to electoral victory later in 1886. The Liberals were out of power for the greater part of the next two decades, returning only briefly from 1892-5. Gladstone used this last opportunity to throw all his energies into the Home Rule Bill of 1893, which was longer than its predecessor and more carefully constructed. The single 'Legislative Body' of 1886 was replaced by an Irish 'Parliament', composed of two 'Houses' meeting separately, except for occasional joint sessions to decide issues of longstanding disagreement. The 'Legislative Council' of forty-eight members would be elected on a restricted franchise designed to protect Protestant minority rights, while the 'Legislative Assembly' of 103 members would be returned by existing constituencies. The powers granted to the Irish Parliament were limited as in the earlier Bill, except for the concession that the Irish police should ultimately be transferred to Irish control. The most important difference between Gladstone's Bills concerned the thorny question of Irish representation at Westminster. The 1893 Bill initially allowed Irish members to vote at Westminster only on Irish and Imperial subjects, but this 'in and out' scheme was abandoned in Committee as too impractical. Instead the provision was amended to allow a reduced number of eighty Irish representatives full voting rights in the British Parliament, despite the problems this might cause.

The Home Rule issue had a profound effect on the development of both British political parties after 1886. It helped to fortify the Conservative Party, because it rallied the forces of Imperialism and the defenders of property. The Liberal Party, on the other hand, was reduced in strength and bitterly divided in the twenty years after Home Rule was first introduced. Gladstone's fanatical devotion to the Irish cause induced him to stay on as leader, when the party might have benefited from a change. Joseph Chamberlain was lost to the Liberal Party as a potential radical leader, capable of making a powerful appeal to the working classes two decades earlier than Lloyd George and Churchill. The secession of the Whigs was inevitable in any case, though the Home Rule issue hastened their departure. In electoral terms the Irish crisis weakened the Liberals until at least 1900, with the defection of the Liberal Unionists, the disruption of the Liberal electoral organisation and the abstentions of former Liberal voters.

From 1886 to 1894, Gladstone stubbornly maintained Home Rule as the focal point of his leadership, paralysing the party's development in other areas by lack of direction. D.A. Hamer has argued that Home Rule acted as a useful substitute for the fundamental unifying programme which the party lacked, disguising factional dissensions over domestic reforms.[1] Yet the preoccupation with Home Rule was itself responsible for diverting time, energy, and manpower from the reforming aims listed in the 1891 Newcastle programme. Home Rule generated immense divisions among Liberals. It gradually alienated left-wing radicals and a section of the working classes, who sought social and economic reforms with a more direct relevance to the needs of the British masses. The Irish question probably also accelerated the gradual movement of middle class voters from the Liberal to the Conservative Party. Irish agrarian violence always alarmed the English propertied classes. They became still more dismayed when Gladstone tried to solve rural unrest by interference with Irish property rights, thereby establishing a dangerous precedent. Moreover, the Home Rule campaign offended the rapidly growing patriotic fervour of the middle class advocates of imperial strength and unity.

After the defeat of the 1893 Home Rule Bill by the House of Lords, Gladstone was prepared for a battle with their Lordships. His colleagues recognised, however, that such a major constitutional struggle should be undertaken only on an issue with greater electoral appeal than Home Rule. The inevitable result was the long awaited retirement of the Grand Old Man. But Home Rule remained a divisive issue in the Liberal Party. Sectionalism was rampant, and the party was demoralised by the personal feuds involved in the struggle for Gladstone's mantle. The feud between Lord Rosebery, John Morley, and Sir William Harcourt ended when Sir Henry Campbell-Bannerman became leader in 1898, as a compromise candidate expected to exercise a conciliatory influence.

Before the 1900 election, Campbell-Bannerman and Herbert Gladstone, the Liberal Chief Whip, decided for the moment to shelve Home Rule as a major electoral issue. Herbert Gladstone was more realistic about the Irish cause than his father. He argued that the Liberal Party as a whole had supported Home Rule in the 1895 election; yet the country gave a great majority to the Unionists, with their alternative policy of 'Local Government and Land Acts which are to kill Home Rule on the lines of "kindness and firmness" '. Given the feeling in the country, and the need to place the Liberal Party 'on a broader basis', Gladstone suggested that Home Rule should 'not rank for the time being, as a practical question of politics'.[2] This decision was reinforced by the chaos in the Irish Nationalist Party, which split into three feuding sections after the fall of Parnell in 1891. Between 1895 and 1905 the Nationalists allowed their alliance with the Liberals to lapse, as active hostility developed on issues such as education and the Boer war.

From 1899 to 1905, then, Home Rule was relegated to a less prominent position at Herbert Gladstone's suggestion. However, friction between the Liberal Imperialist and Gladstonian wings of the party continued to focus on the issue of Home Rule from 1900 to 1905. Lord Rosebery, former Liberal Premier and leader of the Liberal Imperialists, increasingly adopted a Unionist view of the Irish question. He advocated a 'clean slate' policy, wiping Home Rule from the party programme. Rosebery's chief lieutenants, Asquith, Haldane and Grey, were less extreme, though Haldane appeared at times to find Rosebery's reasoning persuasive. Slowly, however, Asquith and Haldane adopted the gradual-ist policy suggested by Sir Edward Grey: 'Things must advance towards Home Rule, but I think it must be step by step'.[3] The Gladstonian wing of the party, led by Campbell-Bannerman and John Morley, had tended to make Home Rule a prominent issue again, partly in reaction to Rosebery's attitude. But when it became necessary to prepare for another election in 1905, Campbell-Bannerman recognised that Home Rule presented a major obstacle to party unity, and he determined to rally the party around Grey's 'step by step' policy. In November 1905, Campbell–Bannerman announced a vague compromise formula at Stirling, which did not specifically disavow Home Rule, but implied that a full measure of Irish self-government would not be introduced in the next Parliament. The Irish Nationalists must meanwhile be satisfied with 'an instalment of representative control', which would lead up to their larger aim.[4]

Home Rule consequently played little part in the landslide electoral victory of 1906, which returned the Liberal Party to power. Asquith agreed with Campbell–Bannerman that they would only obtain a good majority if it was made perfectly clear to the electors that 'it will be no part of the policy of the new Liberal Government to introduce a Home Rule Bill in the new Parliament'. The reasons for this postponement were largely practical rather than ideological. As Asquith pointed out, a Home Rule Bill 'will be at once chucked out by the House of Lords, and will wreck the fortunes of the party for another 20 years'. Lord Crewe advanced another argument, which he considered even more important than the Lords' veto, though it is worth noting that his reservations about Home Rule were probably influenced by his position as Rosebery's son-in-law:

More than ever before the L[iberal] party is on its trial as an engine for securing social reform – taxation, land, housing etc. It has to resist the ILP [Independent Labour Party] claim to be the only friends of the workers. Can it do this, and attempt H[ome] R[ule] as well ?[5]

The Liberal Government has been accused of abandoning Home Rule in 1906, simply because it had a massive majority independent of the Irish Nationalists. Yet the Nationalists had nothing to gain from the introduction of a Home Rule Bill in 1906–9, if the Government was in no position to carry it. The Lords' veto made Home Rule a practical impossibility, and there was no point in repeating the 1892–5 experience. If Home Rule, was ever to pass, the Lords' veto power must first be reduced, but the Irish question was scarcely a popular issue on which to force a constitutional showdown. It was likely that the Government would have to stand or fall over Home Rule when they did eventually introduce it for the third time. Therefore, it made good sense to wait until the Lords' veto could be overthrown, meanwhile building up unity and confidence in the Parliamentary Party, and increasing support in the country through social and economic reforms.

James Bryce, Irish Secretary in 1906, entertained a faint hope that the Irish might be satisfied with less than full Home Rule, in view of the land reforms and local government reforms introduced by the Unionists. This hope was as short-lived as Bryce's term of office. He attempted to carry out Campbell-Bannerman's Stirling pledge through an Irish Council Bill of 1906, which proposed to establish an administrative council with limited powers. This raised a storm of Irish protest. John Redmond and John Dillon, the leaders of the Irish Nationalist Party, were shocked by its inadequacy, and convinced that it was a device to bury Home Rule altogether. The Liberals' compromise formula was abandoned, and Augustine Birrell replaced Bryce at the Irish Office.

Despite the long postponement, the majority of the Liberal Cabinet were not seeking the opportunity to abandon Home Rule entirely. The party had a genuine commitment to Home Rule. This pledge had only been deferred in unpropitious circumstances. The fanatical zeal of Gladstone, and the crusading spirit of the early Liberal converts, were replaced by a more stoical spirit of obligation. Enthusiasm and passion inevitably declined as the years passed, and constant repetition gave the Home Rule arguments the familiar ring of a well-known psalm. A few Liberals retained the old enthusiasm. John Morley was not entirely jesting when he remarked to Rosebery in 1905: 'You will find me very slack about One Man One Vote, Land Values, and Welsh Church. The only thing about which my ardent soul is still ready to *blaze* is Irish Home Rule !!! Your Vesuvius is nothing to it'.[6]

After 1895 the most characteristic attitude among Liberals was a quiet commitment, which should not be mistaken for apathy. Home Rule took its place besides Free Trade as a fundamental item of faith in the Liberal creed. This became very clear when Herbert Gladstone, the Liberal Chief Whip, acting as 'a kind of telephone exchange', elicited the views of his colleagues on the subject between 1899 and 1901. Lord Ripon expressed the hope that: '. . . no step will be taken which will depose Home Rule from the position which it has held for the last 14 years as the fundamental principle of the policy of the Liberal Party for Ireland.' Sir Edward Grey remarked that Liberals had learnt a good deal about Irish history since the Home Rule controversy began, and this knowledge had 'filled us with the spirit of forbearance and sympathy and a deep sense of obligation towards Ireland'.[7] Asquith replied firmly that there was no question 'of those of us who have for 13 years advocated H[ome] R[ule] abandoning our position'. Lord Crewe agreed in 1905 that 'the Liberal party stands by H. Rule as its ultimate object'. Four years later he was still adamant that Home Rule '. . . has never ceased to be the policy of the Lib. Party since 1886 though there have been differences of opinion as to methods, and as to whether, self govt should come about gradually or by a single measure'.[8]

Without some such obligation to fulfil a historic pledge, some sense of commitment to a firm principle, the Liberal Party would surely have abandoned Home Rule entirely in the years after 1894. The reasons advanced for postponing it would have provided ample excuse for dropping it altogether. But Gladstone had committed his party too deeply and the Liberals had suffered too much in the cause of Home Rule. The Stirling announcement of 1905 implied that the Government would feel free to introduce Home Rule after a further election. The subsequent failure of the 1906-7 Irish Council Bill was crucial, because it demonstrated that half measures would not satisfy the Irish.

It was fairly clear that the Liberals would introduce a full Home Rule Bill once the veto of the Lords was overcome, and when they won a further election. This was confirmed by Asquith's Albert Hall declaration, which preceded the election of January 1910. The Prime Minister stated that a full Home Rule policy was the only solution to the Irish problem, and ended the moratorium of the previous three years. Augustine Birrell, the Chief Secretary, assured Redmond that the Cabinet had agreed on the need for a clear statement that Home Rule was *the live policy of the Party, without limitation or restriction*. Lord Morley also informed the Irish leader that:

. . . almost everybody, if not quite, believes in the importance of taking a definite line upon H[ome] R[ule], on the merits, and apart from the points of temporary expediency, marked as the latter may be. Personally – and I am not over easy to please upon this subject – I was entirely satisfied with the sincerity of the Cabinet.[9]

The Liberal Government's decision to introduce a third Home Rule Bill in 1912 was, then, the logical consequence of a long-standing commitment. The veto of the House of Lords had previously been the chief obstacle, but that was removed by the passage of the Parliament Act in 1911. From 1906–9, the Unionist Opposition had continually used its huge majority in the Upper House to reject or substantially amend important Liberal legislation. In 1909, however, the Lords went too far, when they threw out the controversial budget introduced by Lloyd George, the ambitious young Welsh radical who had become Chancellor of the Exchequer the previous year. The budget provided an excellent issue for a showdown between the Liberals and the Lords, though this had not been the deliberate intention. This was a 'popular' budget, in the sense that it was designed to provide a modest redistribution of income, to help pay for social reforms and battleships. By tradition, the Upper House was not expected to reject money Bills. Battle was joined in a highly complex constitutional crisis, which involved two successive elections in January and December 1910, to determine the voters' attitude to the Lords' veto.

The results were not as conclusive as the Liberals had hoped. They lost the massive majority of 1905–6, not a surprising consequence of four controversial years in office. The Government won a narrow victory in both elections, with results which were almost identical. In the December election the Liberals secured 272 seats. The support of the 42 Labour members and the 84 Irish Nationalists produced a ministerial coalition total of 398. The British Unionists won 255 seats, and could rely on the 17 Irish Unionists to vote with them consistently. If the Irish members on both sides are omitted from the calculation, the Liberals had a clear majority of 17 over the British Unionists, and could increase this to 59 as a result of their alliance with the Labour Party. This point requires emphasis, since Unionist propaganda helped to create the myth that the Liberal Government was entirely dependent on the Irish after 1910. The Liberals did not need Irish votes to maintain their majority. Assuming that the Irish Unionists would vote with the British Conservatives, and Labour members with the Liberals, then the Government could rely on a majority of 42, even if the 84 Irish Nationalists abstained.[10] As Walter Runciman reported after the January election: '– we shall exist without the Irish support but only so long as Redmond refrains from voting against us', though he judged the latter to be a remote risk.[11]

The two Liberal victories enabled the Government to pass their Parliament Act, limiting the veto power of the House of Lords. This legislation was only forced through both Houses by August 1911, after two heated elections, and after Asquith threatened to activate George V's promise to create sufficient Liberal peers to swamp the Conservative Upper House. The Parliament Act was linked with Home Rule from the first, and had a critical effect on the development of the Irish issue in the next three years. The most significant provision was that Bills other than money Bills, which were passed by the Commons in three successive sessions (not necessarily of the same parliament), and which were rejected each time by the Lords, should automatically receive the royal assent. Two years must elapse between the first introduction of such a Bill and its Final Reading in the Commons. A provision of great importance for the Ulster problem was that amendments could be made in the normal way during the first parliamentary circuit in the Commons. Changes could only be made thereafter, however, by means of 'suggestions', which required the agreement of both Houses, but which were otherwise ill-defined. The Parliament Act also stipulated that the Upper House could not reject money Bills, and that the maximum duration of a parliament would be reduced from seven to five years. The Government's ultimate aim of reforming the House of Lords along more representative lines was expressed in a preamble, which provoked subsequent Unionist charges that the Constitution was meanwhile suspended.

The passing of the Parliament Act made the introduction of a Home Rule Bill inevitable, for reasons both of principle and expediency. The Liberals emphasised principle and the

Opposition expediency. The Liberals argued, with considerable justification, that they were fulfilling a long-standing party pledge, which the Lords' veto had previously made impossible. The Unionists preferred to dwell on the reduced Liberal majority and the inflated value of Nationalist support in the Commons. The Opposition accused the Government of having made a 'corrupt bargain' with Redmond, whereby the Nationalists supported Lloyd George's 1909-10 budget and the Parliament Bill, in return for the promise of an immediate Home Rule Bill. Even if a specific bargain of this nature was made, which appears not to have been the case, a general understanding along these lines was surely the natural result of the long history of Liberal commitment to Home Rule.

More justification existed for the associated Unionist charge that the Liberals sought and obtained no mandate for Home Rule in the 1910 elections. Nine of the sixteen ministers who issued addresses at both 1910 elections made no reference to Home Rule, and only 84 of the 272 successful Liberal candidates mentioned it in their December 1910 addresses.[12] Home Rule was given little prominence in the Liberal electoral campaigns because they wanted to concentrate attention on the constitutional issue, but the doubtful electoral value of Home Rule no doubt also contributed. However, as Asquith subsequently pointed out, it was well known that the Government wanted to curb the Lords' veto in order to pass a Home Rule Bill. In any case, their opponents ensured that the electorate was under no illusion concerning the Irish implications of a Liberal victory. This point exasperated F.E. Smith: 'The only argument these scoundrels ever use to show that Home Rule was before the country is that *we* said so.' In their more objective moments, the Unionists acknowledged that the Liberals were not just opportunists. Walter Long admitted privately in 1913 that the Government as a whole had been committed to Home Rule in some shape or form since 1906.[13]

Most Liberals were not seriously worried by charges that their return to Home Rule was governed purely by political expediency. Their commitment was too obvious. Alfred Emmott, the Deputy-Speaker, noted after the second 1910 election that 'nearly every Liberal is pledged to Home Rule and the Govt to a man'.[14] The long ordeal of an attempt to pass Home Rule through three parliamentary sessions was a heavy price to pay simply for the sake of eighty-four Nationalist votes. Naturally those votes had some influence on the situation, particularly its timing, but they were far from being the sole consideration.

The Liberal Party had much to lose by reviving the Home Rule issue in 1912. Many of the younger and more radical backbenchers viewed the return of Home Rule to the centre of the political stage in 1911-14 with misgivings. They had inherited the sense of obligation to carry out Home Rule, but they frequently lacked the emotional enthusiasm of Lord Morley's generation. The more creative and dynamic elements in contemporary Liberalism wanted the traditional pledges discharged as rapidly as possible, to allow the social reforming impulses of New Liberalism to resume their progress. Sir Courtenay Ilbert, the Clerk of the Commons, recognised that, for many Liberal and Labour members, Home Rule blocked the way for all the other measures for which they cared more deeply. Radicals such as Lloyd George, Charles Masterman, Charles Trevelyan and Arthur Ponsonby, consequently took a rather impatient, if long-suffering, attitude to Home Rule. The Liberal weekly, the *Nation*, expressed these sentiments fairly accurately, regretting in December 1911 that 'we are to work at questions which were ripe for settlement twenty years ago'.[15] The Liberal Party had more to gain from continued emphasis on socio-economic reforms, whereas Home Rule was likely to be an electoral liability.

2 The Prime Minister and the Irish Secretary

In 1886 and 1893 Gladstone and John Morley established the precedent that the Prime Minister and the Irish Secretary shared joint responsibility for directing Home Rule policy. Since this precedent was not followed in 1911-14, the roles played by Asquith and Birrell require definition. Augustine Birrell had been notably successful as Irish Secetary during the first half of his administration. From 1907 to 1911, he conducted a most effective holding operation on Home Rule, while at the same time reassuring the Irish leaders of the Liberal Party's long-term commitment to Irish self-government. He won the respect and friendship of the Irish leaders, and restored their confidence in the Government's good will, at a time when Irish self-government was very low on the list of Liberal priorities. This achievement was partly due to Birrell's personality and talents, which were well suited to his formidable task. He combined natural ability with unfailing common sense and humour, and his growing love of Ireland also helped him to establish a shrewd and sympathetic working relationship with the Nationalists. Birrell's skilful settlement of the longstanding Irish Universities' question in 1908 and his valuable Land Act of 1909 further helped to appease the Irish while they awaited Home Rule.[16]

By contrast he played a strangely subsidiary part in Home Rule policy after 1912. His public career and private life suffered an agonising decline from about 1912, for reasons almost completely beyond his own control. The Chief Secretary was well aware that his temperament and abilities were ill-suited to the impossible task he was expected to perform from 1912, and he offered his resignation on more than one occasion. Birrell's increasing ineffectiveness and growing dislike of his position after 1912 had several causes. The nature of the Irish Secretary's role altered with the introduction of the Home Rule Bill, becoming more ill-defined, yet more extensive, than ever before. Ideally, from 1912 the Chief Secretary should have combined the talents of an able administrator, capable of managing the massive daily problems of governing Ireland, with those of a forceful trouble-shooter, who could pilot the Home Rule Bill through the crises ahead. But Asquith was unlikely to find a man who combined the very different qualities demanded by the two roles – with the possible exception of Lloyd George, who could hardly be asked to move from the seniority of the Exchequer to Ireland. Failing to secure the services of a superman, Asquith might have been better advised to establish a formal division of power from 1911, appointing two ministers with separate responsibilities for the Irish administration and the Home Rule Bill. Instead, the Prime Minister relied on piece-meal compromises, which made the post of Chief Secretary increasingly intolerable. Birrell was left in charge of the Irish administration, during a period when acute internal crises in Ireland required his full concentration, if they were not to damage Home Rule prospects. The outbreak of cattle disease in 1912-13, and the spread of industrial agitation in Dublin in the autumn of 1913, under the militant leadership of James Larkin, created immense problems for Birrell. Added to these was the constant anxiety caused by the growth of an armed resistance movement in the north to challenge the Home Rule Bill.[17]

In practice, then, while Birrell was preoccupied in Ireland, the Home Rule campaign in Britain was divided between several leading ministers, including Asquith, Lloyd George, Churchill, Herbert Samuel, and Birrell himself. The Irish Secretary was merely to be the mediator between the Nationalists and the Liberals, the spokesman for the Irish in the Cabinet, and the scapegoat if the Home Rule policy misfired. He was not granted supreme control of Irish policy in the years after 1912, and his precise function remained conveniently vague. Birrell was to bear the public responsibility, but not the power.

Birrell's difficulties as Irish Secretary were made almost intolerable because he disagreed with the Cabinet's crucial policy decisions on Ulster and Irish finance, which proved to be the most controversial aspects of the Home Rule question. In addition, Birrell was subjected to the severe personal strain caused by his wife's prolonged illness with an inoperable brain tumour, from 1911 until her death in 1915. At the height of the Ulster crisis in 1913-14, Birrell suffered intensely from the demands of a post which forced him to spend months in Ireland, away from his dying wife. Consequently, the Irish Secretary appeared increasingly ineffective and irrelevant as the Irish crisis mounted from 1912 to 1914. By the second half of 1913, initiative in Irish Home Rule policy almost entirely passed into the hands of Asquith and Lloyd George, while Birrell played little more than a reluctant, passive role in the escalating crises of 1914. Under the circumstances, Asquith would have been better advised to accept Birrell's resignation. Birrell himself did not force the issue because of his exceptional loyalty to Asquith, his profound sense of public duty, and his growing commitment to Ireland and the Nationalists.[18]

Clearly it was the Prime Minister's responsibility to decide whether Birrell was the right man for the Irish Office after 1911. Asquith had several reasons for retaining his services. No obvious alternative was available, who was likely to be any better suited to the task than Birrell, particularly after Churchill refused the post in 1910. Further, in 1911-12 the Prime Minister vastly under-estimated the potential gravity of the Ulster question, and continued to hope that Birrell would be equal to any crises which might arise. Moreover, as Churchill pointed out in 1910, it was in the Government's interests 'that Birrell should stand to his post. The Nationalists respect him and trust him. He has all the threads in his hands. He has been through the unpleasant process of being disillusioned.'[19] Asquith knew full well, in any case, that it would not be easy to find anyone else with the same ability to win the necessary concessions from the Nationalists.

In practical terms, then, the Government's Home Rule policy from 1911-14 was controlled by the Prime Minister, in a manner that contrasted strongly with the complete delegation of authority to the ministers responsible in most other areas. The Ulster policy was peculiarly the Prime Minister's own responsibility, especially since it was forcefully opposed by two of the ministers most concerned with Ireland – Churchill and Lloyd George. In view of the central role played by Asquith, some comments on the strengths and weaknesses of his character will prepare the way for the detailed evaluation of his Irish policy.

Herbert Henry Asquith came from a Yorkshire middle-class family, and gained a First in Classics at Balliol, as a preliminary to a brilliant career in politics and the law. He first entered the Commons in 1886, just missing Gladstone's first attempt to introduce Home Rule, and represented East Fife consistently thereafter, until 1918. His rapid rise to prominence marked him out early in his career as a potential prime minister. Even his private life accorded well with his political prospects after his second marriage in 1894 to Margot Tennant, a celebrated socialite. Asquith became a Queen's Counsel in 1890, and was appointed Home Secretary during

Gladstone's final administration. When the Liberals were returned to power in 1905, Asquith was Chancellor of the Exchequer until he succeeded Campbell-Bannerman as Prime Minister in April 1908. To the mass of Liberal voters and the party rank and file, Asquith frequently appeared cool, distant and reserved. Indeed, this is the impression of Asquith gained from the severe economy of style used in most of his letters to his colleagues, which give the historian a rather one-dimensional view.

Yet he won the loyalty and even the devotion of the widely different personalities who came to know him well in Cabinet. Asquith was serene and imperturbable by temperament, remaining calm and philosophical in the face of political crises. Birrell's affectionate character sketch of Asquith was qualified by the revealing comment that 'I was never able to find any fault with Asquith as a human being except that he was always very much the same.' In many respects he was the ideal leader for a Cabinet composed of so many brilliant, but very different, individualists, for he was remarkably adept at reducing his colleagues 'to a harmonious whole'. Even Asquith's critics were prepared to admit, with Alfred Emmott, that 'intellectually of course he is a marvel'. He possessed an easy mastery of political affairs, outstanding dialectical skill, and an unchallenged authority in Cabinet. He was a first rate chairman, with a talent for reducing a complex, detailed problem to the bare essentials, and for adjudicating impartially between conflicting views. Late in 1913, Churchill told Austen Chamberlain that Asquith was 'supreme' in the Cabinet, but 'very self-contained, reserved and slow to speak, and thought it unfair to use his casting vote until all had spoken'.[20]

John Burns praised Asquith's quiet mastery, attributing the unity of the Cabinet to the tact, temper and wisdom of the Prime Minister. Joseph Pease was even more eulogistic in his admiration for the 'consummate quiet masterhand' of 'our great leader'; by August 1914 he rated Asquith 'the greatest statesman of the Age !'. After the hard session of 1913, the Chief Whip, Percy Illingworth, paid tribute to Asquith's amazing qualities of discernment, decision and courage, which had earned the admiration and affection of his colleagues.[21] The Prime Minister gave his talented ministers great freedom within their own departments, with impressive results in most fields during his peace-time administration. From 1908 to 1911 his Government produced an outstanding series of social reforms, culminating in the 1911 Insurance Act, and presided over a major constitutional reform.

Asquith also had his faults. When he told the Tories to 'wait and see' in March 1910, he unwittingly provided them with a catch-phrase which symbolised his limitations. His tendency to prevaricate, and to create ambiguities in his statements through careful qualifications, often seemed like wilful evasion. Lord Morley in 1912 criticised Asquith's procrastination and indolence in shirking difficulties, confident 'in his ability to furnish at least some provisional solution when the situation created by neglect threatens to get out of hand.' Sir Courtenay Ilbert considered Asquith too easy-going and not inclined to maintain a sufficiently tight control over some of his colleagues. Even the faithful John Burns regretted his hero's 'ingrained indisposition to take risks and incur the responsibility of the moment'.[22]

This style of leadership, however, worked well in most areas of government in peace-time, given Asquith's capable team of colleagues. Before the Irish crisis of 1913-14, the only ominous sign of potential trouble came when Asquith temporarily appeared to lose his nerve during the constitutional crisis over the Lords. In spring 1910, Walter Runciman feared that the Prime Minister was losing any faculty of decision he ever had.[23] The lapse was forgotten after Asquith regained control, but a similar inertia in critical emergencies revealed itself more dangerously during the Ulster crisis and the European war.

Another limitation possibly also influenced his management of the Irish question. R.B. Haldane, for many years a close friend of Asquith, War Minister from 1906-12 and subsequently Lord Chancellor, commented many years later that Asquith was only partially endowed for the Premiership. His great intellectual apparatus was restricted to grasp, understanding and judgment; he stated other people's ideas perfectly, but was not himself a man of imagination.[24] Consequently, Lloyd George and Churchill were perfect foils for Asquith's talents, so long as he was acknowledged master, and agreement existed over aims and method. But potential for division and drift existed when their paths diverged, as sometimes happened over Ireland.

Moreover, Asquith had a well-ordered legal mind, which did not instinctively relate to the play of passions in others. The *Nation* thought his ministry 'a little soul less', lacking Gladstone's 'impassioned energy': 'Mr. Asquith has not always suggested to friendly critics that larger kind of intellectual resource which yokes the device of the hour to long views of policy and broad conceptions of national honor [sic] and interest.'[25] He had difficulty in taking Irish Nationalism and Ulster Unionism entirely seriously, since they involved such a large element of emotional commitment. His temperament and his legal training convinced him that the Irish problem could be solved by the usual constitutional procedures of British parliamentary politics. The Irish, in turn, were suspicious of Asquith's wholly rational approach to the Home Rule cause. His temperament did not allow for passionate enthusiasm but, in any case, it was some time before he could allay the mistrust aroused by his earlier links with Rosebery's anti-Home Rule policy.

Asquith's style of government created further pitfalls, because of the ill-defined manner in which responsibility for the third Home Rule Bill in parliament was divided among various ministers. Despite impressive intellectual force and superb oratorical skill, Asquith lacked personal magnetism over his rank and file. He ruled through his command in the Cabinet and tended to rely on able colleagues and the whips for his control over his party. The *Nation* remarked in 1912 that, on the parliamentary stage, the Prime Minister left to Lloyd George and Churchill 'the wide area of persuasion, agitation, the mustering and direction of popular forces, the maintenance of the old fire in Liberalism'. Even before he became Prime Minister, his wife admonished him to make more effort to impress the common man and attend more frequently in the House.[26] Asquith did not noticeably improve in these respects after he succeeded to the Premiership. He 'left his colleagues more alone than a Prime Minister should'. He was disinclined to cultivate either the party rank and file or the press, thereby incurring the risk of losing touch with changing shifts of opinion in his party.[27]

For the most part, Asquith's strengths were more obvious than his weaknesses, until the outbreak of the European war in August 1914. Before the war, only the Irish question had a similar tendency to expose his limitations so mercilessly. But since many people in Britain only noticed Ireland whenever emergencies erupted, Asquith's failings in Irish policy have attracted less attention than his inadequacies in wartime. Even his colleagues, immersed in the business of their own departments, had more reason to notice Asquith's undoubted abilities in other areas, than his lack of direction in the Home Rule crisis. To some extent Asquith's colleagues failed to criticise his limitations because they shared them. It can be argued that they reflected the broader problems of the Liberal philosophy.

3 Drafting the Bill: A Gladstonian Solution or United Kingdom Devolution ?

Early in 1911, the Government prepared to carry out its promise of Irish Home Rule, after so many years of defeat, frustration and postponement. The Cabinet believed that finance and Irish representation were the two major problems which might wreck their Bill, particularly as these were the gravest weaknesses in Gladstone's measures. There was considerable controversy as to the form the Bill should take to deal most effectively with these problem areas. The most obvious approach was a modification of Gladstonian Home Rule, advocated by the Irish Secretary in March 1911: 'The Bill would be like Mr. Gladstone's Bill of 1893, subject to the alterations and modifications which time had shown to be wise.'[28] United Kingdom devolution was the only alternative to the Gladstonian approach under consideration in 1911, and it received substantial support. Federalism and finance obsessed the Cabinet in 1911. The question of Ulster was scarcely even discussed.

In January 1911, the Cabinet appointed a committee of seven ministers to consider the entire Home Rule question.

The members of the committee were Birrell, Lloyd George, Churchill, Haldane, Herbert Samuel and Sir Edward Grey, with Lord Loreburn as chairman. Their discussions rapidly focused on the two issues of Home Rule finance and United Kingdom devolution, with devolution increasingly monopolising their attention. United Kingdom devolution, more commonly known in these years as 'federalism' or 'Home Rule all round', was generally understood to mean the granting of subordinate assemblies for England, Scotland, Wales and Ireland. These would control essentially local affairs, under the supreme control of the Imperial Parliament, which would be responsible for national questions such as foreign policy, defence, trade and customs. Devolution appealed to the committee as an alternative to the more obvious Gladstonian approach adopted in 1886 and 1893. Its advocates claimed that devolution would solve the Irish Home Rule question, increase regional efficiency within the United Kingdom, and relieve the congestion of business at Westminster. Home Rule all round also had the advantage of providing a logical solution to the thorny problem of Irish representation at Westminster, without giving the Irish an unfair voice in the local affairs of Great Britain. Devolution won considerable support from all members of the committee, except Birrell, and they devoted much of their time to discussion of a possible federal scheme.[29]

Only Churchill and Lloyd George actually presented federal proposals to the committee. Churchill circulated two memoranda in February and March, proposing a full-blown scheme of Home Rule all round.[30] He suggested the rather drastic method of dividing the United Kingdom into ten segments, each with its own Assembly for legislative and administrative purposes. The committee also spent considerable time discussing a far more limited compromise proposed by Lloyd George in February. This suggested that devolution should be the ultimate aim; meanwhile Irish Home Rule should be passed, and Bills relating exclusively to England, Scotland or Wales should be dealt with by grand committees of the regional members concerned.[31]

The committee's enthusiasm for United Kingdom devolution was quite remarkable in view of the problems it presented. It was an exceptionally complicated and controversial approach to the Irish question. The Irish Secretary and the Nationalist leaders were adamantly opposed to any form of Home Rule all round, whether of the Churchillian or the Lloyd George variety. Birrell shared the conviction of Redmond and Dillon that federalism would 'complicate the Irish part of the question', and possibly wreck Home Rule altogether. Apart from the doubtful motives of some of its supporters, Birrell and the Nationalists recognised the enormous practical problems involved in its implementation. Birrell aimed 'to pave the way for Home Rule (on more or less Gladstonian lines), and to do all that in me lay to make any other solution of the problem *impossible*'.[32] During 1911 Birrell acted as watch-dog for Irish interests, since the Nationalists were excluded from the committee's deliberations for almost a year. He protested strongly to the Cabinet in August about Irish Home Rule '– being included in a devolution Federal scheme for Wales & Scotland which the country had never discussed'. He confided in Churchill that he was 'very unhappy' about the Bill: '[If] Home Rule for Ireland is to be put in the same bag with some kind of Home Rule for England, Scotland & Wales, I believe the crash will be prodigious'.[33]

Birrell's quiet, but persistent, stand against Home Rule all round finally won round the Cabinet, but it was a slow process. He found support for the traditional Gladstonian approach from colleagues like John Burns, Lord Morley, McKinnon Wood and Reginald McKenna, who were not members of the sub-committee. Churchill's grandiose scheme for a United Kingdom divided into ten parts was quickly dropped, but the Lloyd George plan lingered on until April 1912. Lloyd George's 'grand committee' proposal was actually inserted in the August 1911 draft of the Bill, but was subsequently omitted, and no reference was made in the final text to any future federal scheme.

Asquith did, however, make a token gesture to the federal idea when he introduced the Home Rule Bill in the Commons on 11 April. He emphasised that the Irish claim came first, but promised that the Irish Bill would be treated as a first step towards wider devolution. The advantages of this approach were two-fold. It was useful to pay lip-service to the federal principle in an attempt to retain the support of the Welsh and Scottish nationalists and those Liberals who were lukewarm about Irish Home Rule. There were approximately eighty Liberal federalists in the Commons, but Asquith subsequently failed to convince them of the reality of his federal promises. Their disillusionment tended to make them extremely critical of the weaker features of the Irish Home Rule Bill during the 1912 debates, especially those provisions which were inconsistent with a federal scheme. Scottish federalists were consequently among the more vocal Liberal critics of Asquith's Ulster policy. They led a backbench revolt against the financial provisions of the Irish Bill in November 1912.

A second function of the Government's avowed federal intentions was to leave open a line of approach to the Unionists, in case deadlock over the Irish Bill at any stage made compromise negotiations a necessity. Thus the Government never entirely rejected the federal idea after April 1912, because its tactical advantages remained significant. By 1912, Home Rule all round had ceased to provide a serious alternative to a purely Irish Home Rule measure for the Liberals. Yet it remained a powerful negotiating gambit, because Home Rule all round was a sufficiently vague and all-embracing formula to mean all things to all men.

Meanwhile, the Cabinet could no longer avoid the task of determining the final shape of the 1912 Irish Home Rule Bill. The Gladstonian approach was adopted largely by default, in the absence of any clearly defined alternative. Once federalism was dropped, there was little time or inclination to look further afield than the second Home Rule Bill of 1893. There was some justification for using the final version of the 1893 Bill as a starting-point, since this had been debated at length before it finally passed the Commons. Considerable alteration was necessary, however, after nearly twenty years, but this did not unduly disturb the leisurely committee. The Cabinet committee on Home Rule was not inclined to constructive hard work. In the eleven months before the Nationalists were brought into consultation, the committee made almost no progress towards drafting a new measure, federal or otherwise. Two supposedly new drafts of the third Home

Rule Bill were printed in June and August 1911, but they reproduced the 1893 Bill so faithfully that the schedules were not even amended to take account of Queen Victoria's death.

Herbert Samuel rather overstated the case in September 1911, when he confided to Herbert Gladstone that 'The Home Rule Bill is in being, but with a good many blanks and square brackets'. When the Nationalist leaders were finally allowed to see the second draft in December 1911, they were informed that it 'was not the result of serious consideration, but had been thrown hurriedly together and was not to be regarded as expressing the settled view of the Cabinet'.[34] This remarkable admission was a damning indictment of the supposed labours of the Home Rule committee over the previous year. The third Home Rule Bill only began to take final shape after January 1912 and the committee played little further part. Birrell at last assumed a leading role, since federalist aspirations were abandoned, and he was allowed to work closely with the Nationalist leaders. He thrashed out the detailed provisions of the measure in the course of frequent discussions with Redmond and Dillon, who visited him almost daily when he was in London. The few innovations of 1911 were abandoned one by one, between February and April 1912.

The process of preparing the Bill was very slow in the early months of 1912. This was partly due to a decline in Cabinet morale, which reached its nadir in March. Government confidence had been temporarily undermined by a serious coal strike, combined with by-election reverses, and the activities of the militant suffragettes. The Cabinet even discussed the possibility of resignation on 6 March, only four weeks before the introduction of the Irish Bill. The Prime Minister warned that they must consider their position very carefully in the light of the by-election figures, particularly as they had major measures still to carry through. It was the seventh year of their existence, and they did not want to be charged with clinging to office when they were losing moral authority. Asquith's unusually pessimistic remarks may have been deliberately intended to arouse his gloomy colleagues from their lethargy. They certainly stimulated a much-needed fighting spirit and ministers' reactions on the Irish issue were most significant.

Morley warned that they must consider the Irish response in the event of their resignation. They were pledged to the Nationalists, and bound to pursue Home Rule, as they did in 1893 with a smaller majority. Lloyd George, Haldane and Churchill advocated pressing on with Home Rule for the sake of the Irish. Loreburn thought they 'must stay & go down fighting', and Birrell pointed out that 'we are bound to the Irish'. This response encouraged Asquith to decide that they should at least introduce their Bills, though their dwindling popularity offered little prospect of getting them passed.[35]

The process finally speeded up at the end of March. In contrast to the leisurely progress of the past year, Birrell, Samuel and Asquith worked exceptionally long hours on the final draft in the last two weeks before the introduction of the Bill. Birrell kept the Irish leaders closely informed of all developments, and attempted to accommodate their preferences wherever possible. Even as late as 6 April, when Birrell sent Redmond the most recent draft of the Bill, he added that 'there are a good many rough edges yet and blanks'. Frantic last minute meetings were held on 9 and 10 April, chiefly between Birrell, Asquith, Redmond and Samuel, to decide final drafting points and polish up those rough edges. The day before the Bill was introduced, Birrell and Samuel each participated in three conferences and a Cabinet, all on the subject of Home Rule. The Chief Secretary then sent a letter of reassurance to Redmond, concluding: 'I pray Heaven we may have a good send off.'[36] Fortunately for the Liberals, the Home Rule debate began in a more favourable political climate, since the coal strike was over and the Cabinet's morale improved.

The final draft of the Government of Ireland Bill was substantially complete in time for its First Reading on 11 April, though it was not printed until four days later. The most outstanding feature of the Bill was the remarkable similarity to the 1893 Bill as amended in Committee. Indeed, the Cabinet took pains to retain the exact format and terminology of the earlier Bill. Any changes had to be firmly justified, as 'a departure from precedent would probably lead to debate in the House'. The Bill provided for the establishment of an Irish Parliament, consisting of a nominated Senate and an elected House of Commons, subject to the supremacy of the United Kingdom Parliament. The Irish Parliament was granted general powers to legislate for the 'peace, order and good government of Ireland', except for those subjects specifically excluded. The latter included matters concerning the Crown, the making of war and peace, the army and navy, defence, treaties and foreign trade. This list followed the 1893 Bill very closely, but an entirely new set of 'reserved matters', such as land purchase, old age pensions and national insurance, were necessary to deal with social reforms since 1893. Certain reserved powers, like control of the Royal Irish Constabulary, might ultimately be transferred to the Irish Government's control, but land purchase was to remain permanently under Imperial control.[37]

The list of restrictions on the Irish Government's powers was very much shorter than in the 1893 Bill. The remaining restrictions were concerned solely to protect religious equality. This was the only safeguard included to deal with the problem of the Ulster Protestant minority. As in the 1893 Bill, provision was made for a joint session in cases of disagreement between the two Irish Houses. The Irish Senate was originally intended to be nominated by the Lord Lieutenant, rather than elected on a property franchise as in 1893. However, the 1893 procedure was subsequently restored as a consequence of one of the few amendments of any importance passed in Committee in 1912. The number of Senators was fixed at forty and the members of the Irish House of Commons at 164. A compromise was reached over Irish representation at Westminster, whereby Ireland should send only forty-two members, although entitled to sixty-four on a strict population basis. The functions of the executive authority in Ireland were defined more precisely than in the brief, vague provisions of the earlier Bills. The Lord Lieutenant would be the head of the Irish executive, representing the Crown. His office was deliberately made non-political by the stipulation that he was to be appointed for a fixed term of six years, unaffected by any change of ministry. The Lord Lieutenant would be advised on Irish matters by the 'executive committee of the privy council', which would be the Irish equivalent of the British Cabinet. Irish ministers would normally be heads of the various government departments and could be dismissed if they lost the confidence of parliament.

The result was a measure which followed the Gladstonian Bill of 1893 as closely as the changed circumstances of the later period allowed, in all respects except finance. The new Bill was essentially a very limited revision of the previous one. From January 1912, when Birrell assumed a prominent role, the main innovations of 1911 were dropped and the framework of the Gladstonian Bill was largely restored. The Chief Secretary made every effort to ensure that the final draft was acceptable to the Irish leaders. Birrell's colleagues were probably eager to cooperate because of the uncertainty of their political position in the early months of 1912. In any case, so long as the Nationalists were demanding nothing more revolutionary than a reversion to the 1893 Bill, the Government could safely accede with a good grace. Most of the concessions made to the Irish leaders were of this nature. They had the double advantage, for the Liberals, of gaining Nationalist approval, as well as promising the security of a measure already passed by the Commons. The Nationalist leaders rarely insisted on major alterations, knowing well the limits of their powers, and fearing that too marked a departure from the 1893 precedent might arouse renewed enthusiasm for the federal alternative. When they did express a preference for a fundamental change which was unwelcome in Great Britain, such as fiscal autonomy, they were refused. Asquith's Government was by no means the slave of the Nationalist leaders, as the Unionists claimed.

The financial provisions constituted the only important section of the 1893 Bill to be entirely transformed. Finance, like federalism, dominated the discussions on the Irish question in 1911. Finance, rather than Ulster, was considered the most serious problem in 1911, and the most likely obstacle to block the path of Home Rule.[38] The financial clauses of the Home Rule Bill were drawn up independently, and were not incorporated into the drafts of the measure until 5 March 1912. The fiscal aspects of Home Rule were not examined by the Home Rule sub-committee in 1911, but first by a specialist committee of financial experts under Sir Henry Primrose and later by Herbert Samuel.

The financial difficulty was acute even in Gladstone's day, but by 1911 it was a far greater obstacle, since the balance of indebtedness had moved against Ireland. In 1886 Irishmen contributed in taxes to the United Kingdom Exchequer well over £2 million more than they received from Government expenditure. By 1910-11, Irishmen received over £1 million more in benefits than they paid in taxes. Irish revenue had increased by only 28 per cent between 1896 and 1911, whereas Government expenditure in Ireland had soared by 91 per cent, mainly due to old age pensions and land purchase. The Primrose committee and most Irish Nationalist economists disapproved of this steadily rising expenditure, which made Irish self-sufficiency and financial autonomy increasingly unattainable. The financial link with Great Britain entailed in Ireland a scale of expenditure which was beyond the requirements of a largely rural population and beyond the natural resources of the country to supply.[39]

The Primrose committee proposed to solve these problems with a bold, simple plan, entirely different from Gladstone's fiscal schemes. The Irish Government should be given full control over all its own revenue and expenditure, except that the Imperial Exchequer should meet the Irish deficit by assuming liability for all Irish pensions already granted. This plan was expected to promote 'an autonomous Ireland, self-contained and self-sufficing so far as its own local administration and finances are concerned'. Unfortunately for the Irish Nationalists, the Chief Secretary was the only minister to support the Primrose committee's recommendation of Irish financial independence. Birrell failed in his attempt to persuade his colleagues to 'give Ireland the Primrose Report and thus secure her support'.[40]

The Primrose committee was merely advisory, and it was not Birrell but Herbert Samuel, who was delegated to frame the fiscal provisions. The Postmaster-General was one of Asquith's brilliant young protégés, and was highly respected in the Cabinet for his quick mastery of complex material and his general quiet efficiency. The other members of the Home Rule committee were only too pleased to leave the financial questions in Samuel's capable hands. Consequently, finance was the only aspect of the forthcoming Home Rule Bill which

45

was thoroughly and efficiently examined in 1911. In October 1911, Samuel studied the Primrose Report, utilised most of its statistics, but entirely rejected its fundamental proposition regarding Irish fiscal autonomy. From the autumn of 1911 he devoted much of his energy to his finance scheme, and deluged the leisurely Home Rule committee with detailed memoranda on finance. Unfortunately, the scheme he ultimately produced was so complicated that it defeated the comprehension of most of his colleagues.

Samuel presented his proposals to the Cabinet on 4 December 1911, and they were incorporated into the latest draft of the Home Rule Bill on 5 March 1912. Samuel's scheme was extraordinarily elaborate, and involved a far greater degree of British control over Irish finance than the Primrose proposals. Until the £2 million Irish deficit was extinguished, the entire proceeds of all Irish taxes, including customs and excise, were to be paid into the Imperial Exchequer. A block grant of about £6 millions would be transferred annually from the Imperial to the Irish Exchequer, to cover all purely Irish expenditure, other than the 'reserved services'. The Imperial Government was to control and pay for the 'reserved services', including old age pensions, national insurance, land purchase and collection of taxes. If the Irish Government chose to take over any of the 'reserved services', then the block grant, generally termed the 'transferred sum', would be increased accordingly. The transferred sum would include a surplus of £500,000 p.a. for the first three years, to provide a working margin for the Irish Government. This surplus would be reduced gradually during the next six years, until it reached £200,000 p.a., at which point it would remain fixed. The financial scheme should be re-examined when Irish revenue exceeded expenditure for three consecutive years. Once Irish solvency was thus established, the Imperial Parliament would consider imposing a fair Irish contribution to common Imperial expenditure. Samuel's decision that Irish customs and excise should remain under Imperial control, as in Gladstone's Bills, was one of the more controversial points. However, the Irish Parliament was granted very limited powers to vary customs and excise duties imposed by the Imperial Parliament, and could also levy any entirely new taxes other than customs duties.[41]

The Samuel scheme presented just as many difficulties as the Primrose plan, without providing a final solution to the question of Irish finance. It was so complicated that few people other than Samuel ever understood it. *The Times* complained that its chief characteristics were 'complexity, entanglement, and obscurity', and even the Prime Minister's speech on 11 April 'left the financial provisions in some obscurity'.[42] The Nationalists detested Samuel's financial provisions, and condemned Imperial control of Irish finance as a 'distinctly retrograde step'. However, Redmond and Dillon finally decided that they must tolerate Samuel's scheme, rather than risk wrecking Home Rule prospects at a late stage.[43]

Samuel's intricate system of checks and balances did not even satisfy the Liberal backbenchers. He had made minimal concessions to the Irish demands for fiscal autonomy by allowing the Irish Parliament to retain extremely limited powers to vary customs and excise duties. These were sufficient to provoke a backbench revolt during the Committee debate on the financial provisions, in November 1912. Between seventy and eighty Liberal members signed a memorandum, early in November, protesting that Ireland's power to vary customs duties blocked the way to a unified federal system. Sixty-four Liberals subsequently failed to vote on one or both divisions on the Finance Resolution on 19 and 20 November. Their opposition was highly effective and the Cabinet revoked the Irish Parliament's power to reduce customs and excise duties, to meet the criticisms of 'a formidable section of the party'. Birrell explained regretfully to Redmond that the Government was 'fully persuaded that a Parliamentary Situation had arisen, which cannot be fairly estimated simply by counting votes in the lobby – and that the concession is really *necessary* . . .'. This backbench revolt was responsible for one of the very few amendments of any importance inserted in the Bill at Committee stage.[44]

The serious problems involved in Samuel's finance scheme were, however, obscured by the increasing emphasis on the Ulster question. As Sir Almeric Fitzroy noted in July 1913: '. . . the Government have escaped substantial criticism on the financial claims which constitute the real flaw in their constructive statesmanship, and might, if properly exposed, have upset their plans'.[45] In terms of the actual events of 1912-14, the most fundamental weakness in Samuel's scheme was that it increased the Government's difficulties in making subsequent provision for Ulster. It tied the Liberals even more firmly to the original Home Rule Bill of April 1912, which ignored the Ulster problem. It was clear that Samuel's complicated system of checks and balances would automatically break down if Ulster had to be excluded at any stage. Samuel himself claimed that: 'It is difficult to see how any workable financial scheme, of any kind, can be evolved, based upon a fiscal separation between Ulster and the rest of Ireland.' Evidently, Asquith and Lloyd George did not share this view when they agreed to Ulster exclusion in 1914, but the complexities of Samuel's scheme added immensely to their problems in revising the financial provisions. Hostile critics claimed that '. . . freedom for Ulster walks hand in hand with financial chaos in this particular Bill', and even interpreted the finance scheme as a 'crafty device to . . . create a dilemma from which Ulster cannot escape'.[46]

The Liberal Government was well advised to dismiss United Kingdom devolution and to concentrate on the immediate problem of Irish Home Rule. It is less certain that the decision to follow the Gladstonian model rigidly, in all but finance, was equally wise. The result was a measure which combined a reproduction of the 1893 Bill with a totally revised financial scheme. The separate examination of the two sections of the Bill was unwise, given the interdependence between financial and other aspects of Home Rule. A complete re-appraisal of the entire measure, such as Samuel applied to the financial provisions, might have been more effective. It might even have induced the Cabinet to consider the implications of the Ulster question, rather than being mesmerised by federalism. Instead, the Bill of April 1912 ignored Ulster, and put forward a complicated fiscal scheme which infuriated enemies and allies alike.

The leisurely manner in which the 1912 Home Rule Bill was prepared was quite remarkable. Some explanation can be found for the lethargy of the Home Rule committee throughout 1911. Loreburn gave no lead, since he was out of sympathy with the Cabinet, and retired in 1912. Birrell took little active part in the committee's rather aimless deliberations up to December 1911, because he objected to the federal emphasis, and the refusal to consult the Nationalists. Samuel was preoccupied with Home Rule finance, Grey with foreign affairs, Lloyd George with insurance and Churchill with his navy. 1911 was dominated by anxiety over the Parliament Bill crisis, industrial disputes, the insurance legislation, and diplomatic difficulties. These other concerns may help to explain the lethargy of the Home Rule committee, but they do not entirely justify it.

1911 was a year of drift on Irish matters, setting an unfortunate precedent for the next two years. The important decisions about the Home Rule Bill were left until the very last minute in 1912. Time which should have been spent in constructive preparation for a major piece of legislation, which was to dominate the political scene for the next three years, was frittered away. The Prime Minister may well have decided from the start that a revised version of the 1893 Bill would be adequate. He gave the committee little guidance in 1911 and may have used it as a harmless way to ventilate potentially embarrassing ideas on Home Rule all round. By delegating responsibility for the Home Rule Bill to this committee, the Cabinet was left free to forget about it until 1912; federalism was exhaustively aired and discarded, and Ulster was ignored altogether. The finance of the Bill only received comprehensive treatment because Samuel was a thorough minister. The Prime Minister's procrastination, and preference for avoiding the hard decisions in 1911-12, accurately foreshadowed his method of dealing with the mounting Irish crisis from 1912-14.

II
THE 'ULSTER QUESTION' FROM 1886 TO APRIL 1912

1 The Origins and Significance of the 'Ulster Question'

The 'Ulster Question' was the customary term used to describe the problem posed by the existence of a large Protestant community in the province of Ulster, totally opposed to the Home Rule demand of Nationalist Catholic Ireland. The total population of Ireland according to the 1911 Census was 4,390,219, of whom one-quarter were Protestants. The vast majority of these Irish Protestants were concentrated in the six north-east counties of Ulster, where they controlled the political power and economic wealth.

Ulster was colonised in the seventeenth century by English and Scottish Protestant settlers, who were strongly attached to Britain in outlook and traditions. There were marked differences in temperament, race, religion and history between Ulster and the rest of Ireland. From at least 1886 onwards, the Ulster Protestants had feared and mistrusted the prospect of Home Rule, because they believed it threatened complete destruction of their way of life.

The complexities of the problem were increased by the uneven geographical distribution of the two major religious groups in Ireland. In the nine county province of Ulster, Protestants and Catholics were fairly evenly balanced numerically. The proportion of Protestants in the whole of Ulster rose from approximately 52 per cent in 1885 to just over 56 per cent between 1901 and 1911.[1] The Protestants were in a distinct minority in the three south-west Ulster counties of Cavan, Monaghan and Donegal. They were concentrated in the six north-east counties of Ulster, where about 66 per cent of the population were Protestant in 1901. This concentration was most pronounced in the four counties of Antrim, Armagh, Down and Londonderry, whereas Fermanagh and Tyrone were more evenly balanced.

In the three southern provinces of Leinster, Munster and Connaught, Protestants formed only about 10 per cent of the total population, but their influence was greater than their numbers suggested. For years they had been the dominant aristocracy, though their power and social position were gradually reduced as the southern landlord interest declined. The southern Unionists were also distributed unevenly. They constituted 14 per cent of the Leinster population, compared with only 6 per cent in Munster, and 4 per cent in Connaught. More than half the southern Protestants lived in the Dublin and Cork areas, leaving few Protestants scattered throughout the rest of the south and west.

The problem was accentuated because the three southern provinces remained predominantly agricultural, whereas the four north-east counties of Ulster underwent rapid industrial expansion after 1800. These Ulster counties benefitted from the Act of Union, depending on Britain for the large markets which were the basis of their prosperity in the linen, shipbuilding and engineering industries. The Ulster Protestants feared that their industrial prosperity would be ruined by an incompetent and prejudiced economic policy controlled from Dublin, imposing protective tariffs and excessive taxes. Their opposition to Home Rule was strengthened by their conviction that it could not work without Ulster, since the resources of the north were indispensable to the economic viability of Irish self-government.

Ulster Protestants were conscious of a separate sense of identity, which isolated them from the Catholic majority and also from the scattered Protestants in the south. This was a product of the special loyalties created by a common sense of race, religion and culture, strengthened by the historical traditions of evangelical Protestantism. Segregation of Protestants and Catholics was fairly rigid; passions were easily inflamed in the Belfast area, where children of both religions were brought up in an atmosphere of bigoted, sectarian rivalry. Protestants clung to the traditional ideas of the Protestant ascendancy. They were not prepared to surrender their privileged position for one of inferiority, or even equality, under a Catholic-dominated Dublin Parliament. Protestants forgot their own differences and united in the face of an assumed Catholic threat. Though the influence of the Catholic clergy on the Nationalist Party declined during the nineteenth century, Protestants continued to fear that Home Rule meant 'Rome Rule' and religious persecution. After 1886, political and religious lines of division increasingly coincided. Contemporaries generally equated Protestantism with Unionism, and Catholicism with the Home Rule policy of the Liberal and Nationalist Parties. Former Protestant Liberals tended to become Unionists, and Protestants sank their earlier denominational and political rivalries in a common defence of the Union.

2 Gladstone and the Ulster Challenge

Gladstone did not ignore the Ulster question in 1886. Certainly he underestimated its dimensions, but so did most British politicians. The Ulster challenge was strong and serious, even in 1886.[2] The Ulster Unionists openly threatened civil war if the first Home Rule Bill was passed, claiming that 'the dictates of that Irish Parliament would be resisted by the people of Ulster at the point of the bayonet'. A united Conservative-Unionist party replaced the traditional rivalry between Conservatives and Liberals in Ulster, and a distinct Ulster Unionist Party was organised at Westminster. Popular demonstrations in Ulster against Home Rule reached their climax with the Belfast visit of Lord Randolph Churchill, who raised the famous war-cry: 'Ulster will fight and Ulster will be right'. Ulster passions were genuine and they were already aroused before Churchill's visit. Parnell was almost certainly wrong in claiming that the agitation would have evaporated without encouragement from England.[3]

The Protestant *Belfast Newsletter* proclaimed that the loyalists were not afraid of civil war and would incur any risk rather than submit to being ruled by boycotters and moonlighters. *The Times* considered the warlike threats of Ulster perfectly genuine and insisted that the organisation of resistance in Ulster was no merely local affair, but a general movement. There is evidence of a rapidly growing organisation and firm intention behind the impassioned speeches and the sometimes ridiculous propaganda. Serious riots in Belfast from June to September 1886 further illustrated the intensity of feeling, which had reached fever pitch by the time the Home Rule Bill was defeated. The Royal Commission which subsequently investigated these riots concluded that the highly explosive condition of public opinion over Home Rule was a major cause.[4] An anonymous article in the *Fortnightly Review* emphasised that the riots would have taken a more ominous form had the Home Rule Bill been passed: 'There would have been no riots but there would have been civil war'.[5] Two factors prevented the Ulster challenge from becoming as critical in 1886 or 1893 as it became in 1912-14. Ulster's opposition lacked the united leadership and highly developed organisation provided later by Sir Edward Carson. It also lacked immediate pressure, because the Ulstermen knew the first two Bills would never pass the veto of the House of Lords.

Gladstone's decision to make no special provision for Ulster in 1886 was not based on complete ignorance of the problem, or a deliberate attempt to suppress it. John Morley revealed that Ulster was one of the 'knottiest points' discussed in the Cabinet. However, the Irish Secretary's personal view that the Ulster agitation was largely artificial[6] seems to have influenced the Cabinet more strongly than the well-informed advice of James Bryce, who took the Ulster threats seriously. Bryce was a prominent Liberal and an Ulsterman, who explained his views in the February 1886 issue of the *Nineteenth Century*, after two recent visits to Ulster. He warned that a serious risk of collision existed unless Ulster was given some measure of local autonomy to protect the Protestant minority and Ulster's economy: 'England ought to realise that here lies a difficulty which she cannot evade without dishonour nor neglect without the risk of civil war'. Bryce presented his case more formally to the Cabinet early in March, but his advice was rejected.[7]

By 20 March 1886, Gladstone decided that the question of special treatment for Ulster should be left open for consideration during the parliamentary debate. When he introduced the Home Rule Bill early in April, he declared that the Government was prepared to give careful thought to any practicable plan for Ulster which received general approval.

53

Gladstone explained that none of the various schemes suggested had seemed entirely justified, particularly in view of the widespread Nationalist sentiment expressed at the 1885 election.[8] Instead Gladstone inserted safeguards for the Protestant minority into the Bill, providing that the second 'Order' in the Dublin Parliament should have a veto on the first, and should be partially elected on a high property franchise. The Irish Parliament was also forbidden to pass discriminatory legislation on religious matters. Such safeguards failed to satisfy the Irish Unionists, both in 1886 and 1893, when again no special provision was made for Ulster.

There was considerable justification for this line of action on Gladstone's part in 1886. Many Liberal and Nationalist politicians shared Labouchère's view that Ulster's threats were 'a game of brag'. Nationalist derision even took the form of an advertisement in *The Times* for '25,000 old women with broomsticks to march against the Orange men'. Moreover, as Gladstone explained in his concluding speech on the Bill, since Parnell and the Ulster Unionist leader had both rejected partition, there seemed no reason to pursue it further.[9] In all fairness to Gladstone, he gave the Ulster question as much consideration before the 1886 Bill was introduced as did Asquith's Government twenty-five years later, despite the vastly different circumstances.

By 1911 the extent of Ulster's hostility to Home Rule should have been perfectly clear to the Cabinet. The Ulster Unionist organisation had been made more effective in response to the 1893 Home Rule Bill, which followed its predecessor in treating Ireland as a single unit. The Ulster Defence Union was established in 1893 as the supreme Ulster Unionist authority to prepare for resistance to Home Rule. Demonstrations and armed preparations again took place, but the House of Lords still stood between the Ulster Unionists and a Dublin Parliament. Ulster Unionist forces were again reorganised after the shock of the 1904–5 'devolution crisis', when members of Balfour's Unionist Government were suspected of harbouring Home Rule sympathies. By 1905 the Ulster Unionist Council had been formed to direct the forces in preparing to resist any future encroachments on the Union.[10]

Even more ominous was the adoption of Sir Edward Carson as the new leader of the Ulster Unionist Council in July 1911. Carson has been well described by Roy Jenkins as a southern Irishman who 'combined great personal charm, hypochondriacal neurasthenia, a huge law practice, and a strong taste for melodrama'. Carson was determined to stamp out apathy on the Home Rule question, as he told Lady Londonderry: 'I will make a big effort (my last in politics) to stir up some life over this Home Rule fight . . . I will lead for myself this time'. When he launched the campaign against Home Rule in July 1911, with Captain James Craig, Carson emphasised that he would only lend his name and powerful support to a movement which was serious in its determination to resist Home Rule. 'I am not for a mere game of bluff,' he wrote to Craig, 'and unless men are prepared to make great sacrifices which they clearly understand the talk of resistance is no use'.[11]

The Government was soon acquainted with Carson's intentions, which were only too well publicised. A vast Ulster Unionist demonstration at Craigavon, on 25 September 1911, indicated the strength of the Carson-Craig partnership and their rank and file support. Carson threw down his challenge to the Government: 'We must be prepared . . . the morning Home Rule is passed, ourselves to become responsible for the government of the Protestant Province of Ulster'. In January 1912, Leopold Amery reported to Bonar Law the impressions gained during a two week tour in Ireland:

Ulster I think we can count on absolutely. They are determined from top to bottom . . . and are quietly working out all their plans for keeping order and carrying on the local administration within their own area . . . If attacked, they will fight . . .[12]

Thus, long before the third Home Rule debate began at Westminster, the Unionists publicised their intention to carry the battle outside parliament in order to win public support. The Parliament Act prevented the Unionists winning victories inside the House, where their attack would be splintered against an automatic Government majority. When Bonar Law became leader of the British Unionist Party in November 1911, a more aggressive and partisan approach to politics replaced Balfour's moderation and broader perspective. Bonar Law was determined to provide firm leadership, especially since he was taking over a shattered party in the aftermath of the humiliations of the 1910 election defeats and the Parliament Act. The impact was all the greater in that Bonar Law's unexpected rise to power coincided with the advent of Carson. Bonar Law warned Lord Emmott that the 1912 session would be a very nasty one, and he rather expected that every Unionist would be suspended before the Home Rule Bill left the Commons.[13] The Ulster Protestant campaign against Home Rule had received the official sanction of the British Unionist Party.

3 A Tragic Omission: The Neglected Ulster Dimension, January 1911 to February 1912

Despite all the warnings since 1886, Asquith's Government almost entirely ignored the Ulster problem throughout the twelve months preceding the introduction of the third Home Rule Bill in April 1912. Contrary to the accepted view, there is little to suggest that 'Asquith was aware from the beginning that Ulster would be his most formidable difficulty'.[14] There is no evidence that the Cabinet even considered the Ulster problem until February 1912. Finance and federalism dominated the Government's Home Rule discussions up to April 1912, and most ministers remained sublimely ignorant that Ulster might wreck their Bill.

The Ulster question clearly created a dilemma for Liberals who accepted the Gladstonian concept of self-determination for a united Ireland. The existence of the large Protestant Unionist community in north-east Ulster raised important questions about minority rights and about the possible necessity of imposing Home Rule by force on a recalcitrant Ulster. There were no answers to these aspects of the Irish question which did not in some way conflict with fundamental Liberal principles. The complexity of the problems involved made it all the more vital that they should be thoroughly examined before the final form of the third Home Rule Bill was settled.

Yet Asquith's Cabinet completely failed to comprehend the

extent of the Ulster problem. The Government missed the opportunity to incorporate special provision for Ulster into the Home Rule Bill when it was first introduced, and the best chance to seize the initiative over Ulster was thereby lost. The cabinet committee on Home Rule assumed throughout 1911 that the whole of Ireland should be treated as a single unit. But, if there was a case for continual discussion of Home Rule all round, there was a far stronger case for some examination of the Ulster question. No evidence exists to indicate that the Government even weighed the arguments for and against Ulster exclusion until February 1912, when it was already too late to alter the framework of their Bill. This failure to assess the Ulster problem, and to examine the possible methods of dealing with it, is surely a severe indictment of the Government. It seemed far easier to treat Ireland as a single unit, following Gladstonian precedent, in the hope that Ulster's challenge was hysterical bluff which would ultimately evaporate.

The Liberal press largely ignored the Ulster question up to spring 1912. The occasional references to Ulster's preparations for resistance were punctuated by the same derision as in 1886 and 1893. The radical weekly journal, the *Nation*, frequently provided well-informed comment on Cabinet aims and attitudes through the close links of its editor, H.W. Massingham, with prominent Liberal politicians and intellectuals. It faithfully expressed the views of the radical wing of the Liberal Party, opposing Grey's foreign policy, and applauding the progress of New Liberalism under Lloyd George's energetic leadership. The Government's Home Rule policy was loyally supported as the fulfilment of an obligation to 'old Liberalism', which should be settled as rapidly as possible to make way for the social reforms of the New Liberalism. The *Nation* reflected the Government's attitude to the Ulster challenge. In September 1911, it ridiculed the 'Playboys of Northern Ireland' as they gathered to hear 'Robespierre-Carson' openly inciting them to 'sedition and outrage'. The *Nation* then ignored Ulster again until January 1912, when readers were briefly informed that Ulster's threats left Britain sceptical and cold. However, a letter from Massingham to Redmond, in February 1912, suggests that the editor was more concerned about the Ulster question than his paper revealed. Massingham mentioned that English anxieties about Home Rule focused on the Ulster question and the fear of intolerance: 'I found more evidence of this feeling than just now I thought it wise to publish.'[15]

Readers of the Unionist press were told a different story. Monypenny wrote a series of articles for *The Times* early in 1912, concluding that the Protestant Ulster counties would go to any length in resisting Home Rule. Buckle, the editor of *The Times*, was equally impressed by Ulster's threats. The Unionists assumed that the Government's silence on the subject of Ulster must be a deliberate policy, resulting from their fear of the Ulster threats. F.S. Oliver later remarked to Bonar Law: 'Those of the Government who understood anything about the Irish Question were frightened by the Ulster difficulty in January 1911 before they had even begun to touch the subject.'[16] It was inconceivable to the Opposition that the Government could underestimate the Ulster challenge to the extent of ignoring it so completely.

4 Ministerial Misgivings on Ulster: Birrell, Churchill and Lloyd George, 1911–12

The only members of the Cabinet who were far more deeply concerned about the question of Ulster, in the months before April 1912, were Birrell, Churchill and Lloyd George.[17] Of these, the Chief Secretary was the only minister who anticipated the full significance of the Ulster problem as early as August 1911. He explained his personal views on Ulster at some length in a significant letter written to Churchill from Dublin, late in August:

Ulster has cried 'Wolf' so often and so absurdly that one is inclined to ridicule her rhodomontade, but we are cutting very deep this time and her yells are genuine . . . Great ferment and perturbation of spirit exists – mainly fed amongst the poor folk by hatred of Roman Catholicism and amongst the better to do by the belief that under a Home Rule régime Ireland will become a miserable, one-horsed poverty stricken, priest ridden, corrupt oligarchy.

Birrell believed that the Ulstermen were not bluffing, though he admitted that he could not predict the exact dimensions of the potential trouble in Ulster.[18]

The Ulster question posed problems for all Liberals, but in Birrell's case the conflicts involved were increased by his own peculiarly difficult position as Chief Secretary. On the grounds of personal preference and deeply-rooted sentiment he shared the Irish Nationalists' desire for a united Ireland. But in practical terms he recognised that some form of exclusion of the predominantly Protestant areas of Ulster might be the only way to secure Home Rule for the rest of Ireland. Thus he was the first Liberal minister to suggest the possibility of a compromise solution, similar to that later proposed by Lloyd George in November 1913 and subsequently adopted in the Government's Amending Bill of March 1914. This idea appears to have been mentioned for the first time in Birrell's letter of August 1911 to Churchill, which was also shown to Lloyd George on Birrell's instruction:

. . . were the question referred to Ulster county by county, it is probable that all Ulster save Antrim and Down would by a majority support Home Rule and it might then be suggested and agreed to that for the transitional period, say 5 years, Antrim and Down might stand out and that at the end of that time there should be a fresh referendum to settle their fate. If this was done, there could be no Civil War.[19]

The scheme for temporary Ulster exclusion by county option and referendum, usually attributed to Lloyd George or Churchill, probably originated, then, with the Irish Secretary himself. There is no evidence to support Churchill's claim that he and Lloyd George advocated Ulster exclusion as early as 1909,[20] and it seems most unlikely that they put their proposal to the Cabinet before February 1912.

However, although Birrell was one of the few ministers to recognise at an early date that Ulster exclusion might be necessary, he did not feel free to press it formally on the Cabinet or the public. His references to Ulster in public speeches in 1911 were brief, cautious and far more optimistic than his private remarks to Churchill.[21] Because of his official position as Irish Secretary, with all that implied in terms of deep commitment to the Nationalists, any such proposal from Birrell would have been regarded as the worst form of treachery by the Irish leaders: it might well have entirely destroyed their confidence in the Liberal Party's good faith. It seems possible, therefore, that Birrell may have deliberately placed his suggestion before the two ministers most likely to force the issue further.

Lloyd George and Churchill were the two ministers, other than Asquith and Birrell, who had the greatest impact on the Government's Irish policy from 1911-14. Churchill played the more vocal and active role, while Lloyd George intermittently exercised a more powerful influence behind the scenes, especially after October 1913. Both these extraordinary men shared the *Nation*'s attitude to Irish Home Rule. It was a long-standing party commitment, which must be honoured as quickly as possible, allowing the Liberal Party to proceed with more relevant and socially progressive causes. Neither man was notably enthusiastic about Irish Home Rule as a great Liberal cause *per se*. They were both irritated by the parliamentary time and the ministerial energy it diverted from other issues. Churchill's view of the priorities due to these other causes admittedly altered after he moved in 1911 from the Board of Trade to the Admiralty, transferring his enthusiasm from social reform to naval expansion.

Lloyd George was supremely talented, full of restless energy and dynamic resourcefulness. His talents led to a spectacular rise to power, as Chancellor of the Exchequer in 1908 and potential successor to Asquith by 1914. He was a radical and champion of the people – a man of action, guided by instinct more than intellect. He was adaptable and proved to be a masterly negotiator, skilfully combining force with gentle persuasion. Inevitably he made enemies, who thought him ambitious, opportunistic and unscrupulous, but his colleagues generally felt that his outstanding abilities far outweighed his deficiencies.

The Chancellor of the Exchequer intervened rarely in Home Rule policy until the autumn of 1913. When he did play a part, it was usually in connection with the Ulster problem. Lloyd George never became as emotionally involved with Ulster as Churchill, but he held strong views on the subject. His Welsh background gave him an instinctive sympathy for the cause of any struggling minority. In the case of the Ulster Protestants, this sympathy was strongly reinforced by Lloyd

George's nonconformity. Probably even more important, he viewed the Ulster problem as a potential stumbling-block to the speedy achievement of an Irish settlement. It must be dealt with quickly and effectively, so that Lloyd George could devote all his attention to social reforms, such as the land campaign which obsessed him from 1912-14.

While the Home Rule Bill was being drafted, then, Lloyd George was convinced that the Ulster problem should be squarely faced, rather than ignored. His views received less public attention than those of Churchill, but Lloyd George was prepared to press them equally forcefully on the Cabinet in February 1912. He also discussed them with some of his colleagues beforehand, though only one fragmentary piece of evidence survives. On 30 January, the Chancellor had lunch with McKinnon Wood, the Scottish minister, and Richard Holt, a Liberal member. Holt noted in his diary:

Had a good talk about Ulster and Home Rule – all agreeing that Home Rule was neither popular nor unpopular in Great Britain and that it could not be imposed upon Ulster by force and that if possible the Protestant counties in Ulster should be exempted.[22]

If Lloyd George had his critics, the First Lord of the Admiralty had many more. As a former Conservative, Churchill was mistrusted by many politicians on both sides of the House. He was considered in some quarters to be irresponsible, unreliable and unpredictable. His colleagues were not always convinced that his undoubted abilities compensated for his infuriating limitations. Haldane commented that Churchill tended to act first and think afterwards, despite his energy, imagination and courage. Yet he was recognised as a brilliant parliamentary speaker, with immense intellectual gifts, which might approach genius, given greater discipline and maturity.[23]

When Churchill took over a new responsibility or adopted a new cause, he responded enthusiastically to the challenge, with all the force and ability of his powerful personality. This was the case with his advocacy of Ulster exclusion. As a convert from Unionism he was never a wholehearted Home Ruler. He was even more impatient than Lloyd George to settle the Ulster difficulty in whatever manner would be most effective to dispose of the Home Rule issue. Moreover, Churchill's sense of history attracted him inevitably to the Ulster question, because his father had first played the Orange card, with the resounding cry that 'Ulster will fight and Ulster will be right'. On 4 October, 1911, he informed his Dundee constituents that: 'It is our duty to exhaust every effort which sympathy and earnestness can inspire to understand the reasonable difficulties of Ulster and to allay unfounded alarm.'[24]

By January 1912, Churchill was evidently exasperated by his colleagues' silence on the Ulster question, and decided to rectify the matter by a personal visit. His plan to speak in the Ulster Hall in Belfast, where his father had declared against Home Rule twenty-six years earlier, was particularly provocative. Churchill's visit was interpreted as a deliberate Government manoeuvre to carry the war into the enemy camp. Carson was deeply concerned that it would be impossible to control the inflamed situation which Churchill would provoke, and he believed the Government knew this. Professor Dicey, the eminent Unionist jurist, thought Churchill had set a trap, intending to incite the Unionists to violence.[25] Lord MacDonnell assumed that: 'The Home Rule fight has begun. Carson is leading the Ulster host and Churchill and Birrell are going next month to stump Ulster with Redmond Dillon and Devlin.' This was far from the truth. Churchill had consulted none of his colleagues except Lloyd George. Birrell was particularly exasperated at not being informed, warning Churchill to 'leave Ireland alone in the future'.[26]

The Ulster Unionist Council decided to prevent Churchill speaking at the Ulster Hall on 8 February. The *Nation* condemned the Ulster 'anarchists', who had 'smeared the rugged surface of their ruffianism with the slime of moral indignation', by their refusal to allow Churchill to use the Ulster Hall. After considerable controversy, Churchill agreed to transfer his meeting to a marquee at the Celtic Road football ground in a Catholic district of Belfast. Churchill justified his visit in an interesting letter to Redmond on 13 January. He claimed that it was useful for a minister to set at rest any genuine apprehensions felt by the Ulster Protestants: '. . . it will be a great gain even to give the appearance that a fair and reasonable discussion of the subject has begun in Ulster.' Some of Churchill's colleagues were less convinced of the value of the enterprise. Lord Morley deplored Churchill's recklessness, which had destroyed the last chance to introduce the Home Rule Bill in a calm atmosphere.[27] After all the fuss, the meeting was rather an anti-climax, not improved by the effects of a rainstorm on Churchill's large marquee. Nevertheless, it was scarcely surprising that Lloyd George was advised against making a similar visit to Belfast only a few weeks later: 'It would set the town on fire, inflame slumbering passions, and play old Harry with the prospects of Home Rule.'[28]

5 A Cabinet Decision Against Ulster Exclusion, February 1912

On 6 February 1912, Lloyd George and Churchill presented the Cabinet with a formal proposal for Ulster exclusion. The sources for this vital Cabinet are fragmentary and not entirely consistent. Asquith's Cabinet letter to the King provides the longest account, but omits personality clashes and major differences of opinion. The Prime Minister's version must, therefore, be used in conjunction with the brief references and recollections of other ministers. Lloyd George and Churchill proposed that an option should be given to the predominantly Protestant Ulster counties to contract out of Home Rule. This option might be included in the initial Bill, or by amendment at some subsequent stage. All sources agree to this point and state that the plan was rejected.

According to the Cabinet letter, a majority of ministers finally acquiesced in the alternative proposals suggested by Crewe and strongly recommended by Asquith. These provided that, while the initial Bill should apply to the whole of Ireland, the Irish leaders should be informed that the Government remained free 'to make such changes in the Bill as fresh evidence of facts, or the pressure of British opinion, may render expedient'. The possible consequences of this policy were outlined:

. . . if, in the light of such evidence or indication of public opinion, it becomes clear as the Bill proceeds that some special treatment must be provided for the Ulster counties, the Government will be ready to recognise the necessity, either by amendment of the Bill, or by not pressing it on under the provisions of the Parliament Act. In the meantime, careful and confidential inquiry is to be made as to the real extent and character of the Ulster resistance.[29]

There is no doubt about the positions adopted by Lloyd George, Churchill, Crewe and Loreburn. Churchill subsequently reminded the Prime Minister: 'I have always wished to see Ulster provided for and you will remember how Lloyd-George and I pressed its exclusion upon the Cabinet (and how Loreburn repulsed us in the most blood thirsty manner).' Lloyd George also recalled that Loreburn was 'most violent' in his opposition.[30] Churchill and Lloyd George asked their colleagues what would happen if Ulster rebelled, if military forces were ordered into the province, and whether they were ready to shoot down people in the streets of Belfast to enforce Home Rule on Ulster. 'The reply was that it might be so, but that "sufficient unto the day".'[31]

The views of other ministers are more difficult to reconstruct. Asquith subsequently claimed that Morley joined Loreburn in vehement opposition to Ulster exclusion. Charles Hobhouse's diary is one of the more reliable sources for this Cabinet since it was written up soon afterwards. The entry records that Lloyd George 'was backed by Asquith, Churchill, Haldane and myself. Birrell vowed he would not touch any Bill different to that of '86 and '93.'[32] This is surprising, since it places Birrell firmly in the anti-exclusion camp, while Asquith's position does not tally with the Prime Minister's own account to the King. Birrell's behaviour is the more readily explained. His letter to Churchill of August 1911 showed that he privately sympathised with the appeal for Ulster exclusion advanced by his two younger colleagues. Birrell may even have been the original source of the plan. But the Chief Secretary's ambivalence about the Ulster question led him to adopt the role of spokesman for the Nationalists in public statements and even in Cabinet, when pressed to comment.

Asquith's Cabinet letter suggests that he gave strong support to Crewe in rejecting exclusion, whereas Hobhouse places him in the Lloyd George camp. Both accounts may be correct in that the Prime Minister probably moved from one position to the other in the course of a lengthy, heated discussion. Hobhouse later made a revealing comment on Asquith's general behaviour in Cabinet:

. . . he has little courage; he will adopt the views of A with apparent conviction and enthusiasm, but if the drift of opinion is against A he will find an easy method of throwing him over. He is nearly always in favour of the last speaker, and I have never seen him put his back to the wall.

Another entry noted that 'the P.M. as usual crossed over to the winning side',[33] and this is probably what happened on 6 February. It seems likely that Asquith initially supported Lloyd George, Churchill, Haldane and Hobhouse in the exclusion camp. Then Loreburn, Crewe and Morley, aided by an uncertain Birrell, persuaded the majority to reject exclusion, and the Prime Minister followed the mood of the meeting.

Several interesting points emerge. Only Lloyd George, Churchill, Loreburn and Crewe held particularly strong views on Ulster exclusion on 6 February, and they were in opposite camps. Two months before the introduction of their Irish Bill, the Prime Minister and the Irish Secretary provided neither leadership nor guidance on the most controversial aspect of their legislation. Two ministers, at least, were far from happy about the decision. Churchill was not prepared to admit defeat, and had no intention of letting the matter drop. Precisely a month later he introduced the question again in Cabinet, as Harcourt noted: 'Winston – recurring to idea of separate treatment of Ulster', but to no avail.[34] However, Churchill was not so easily deterred and his colleagues had not heard the last of his views on Ulster exclusion. Lloyd George acquiesced more quietly than Churchill, partly, no doubt, because he was eager to return to matters which held more interest for him.

6 The Failings of Asquith's Ulster Policy

The general justification for Asquith's policy of 'wait and see' deserves to be re-examined in the light of the evidence now available. Several major questions are raised by this vital

Cabinet decision against making initial provision for Ulster.

The Prime Minister's policy of ignoring Ulster until events forced him to do otherwise can be defended on general and historical grounds. The Liberal Party had always advocated Home Rule for a united Ireland, which was the aim of both Gladstone's Bills. A departure from traditional policy had to be justified more forcefully than a maintenance of the status quo. Moreover, the Irish Nationalists strongly reinforced the Cabinet decision by their vehement opposition to any form of Irish partition and by constantly minimising the strength of the Ulster challenge. The inevitable opposition of the Ulster Unionists to Ulster exclusion, and the existence of large Catholic, Nationalist minorities in the north, added further complications. There was also the fear that Home Rule was not economically viable unless Ulster was included. Another practical difficulty of some significance was entirely of the Cabinet's own making. The Home Rule Bill had been drafted largely before February 1912, without taking the Ulster problem into consideration at all. This did not necessarily mean that it was an impossibility to draft a Bill making special provision for Ulster. It did mean, however, that any plan for Ulster exclusion would require drastic revision of this particular Bill, especially its complicated financial provisions.

Roy Jenkins has provided a most persuasive defence of Asquith's Ulster policy. Apart from the points just mentioned, he emphasises two further arguments. The first two parliamentary circuits in 1912 and 1913 were dummy runs: 'Why should anyone settle until they saw what the disposition of forces was likely to be when it came to the final confrontation?' Secondly, Jenkins claims that no arrangement for Ulster exclusion would in 1912 have destroyed the opposition to Home Rule. The British Unionists were largely playing 'the Orange card' to wreck the entire Home Rule Bill and smash the Liberal Government: 'They would have swallowed the concession as though it were nothing and looked for a fresh battleground . . .'[35]

These arguments are undoubtedly powerful, but they overlook several important points. First, Asquith's Government had not examined the situation in Ulster in February 1912 sufficiently thoroughly to be sure that their decision was wise. This point will be considered further later. Secondly, there would have been stronger moral justification for Asquith's policy had he really believed that Home Rule for a united Ireland could ever be passed. But he evidently recognised from the start that the Bill would never pass without an amendment making some provision for Ulster. This was indicated in his February 1912 Cabinet letter, and confirmed by an interesting letter he wrote to Churchill in September 1913:

I always thought (and said) that, in the end, we should probably have to make some sort of bargain about Ulster as the price of Home Rule. But I have never doubted, that, as a matter of tactics and policy, we were right to launch our Bill on its present lines.

If this was the case, then Asquith did not fully consider the consequences of leaving such a compromise until the last minute, and the advantages of taking immediate action. Churchill, at least, failed to understand the logic of the policy: 'We had been met by the baffling argument that such a concession might well be made as the final means of securing a settlement, but would be fruitless till then.'[36]

The most important argument against Asquith's Ulster policy was that it overlooked the advantages to be gained from the Parliament Act by dealing with Ulster immediately. If Asquith had seriously examined the implications of the Parliament Act, he could have ensured that the last two parliamentary circuits, rather than the first two, would be the dummy runs. Special provisions for Ulster would automatically pass within three years, under the terms of the Parliament Act, if they were incorporated into the initial Bill or introduced as Government amendments during the first circuit. The Government did not need the consent of the Opposition up to the end of the 1912 session and could, therefore, largely impose their own terms for Ulster.

The strategy adopted by Asquith, and so adroitly defended by Jenkins, contained one fundamental weakness. Amendments to meet Ulster's grievances could only be incorporated into the Home Rule Bill, after it left the Commons for the first time, by means of 'suggestions' which required Unionist agreement. If no settlement could be reached, the Government could only introduce its own amendments for Ulster by introducing a separate Bill; this would obviously not come into operation, under the Parliament Act, until much later. Thus, by waiting to see the final state of play before negotiating terms for Ulster, Asquith lost an important tactical advantage and placed himself in an unnecessarily weak position. At whatever time he chose to agree that concessions for Ulster were required, he would be admitting that his original measure was far from perfect. His equivocal attitude also made compromise negotiations with the Unionists almost inevitable, at some later stage, if the effective operation of Home Rule was not to be postponed indefinitely. Asquith's policy placed his Government in an exceptionally vulnerable position over Ulster. This was demonstrated most strikingly in June 1912, when a Liberal backbencher proposed an amendment to exclude part of Ulster. The Government was exposed to the embarrassment of criticism from its own backbenches on a particularly delicate issue, which gave maximum opportunity for the wrecking tactics of the Opposition.

The Prime Minister would have been far wiser to dictate his own terms for Ulster from the start and retain the initiative, instead of waiting for concessions to be forced upon him. Any proposal for dealing with Ulster involved difficulties, but these might have been reduced by different timing. If there was justification for introducing Lloyd George's scheme of temporary Ulster exclusion by county option in March 1914, there was far greater cause in April 1912. It would then have been part of the initial Home Rule Bill, obtaining the same benefits from the Parliament Act. This procedure might have eliminated the need for endless negotiations with the Unionists in 1913-14, which culminated in the rejection of a separate Amending Bill for Ulster. Lloyd George's 1913-14 proposal contained nothing particularly original. In general principle it was very similar to Birrell's suggestion of August 1911, which was probably the basis for the Cabinet proposal of February 1912, made by Lloyd George and Churchill.

However, the Liberals would probably have been well advised to propose something less than Ulster exclusion in April 1912. The scheme known as 'Home Rule within Home

Rule' had much to recommend it as a starting point. This took various forms, but usually included administrative autonomy for part of Ulster, and possibly also a legislative veto, within a Home Rule framework for all Ireland. This would have been acceptable to most Liberals, and would have been far easier for the Nationalists to concede, since it did not violate the principle of a united Ireland. Certainly, by January 1913, John Dillon indicated that he would be prepared to accept such a solution, and Redmond followed suit later in the year.[37] The Unionists would almost certainly have opposed it, but their agreement was not essential in the 1912 session. Moreover, 'Home Rule within Home Rule' did not exclude the possibility of further concessions if these proved necessary.

If such a proposal had been incorporated into the original measure, it would have undermined the most persuasive aspect of the Opposition case. The Unionists could not then plausibly accuse the Liberals of ignoring the genuine grievances of the Protestant minority. This was the only aspect of Unionist propaganda against Home Rule which held powerful appeal to British public opinion. This point is ignored by Jenkins, when he argues that an early concession over Ulster would only result in further demands involving a 're-grouping of forces against other aspects of the bill'. No other issue could have aroused the same degree of British public support or justified threats of an Ulster rebellion. The only obvious alternative battleground was that of finance. The financial provisions were undoubtedly a grave source of weakness in the Bill; but they were scarcely likely to arouse a public outcry of sufficient proportions to destroy Home Rule, or create a civil war. In any case, though Unionist agreement was naturally preferable to hostility, it was essentially irrelevant to the passage of a measure under the Parliament Act, so long as the grounds for civil war were removed.

Making provision for Ulster in the 1912 circuit, rather than at a later stage, had a further advantage from the Liberal viewpoint. During the negotiations of 1913-14 there were two major obstacles to an agreed settlement of the Ulster question – the opposition of the Nationalists on the one hand, and the opposition of the southern Irish Unionists on the other. Bonar Law and Carson might be individually prepared to consider

Ulster exclusion, but their negotiating freedom was restricted by the hostility of the southern Unionists, who had powerful advocates in such men as Walter Long and Lord Lansdowne. The southern Unionists had nothing to gain from compromise, and continued to block the way, when an agreed settlement over Ulster was essential to the peaceful passage of Home Rule. But this obstacle, at least, could have been avoided by inserting provision for Ulster into the original Bill. The southern Unionists would not like it, but the British and Ulster Unionists could rightly claim that they had no choice in the matter. Moreover, the introduction of a Government plan for Ulster in 1912 was likely to split and weaken the Unionist forces. The southern Unionists would be totally opposed, but the attitudes of their brethren in Ulster and Britain would be more ambivalent. If the Ulster Unionists continued to threaten civil war, they might well forfeit the sympathy of the public and the support of the Unionists in Britain.

Admittedly, the opposition of the Irish Nationalists would remain an obstacle, regardless of the timing of an Ulster compromise. Naturally the Government preferred to avoid inflaming relations with their eighty-four Irish Nationalist allies at an early stage. Undoubtedly the Nationalists would have opposed Ulster exclusion in 1912 as vehemently as they fought it from 1913-14. Yet the fact remains that they were forced to acquiesce in 1914 'as the price of peace'. They could probably also have been induced to agree in 1912, had it been put to them as the price of Home Rule, especially if the initial proposal had been 'Home Rule within Home Rule'. Though the Liberals were partially dependent on the Nationalists, they could survive, so long as the Irish only abstained and did not vote in the Opposition lobby. The Nationalists were far more dependent on the Liberals for the grant of Home Rule. Birrell recognised in 1911 'how tremendously important it is for Redmond and his friends not to fail and how far they will go to meet us if they can'. He did not think Redmond would be very hard to deal with, because he was pledged to the hilt to pass Home Rule. In a similar vein, Earl Grey believed that Redmond would be obliged to take whatever Asquith offered him.[38] An anonymous Unionist contributor to the *Quarterly Review* believed the Nationalists could be induced to acquiesce in vital concessions over Ulster: 'They have a better chance now of attaining their supreme object than they ever had before, and they are not likely to throw it away'. Naturally, the official Nationalist Party gave no hint that they would be open to any form of concession over Ulster in 1911-12. But the rebel independent Nationalist, William O'Brien, informed Asquith that the Nationalist leaders had 'pledged their credit beyond recall to carrying a Home Rule Act in the present Parliament', and they would be prepared to concede necessary revisions.[39] In the last resort the Nationalists were likely to accept a modified Home Rule Bill from the Liberals, rather than force an election which would wreck their prospects of Home Rule altogether.

Moreover, it might have been wiser for the Government to force the Nationalists to accept a major compromise at the start, however reluctantly. Instead, a continual series of smaller concessions was wrung from them later. Each one was more humiliating than the last and eroded the Irish leaders' confidence in Asquith's good faith. One hard bargain would have been much better than a series of broken promises. It would not have been easy for either party to agree to insert provision for Ulster into the initial 1912 Bill. The Nationalist leaders would have to face intense criticism within Ireland, and the Government would scarcely relish the prospect of keeping their reluctant Irish allies in line throughout three parliamentary circuits. But the Nationalist leaders were in a far stronger position to win round support in Ireland in 1912 than they had become by 1914. By introducing a Home Rule Bill for a united Ireland, the Government raised expectations which could not be fulfilled, so that any subsequent concessions were seen as treachery to the Nationalist cause. Meanwhile Ulster prepared for civil war and feelings on both sides hardened, as the influence of the extremists in Ireland increased.

From the Government's point of view, it was probably worth taking the risk of offending the Nationalists in 1912, in order to gain the benefits of pushing an Ulster solution through under the Parliament Act. The Government would thereby retain the initiative in deciding the terms for Ulster, and negotiations for an agreed settlement with the Opposition could be avoided. The southern Unionists would be in no position to veto a compromise and the case for an Ulster rebellion would be undermined. The Ulster Unionists could not be expected to like such a settlement; but their justification for opposing it, and their appeal for British support, would be substantially weakened, if the Government could show that it had made a reasonable attempt to deal with their grievances.

7 Cabinet Ignorance and Ulster Information: The Irish Police Reports, 1911-12

It might be argued that the Government could not have excluded Ulster in 1912, because they did not become aware of the seriousness of the opposition there until late in 1913. It may well be true that the Cabinet was ignorant of the full dimensions of the Ulster situation in February 1912. But there was little excuse for such complete ignorance in view of Ulster's opposition to the two earlier Home Rule Bills, and the current publicity surrounding preparations for resistance. There was no excuse for the total failure to make a thorough examination of the Ulster situation in 1911, when the Home Rule committee was meeting to prepare the Bill. If special provision for Ulster had been considered advisable, then the entire Bill would have had to be framed in the light of that decision. The Cabinet discussion on the possible exclusion of Ulster in February 1912 was essentially unreal. It took place at far too late a stage for the evidence to be examined, or for the suggestion to be effectively incorporated into a major Bill to be introduced only two months later.

The Government should have acquainted itself more fully with the existing situation in Ulster before discussing the problem in February 1912. Yet there is no evidence that the Prime Minister even asked the Chief Secretary for such a report throughout 1911. Birrell did not present the first report on the Ulster situation to the Cabinet until after the fateful meeting of 6 February. This suggests, at the very least, that ministers were hardly sufficiently well-informed to take that important decision when they did. They might have been better advised to read the police reports and other material circulated by Birrell before arriving at such a critical conclusion.

The Chief Secretary can obviously be severely criticised for not sending earlier reports to the Cabinet. Charles Hobhouse, who considered Birrell a hopeless administrator, commented after the 6 February Cabinet that the Irish Secretary 'had made no inquiry into the real condition or intentions of Ulster, and roundly declared such to be useless'.[40] This was ungenerous and not entirely justified, since Birrell had been examining police reports for Ulster with considerable care since April 1911. Though he had a good deal of information, its value was very mixed; his own uncertainty about the conclusions to be drawn probably made him reluctant to offer guidance to the Cabinet. Birrell had to overcome many practical problems in assessing the gravity of the Ulster problem. His enquiries were hindered by the rudimentary and haphazard espionage methods employed by the 'Crime Special Branch' of the Royal Irish Constabulary. Reports from county inspectors were based on the observations of their local police, who in turn depended upon civilian informants, whose reliability was uncertain. An equal problem was posed by the fact that the local police in the predominantly Protestant areas of Ulster were likely to sympathise with the Unionist movement they were supposed to be investigating.

These deficiencies were well known to the Chief Secretary, but they were too deep-rooted to be easily altered. Assessment of the real danger in Ulster was made even more difficult by the knowledge that the Ulster Protestants would naturally seek to exaggerate the extent of their preparations, particularly if they really were just bluffing. The Ulstermen made little attempt at secrecy, usually quite the contrary. Police arrangements to have Ulster's activities 'discreetly watched' probably did not upset them unduly. Indeed, those participating in the drilling occasionally supplied the police with the required information.

When Churchill offered to place his secret service machinery at Birrell's disposal in August 1911, Birrell politely refused. The Chief Secretary had already 'directed further investigations to be made as to whether any suspicious acts of preparation are on foot'.[41] The police reports from April 1911 to February 1912 indicated a gradual escalation of drilling, but little evidence of any large-scale purchase of arms. Up to

September 1911, the reports were generally negative. The district inspector of county Fermanagh, for example, believed it was simply 'bluster and bravado' intended to impress British newspapers. The tone of the reports altered after the Unionist demonstration at Craigavon in September 1911, because the majority of marching Ulstermen had quite obviously been drilled. In February 1912, Birrell circulated to the Cabinet a general report on drilling in Ulster, which showed that drilling was being practised in all Ulster counties except Donegal and Monaghan. About 12,000 people were involved, but in most cases they were unarmed. [42]

Birrell also obtained the opinion of the Irish law officers in February 1912, concerning the legality of arming and drilling. If it could be proved that arms were being obtained in order to resist a parliamentary statute by force, or to promote civil war, the parties responsible were guilty of sedition and might be indicted. If action was required, the suspected parties should be arrested and their arms seized, but it would be difficult to prove that the purpose was seditious. The case of drilling was rather different. Under an old statute, unlawful military training was forbidden, unless held under the authority of two county magistrates. These magistrates in Ulster would inevitably give the necessary authority; legal prosecution would end in failure, merely providing welcome publicity for the participants. [43]

Such information formed the basis of the Chief Secretary's reports to the Cabinet in February 1912, but it was plainly conflicting and inadequate. Birrell therefore sought additional advice from leading civil servants in Ireland who had personal knowledge of the Ulster situation. He was probably influenced to some degree by the persistently optimistic view of his permanent Under-Secretary. Sir James Dougherty continued to believe that Ulster was bluffing throughout the years 1912-14, regardless of mounting evidence to the contrary. However, Birrell clearly attached more weight to the opinions of Sir David Harrel, who had formerly been Chief Commissioner of the Dublin Metropolitan Police and Irish Under-Secretary from 1895 to 1902. The Chief Secretary was evidently so worried by the Cabinet decision of 6 February 1912 that he discussed the Ulster situation with

Harrel two days later, asking Harrel to put his views in writing for the Cabinet. Sir David pointed out that the Ulstermen were, so far, protesting as effectively as possible in order to influence the British electorate. They were quite serious, and 'in a general far-off way' might be thinking of a time when it might come to a fight in the open. On the whole Harrel did not consider that 'platform speeches will materialise into deliberate and armed resistance to authority'.[44]

Birrell was no doubt reassured by Harrel and Dougherty, whose views suggested that his own fears, like those of Lloyd George and Churchill, were unnecessarily alarmist. They probably helped him to stifle his misgivings about the Cabinet's decision to make no special provision for Ulster, and to express his acquiescence in that decision more confidently. Less than a year later, however, Sir David Harrel's view of the Ulster situation had swung round to the Lloyd George–Churchill standpoint. The acute differences of opinion between Harrel and Dougherty thereafter were reflected in Birrell's own inner conflict, which the Chief Secretary was never able to resolve.

It could, perhaps, be argued that the Cabinet would merely have been confused if they had seen Birrell's inconclusive police reports before, rather than after, their vital decision of 6 February. That decision can certainly be justified, as Roy Jenkins has shown. It would have reflected greater credit on Asquith's Cabinet had it represented a carefully planned strategy, based on the fullest available information. Instead it was a decision taken almost by default with the false confidence generated by ignorance.

8 Conclusion: The Ulster Question – Liberal Failure by Omission

Asquith's Government entered the Home Rule battle in April 1912 totally unprepared to deal with the Ulster question. No more attention had been devoted to the issue in 1912 than in 1886. Up to the time the Home Rule Bill was introduced in parliament, the Prime Minister and most of his colleagues almost entirely overlooked the problem of Ulster. The Cabinet committee which drafted the measure was absorbed by United Kingdom devolution and the financial provisions. Up to April 1912, the Ulster issue was scarcely mentioned in the private correspondence and diaries of prominent Liberals — in stark contrast with the monotonous repetition of the Ulster theme in Unionist correspondence.

The only ministers who were seriously concerned about the problem of north-east Ireland were Birrell, Lloyd George, Churchill, and possibly Grey. Lloyd George and Churchill were annoyed that the Ulster question should remain a potential obstacle to a Home Rule settlement, and a gift to their Unionist opponents. But Lloyd George had little patience with Asquith's uncertain Ulster policy and took almost no part in its control from February 1912 up to autumn 1913. The Chancellor turned his attention back to insurance and land reform, while Grey was equally preoccupied with foreign affairs. Birrell remained very uneasy, despite his acquiescence in the February 1912 decision. Only Churchill continued to exert pressure on his colleagues to reconsider their Ulster policy.

The Government's failure even to examine the Ulster situation, before April 1912, was an important error of omission. The decision to make no provision for Ulster in the Home Rule Bill involved a massive and dangerous gamble. It assumed that Ulster's grievances were exaggerated, and that the Ulstermen would not actually carry out their threats of rebellion. The fact that the Cabinet almost certainly did not appreciate the degree of risk involved hardly exonerates them from criticism.

Asquith's Ulster policy is perfectly explicable in terms of the Prime Minister's personality and characteristic political behaviour, as illustrated by Sir Almeric Fitzroy's comment in January 1912:

Lord Morley confirmed all I have heard of Asquith's indolence in shirking a difficulty, confident in his ability to furnish at least some provisional solution when the situation created by neglect threatens to get out of hand. [45]

But such a cavalier and casual treatment of the Ulster problem was dangerous. While Asquith's Cabinet concentrated on other aspects of Home Rule between February and April 1912, the noisy Unionist campaign gave it top priority. On 9 April

1912, an impressive Unionist demonstration took place at Balmoral near Belfast. Bonar Law and Walter Long pledged the full support of the official Unionist Party in the cause of Ulster, after an enthusiastic military march-past of 80,000 men. Bonar Law denounced the Liberal attempt to pass Home Rule as 'naked tyranny' and threatened to do 'all that man can do to defeat a conspiracy as treacherous as has ever been formed against the life of a great nation'.[46] Two days later, Asquith introduced the Home Rule Bill in the House of Commons. The Liberals hoped for the best, though they were disastrously unprepared to face the Unionist onslaught on the Ulster question.

III
THE FIRST PARLIAMENTARY CIRCUIT

'It is absolutely incredible that the Minister in charge of the Bill, and still more that the Prime Minister, could have left their treatment of the proposed exclusion of Ulster to the inspiration of the moment, or even, and this is more absurd, to the trend of the Debate, as the trend of the Debate developed in the House of Commons.' (F.E. Smith, 18 June 1912, *Hansard*, XXIX, 1505).

The parliamentary debate on Home Rule has been ignored by historians, but it deserves serious attention. This first parliamentary circuit was particularly crucial, since it afforded the second and last opportunity for the Government to incorporate special provision for Ulster into the Home Rule Bill. The Parliament Act provided that the Commons could amend a Bill before it was sent to the Lords for the first time. After that the Bill could only be altered by means of 'suggestions' which required the Lords' agreement. Provided the Nationalists did not actually vote with the Opposition, a Government amendment on Ulster would have passed in 1912, automatically becoming law in 1914 under the terms of the Parliament Act. After the first circuit ended in January 1913 any such amendment required Opposition agreement, allowing the Unionists to dictate their own terms and creating the danger that an acceptable compromise might not even prove possible.

The 1912 debate in the Commons allowed each party to put its case for or against Home Rule, before passions in Ireland became so inflamed that emotion became stronger than reason. The Unionist case concentrated from the first on the Ulster question. The Government, by contrast, attempted to ignore the Ulster issue altogether. Unionist pressure and criticism from the Liberal backbenches rapidly forced ministers to consider the Ulster problem more seriously. The problems of dealing with the Ulster question in Parliament rapidly became clear. Most members of both main parties were sincere in their public attitudes to Ulster in 1912, but they were frequently unable to acknowledge the sincerity of their opponents. Their viewpoints were based on fundamental assumptions so totally at variance that they did not allow meaningful discussion. The Unionist position involved elements of hysteria and fanaticism, while that of the Liberals was too often based on ignorance and uncertainty. Each party waited to see if the other would introduce an amendment in Committee making special provision for Ulster. But if the Government took the initiative in moving such an amendment, it would imply that their original Bill was badly deficient. The Unionists were scarcely eager to move an amendment which involved tacitly accepting Home Rule for most of Ireland, and helping the Government to solve the embarrassing Ulster question. Moreover, the British parties had to consider the hostility of the Ulster Unionists to Home Rule and the fierce opposition of the Nationalists and southern Unionists to any form of Irish partition.

The Home Rule debate opened at a time when the Liberal Party's confidence had been substantially restored after several depressing months. In January 1912 many Liberals were generally gloomy about their political prospects, particularly as they believed the parliamentary session was heavily overloaded. The other two major measures to be introduced under the Parliament Act, the Franchise Bill and the Bill to dis-establish the Welsh Church, were almost as controversial as Home Rule. Sir Courtenay Ilbert, the Clerk of the Commons, was very depressed early in February; the Insurance Act was unpopular, by-elections were going badly, industrial unrest was still a problem, and the Cabinet was sharply split over female suffrage.[1] During the next two months the political outlook brightened considerably and Asquith was praised for having overcome the coal strike and restored his party's confidence.

Contemporary impressions of the Home Rule debate varied considerably. Gladstone's daughter was acutely aware of the nostalgic influence of the past when Asquith rose to introduce the Bill: 'All through one saw another figure, heard another voice. There was an overpowering sense of *his* presence – if it had not been for 1886 and 1893, today could not have witnessed this Bill.' Henry Lucy inevitably recalled 'memories of days and Bills and men that are no more', and Charles Masterman felt that 'every kind of ghost seemed to rise up of the old days and the old fights'. John Burns calculated that sixty-seven of the existing members sat in the Commons in 1893. These survivors viewed the earlier struggles through the rose-tinted spectacles of advancing years, and found the 1912 debate less exciting. The sense of drama and novelty had gone. Observers of all ages commented on the monotony and repetition. Professor A.V. Dicey was doubtful 'whether human ingenuity could now produce on Irish Home Rule either a new argument or a new fallacy', and speakers commonly complained that everything had already been said.[2]

1 Debates on First and Second Reading, April–May 1912: The Unionist Challenge on Ulster and the Government's Reluctant Response

The First Reading was a three-day full-dress debate from 11-16 April, which naturally attracted considerable attention. Government supporters generally condemned the 'unmannerly Tories' and the 'calculated rudeness of the Orange Gang led by Capt. Craig'. Enthusiasm diminished rapidly, however, as the initial novelty vanished. By the end of the First Reading, John Burns was already complaining that the House was 'not at all excited nor interested in Home Rule. A jaded House, overworked Ministry, stale subject, indifferent public.' Several observers commented on the lack of enthusiasm on the Liberal benches, caused because 'Liberals have so long thought it the right thing to do'. This apathy helps to explain the strange dearth of comment on the debate in the private letters and diaries of Liberal politicians. Interest declined still further during the Second Reading, which was allocated seven Parliamentary days between 30 April and 9 May. The *Western Daily Mercury* lamented that the debate was demonstrating 'an unrivalled capacity for dullness', and the *British Weekly* marvelled that so many members possessed the facility for saying nothing at extreme length.[3]

The Unionists displayed far more interest in the Home Rule

debates from the start, because they loathed the Bill so intensely and felt particularly strongly on the question of Ulster. The Unionist case started from the fundamental assumption that any kind of Home Rule was unnecessary and wrong, and that this particular measure was confused and unworkable. The Opposition contended that Ireland merely required further development of the social and economic reforms carried out since 1890, particularly the completion of land purchase. They maintained that Home Rule would inevitably lead to the separation of Ireland from Great Britain and encourage the disintegration of the Empire.

The question of Ulster was, from the first, one of the most fundamental Unionist arguments against the Home Rule Bill. The Unionist case on Ulster was explained explosively and exhaustively throughout the First and Second Reading debates. The *Nation* commented that the Opposition chose 'to stake its entire case upon the wild advocacy of extreme Ulsteria'.[4] The Unionist position on Ulster was consistent, forceful and clear. Seven of the fifteen Unionist speakers on the First Reading and about a dozen Second Reading speakers either represented Ulster constituencies or had strong personal connections with the province. Attention was deliberately concentrated on the one issue of Ulster. The problem of the Protestant Unionist minority in the south and west of Ireland was carefully ignored by almost all Unionist speakers during these early stages of the debate.

The starting-point of the Unionist case on Ulster was that Ireland consisted not of one nation, but two. The Ulster Protestants were separated as much by race, religion and history from the Catholic Nationalists as the latter were from the people of Great Britain. Walter Guinness declared that '. . . in Ireland you have two camps, two races, and two religions', separated for six centuries by bitter differences, which were accentuated because racial and religious cleavages largely corresponded. As Leopold Amery pointed out, any recognition of an 'Irish' nationality involved depriving Ulster of her British nationality. Carson and Bonar Law drove this point home by contending that all the arguments for giving Home Rule to Ireland could just as well be applied to granting separate treatment for Protestant Ulster. The Unionists claimed that religious persecution of the Protestant minority by a Catholic dominated Dublin Parliament was inevitable because of the deeply-rooted religious feud. The Irish Protestants firmly believed that Home Rule involved a threat to their liberty, security and religion and could conceive of no safeguards which could effectively protect them.[5]

Considerable energy was devoted to constant repetition of the theme that the Ulster Protestants viewed the Bill 'with loathing and bitter resentment'. The Unionists insisted they were prepared to use all means to resist the attempt to impose Home Rule on Ulster. Captain O'Neill warned the Government to remember there was a party in Ulster 'determined to go to any length rather than submit to this Bill'. Moreover, several prominent British Unionists gave full support to Ulster Unionist threats. L.S. Amery declared that 'this measure is so great a crime that the people of Ulster are justified in resistance to it by any means at their disposal'. Bonar Law insisted that Ulster would not submit to Home Rule, and Ulstermen were prepared to die for their cause. The Unionists also claimed that the Liberal Government would bear full responsibility for the inevitable bloodshed if they tried to force Home Rule on Ulster. Ministers were told that 'if you go on with this Bill, it means Civil War', and that if these grim warnings were ignored, 'the blood of the explosion will be on their own heads'.[6]

The Ulster Unionists were undoubtedly genuine in their determination to resist Home Rule, but at this stage there was an element of unreality in their threats of civil war, based on the Unionist conviction that a Liberal Government would never dare to coerce Ulster. Bonar Law declared that it was a practical impossibility for a Liberal Government to order the armed forces to shoot down men whose only crime was loyalty, and he believed the Bill would be shipwrecked on that rock. Austen Chamberlain also warned that British public opinion would not tolerate the coercion of Ulster and that 'you and your Bill together, will go to wreck in the storm you have caused'.[7] Throughout the First and Second Readings then, the Unionist position was simple opposition to Home Rule. They were encouraged in this by their assumption that Home Rule would never pass, if only because they believed the Government would shrink from forcing its measure on Ulster. At this stage they hoped that their opposition would induce the Government to drop Home Rule altogether, eliminating the necessity to consider a compromise settlement for Ulster.

The Liberal position on the Ulster question, by its very nature, defies similar analysis in terms of a series of coherent, logically developed arguments. The Liberals were incapable of any common, well-defined response to counter the Opposition onslaught, since they had given little sustained consideration to the Ulster problem before April 1912. They were almost totally unprepared to meet the Unionist challenge on Ulster in the First Reading debate and Ulster was scarcely mentioned by the six Liberal speakers. The Liberal silence on the Ulster question on First Reading indicated ignorance, uncertainty and lack of forethought. The problem was compounded because any Liberal admission that Ulster might have a genuine case involved the implication that the Bill was defective on a fundamental point. The Unionists naturally made capital out of this, increasing their pressure, until the Liberals were forced to make reluctant attempts on Second Reading to answer the Opposition case more fully. The Ulster question fairly rapidly became the dominant issue of the Second Reading debate.

On the First Reading, two out of the six Liberal speakers entirely ignored Ulster, two made exceptionally brief references to the problem, and only Asquith and Birrell attempted to consider it at all seriously. When he introduced the Bill on 11 April the Prime Minister attempted to justify his Ulster policy in a brief statement which reflected his public attitude up to March 1914. Asquith declared that he had never underestimated the determined hostility felt by north-east Ulster to Home Rule: 'But we cannot admit, and we will not admit, the right of a minority of the people, and relatively a small minority . . . to veto the verdict of the vast body of their countrymen'. The Chief Secretary's speech, which wound up the First Reading on 16 April, was even more unsatisfactory. Birrell devoted one-third of an uninspired speech to the Ulster problem, which he could hardly avoid in view of the inflamed speeches by Walter Long and Bonar Law which preceded his own. Birrell denied the charge that the Catholic majority would persecute the Ulster Protestants and protested against threats of 'hypothetical and anticipatory treason' before any coercive action took place. He insisted that Ulster had no cause for alarm.[8] The Opposition was far from satisfied by the Government's treatment of the Ulster problem on First Reading. *The Times*, as usual, was sympathetic to the Unionist viewpoint, complaining that Government policy was 'to brush Ulster aside'. But *The Times* found consolation in the belief that Ulster's determined stand was producing 'gloomy forebodings' in Government circles: 'misgivings and scruples notoriously haunt the consciences' of several Liberal supporters, '. . . we question whether the uneasiness of the Liberal soul will not become greater as time goes on'.[9]

The First Reading division, taken on 16 April, gave the Unionists little encouragement and merely hinted at the existence of some Liberal misgivings about Ulster. The First Reading passed by 360 votes to 266, indicating that the Opposition turned out to vote in greater force than the ministerialists. Even *The Times* correctly predicted that any cross-voting or deliberate abstentions on the part of the Government supporters would be confined to two or three recalcitrants. The Liberal coalition was reported as being solid, with 'no caves, nor hole and corner meetings' as in 1886 and 1893. Admittedly eight Liberal members were absent unpaired, but only three of these were regarded as hostile to the Bill.[10] These three were Sir George Kemp, Captain D.V. Pirie and Thomas Agar-Robartes, all of whom explained their abstentions in their Second Reading speeches. Sir Clifford Cory was the only Liberal member so adamantly opposed to Home Rule that he actually voted against the Bill on First Reading. But at this stage these were still isolated and unexplained straws in the wind.

Government whipping was more efficient on the Second Reading, so that the division on 9 May revealed even less of the growing uncertainty about Ulster in some sections of the party. The Second Reading was carried by 372 votes to 271, showing an increased majority of seven over the previous division. This time Sir George Kemp was the only Liberal member known to have deliberately abstained, while Sir

Clifford Cory was again the one Liberal to vote with the Unionists. The *Nation* congratulated the ministry on the excellent majority of 101, 'representing the practically undivided force of the Liberal, Labor [sic], and Nationalist parties'.[11]

But the Second Reading debate had already indicated that this excellent division list was deceptive. Unionist pressure forced the Liberals to make more specific statements about Ulster in the course of the debate, which lasted intermittently from 30 April to 9 May. Signs of uneasiness were revealed by the Liberal front bench, as well as the rank and file. The Government was obliged to show its hand more openly and several cracks appeared in the ministerial front, which had previously been thought solid. Two leading ministers conceded that some sort of compromise might be required to deal with the Ulster problem. Moreover, those Liberal members with reservations about Home Rule took this opportunity to explain their positions. Several Liberal backbenchers stated explicitly that Ulster exclusion was the only solution. The exclusion of Ulster was thus proposed for the first time from the Liberal benches on Second Reading.

The weak links in the ministry's previously united public front were Churchill and Grey. In the course of a powerful speech on 30 April, Churchill admitted that the 'perfectly genuine apprehensions' of the Ulster Protestants constituted the only serious obstacle to an Irish settlement. It was impossible for the Government to ignore the sincere sentiments of such a well-defined community, especially as the Ulster Protestants exercised such a powerful influence on the Unionist Party. Churchill asked whether the four Protestant counties of north-east Ulster claimed separate treatment for themselves, either by obtaining a parliament of their own, or by remaining under the Westminster Parliament. He declared that it would be disastrous for Ireland if the Ulster Protestants took either of these courses, but if the Ulstermen refused this great challenge they had no right to obstruct Home Rule for the rest of Ireland: 'Half a province cannot impose a permanent veto on the nation'.[12]

It is unlikely that the Prime Minister had advance warning of these highly controversial remarks. This was one of the many occasions when Churchill chose to act independently on the Irish question. Asquith may have been embarrassed, but cannot have been altogether surprised. He knew Churchill's views on Ulster and was familiar with the eccentricities of the First Lord's volatile personality. The Opposition noted the contrast between Churchill's attitude to Ulster and that of his colleagues, but they had no idea whether Churchill's words heralded a change of heart on the part of the Cabinet. A.J. Balfour observed that it was extraordinary procedure for the Government to admit that Ulster was a formidable problem and yet wait until Second Reading to ask the Opposition how they proposed to deal with it. Finally, Balfour challenged Sir Edward Grey, who followed him on the third day of the debate, to tell the House whether he agreed with Churchill that Ulster could not be ignored; Grey should explain how he proposed to solve the riddle left unanswered by Churchill.[13]

Balfour's remarks no doubt left several ministers feeling uncomfortable and induced Grey to attempt a reply to the challenge. No evidence survives to show Grey's attitude towards Ulster exclusion at the February 1912 Cabinet, but by the time he spoke on Second Reading on 2 May, he had evidently moved some way towards the position held by Churchill and Lloyd George. Grey insisted that Ulster's cooperation was important to the successful operation of Home Rule, and he made an important statement which was to be frequently quoted in subsequent debates: 'If Ulster defeats the solution which we propose or makes it impossible, we cannot afford to continue the present state of affairs. Some other solution will have to be found which will free this House and put the control of Irish affairs in Irish hands . . .' As the Opposition were quick to point out, however, Grey said no more than Churchill to suggest what that 'other solution' might be. No further enlightenment was provided by the remaining six ministers who spoke on Second Reading. They either continued to ignore Ulster altogether, or sought the usual refuge in reassuring platitudes, or dismissed Ulster's threats as mere 'midsummer madness'.[14]

The Government had revealed itself far from united on the question of Ulster and decidedly uncertain how to follow through the negative policy determined in the February

Cabinet. No attempt was made to follow up the hints of Churchill and Grey that an alternative solution might have to be found. Indeed, Asquith appeared to believe that the onus for proposing a settlement of the Ulster problem lay with the Unionists. The Opposition were confused and finally concluded bitterly that Churchill had misled them as to the Government's intentions. Sir Almeric Fitzroy noted in his diary that the Second Reading debate had not strengthened the position of the Government:

. . . upon the question of Ulster the hints at concession which prominent Ministers have given are evidence of incertitude that cannot fail to have disastrous effects. It is difficult to see how such offers could be made unless the Government are seriously frightened by the attitude of the Ulstermen; and how then is it reconcilable with prudent statesmanship to leave such a factor out of calculation in formulating a plan for the self-government of Ireland?[15]

2 Dissident Backbenchers: Nonconformity, Federalism and the Celtic Fringe

Though the Second Reading division list revealed little evidence of dissension in the Liberal ranks, the speeches told a different story. It was scarcely surprising that the rank and file were bewildered and uncertain, given the absence of any clear ministerial lead on the Ulster question. But whereas Churchill and Grey had to content themselves with broad hints, a number of Liberal backbenchers expressed strong criticism of the Government's Ulster policy.

Sir George Kemp and Sir Clifford Cory were the most extreme. They could not stomach Home Rule at any price. Kemp opposed Home Rule as firmly as did Cory, though he refrained from voting against the Government. Instead, Kemp explained his position in his Second Reading speech, while abstaining on all crucial Home Rule votes taken before his resignation in July 1912. Unlike Cory and Agar-Robartes, who had always been at least nominal Liberals, Kemp had been a Liberal Unionist until he resigned over tariff reform in 1905. He was reluctantly persuaded to stand as the Liberal free trade candidate for the vital marginal seat of Manchester North-West in the 1910 elections. Soon after his victories

Kemp expressed his desire to return to his work as a Lancashire textile manufacturer, especially as his views on Ireland were entirely Unionist. The Cabinet had to weigh the inevitable loss of his seat against the damage which might be caused by Kemp's opposition in the Home Rule debates. Again and again he was persuaded to postpone his resignation from 1910 to 1912 by the promise of a rather elusive peerage. This promise was not made conditional on his Home Rule vote, but Asquith evidently hoped that Kemp would remain silent in the debate. However, Kemp finally decided to speak against the Bill on Second Reading because of the Government's Ulster policy. He told the House that he would have remained silent about his opposition to Home Rule if only Ulster had been allowed to contract out of the Bill. Kemp believed the Protestants of North-East Ulster were just as much a nation as the rest of Ireland. They would resist Home Rule to the point of fighting, and it would not 'be right of us as a nation to try and force it upon them'. [16] Fortunately for the Government, Sir George Kemp's convictions were too widely respected to allow the Opposition to reap political advantage from his speech, or the Liberals to indulge in recrimination. Kemp's position in the Liberal Party was quite unique and his belated promotion to the peerage in 1913 should not be interpreted as the convenient removal of a party rebel.

The opposition to Home Rule of Sir Clifford Cory and Thomas Agar-Robartes was a more obvious open rebellion from within the Liberal ranks. Both men represented Cornish constituencies, and their reasons for opposing Home Rule developed out of this Cornish background. Cornwall and Devon were centres of stern nonconformity, encouraged by a vigorous Methodist revival. Wesleyanism, the militant, political sect of Methodism, was virulently anti-Catholic and Wesleyanism was predominant in Cornwall. Cornish Wesleyans identified Irish Home Rule with 'Rome Rule' and were adamantly opposed to both. Cornwall was strongly Liberal, but its hostility to Home Rule had encouraged the development of Liberal Unionism in the region from 1886. Sir Clifford Cory voted consistently against Home Rule from 1912 to 1914, though he did not actually speak against it in the House until February 1914. This somewhat bigoted speech left no doubt that a fierce anti-Catholicism was at the root of his hostility. Though Cory was at least nominally Liberal, he took care to explain at each election that he opposed Home Rule. The strong Protestant Liberal Unionism of St. Ives allowed him to win all three elections between 1906 and 1910 on a remarkably individualistic platform. Both Cory and Agar-Robartes had also been keen Liberal Imperialists, and their religious hostility to Home Rule was reinforced by their strong connections with Lord Rosebery and Sir Robert Perks. Their imperialism, their ardent nonconformity, their Roseberyite hostility to 'New Liberalism' and their open opposition to Home Rule, formed a combination which set them apart from most other Liberals. Cory's hostile votes on Home Rule in 1912-14 were no surprise to his party. The *Nation* described him as a nominal Liberal who had ceased to be a Liberal by April 1912.[17]

Thomas Agar-Robartes was not at first ready to speak quite as strongly as Kemp or Cory against Home Rule, but gradually he adopted the same position. As Lord Clifden's eldest son, he was the heir to a great Cornish estate. He sat for St. Austell, the safest Liberal seat in the south-west, from 1908 till his death in 1915. He was popular in the House and had many friends on the Unionist side. Agar-Robartes opposed Home Rule because he was an ardent nonconformist and a former Liberal Imperialist, with a strong devotion to Lord Rosebery. His views on Home Rule were fairly well known and his hostile speech on Second Reading was not unexpected, if unwelcome. He told the House on 2 May that British people were 'bored to tears with the Irish question', and wished to be rid of it, so they could turn to their own affairs.

The emphasis Agar-Robartes placed on the Ulster problem was not anticipated. He declared that he would provisionally support the Second Reading, but would vote against Home Rule at later stages, unless the Government met the grievances of the Ulster Protestants. He dismissed the 'simple' argument that the Ulster Protestants were bluffing and denounced the Government's attempts to ignore the genuine convictions of the Irish Protestants. Amidst a roar of Opposition cheering, Agar-Robartes declared that there was only one way out and that was 'to leave the North-East of Ulster out of your scheme'.[18] This speech was highly significant, because it foreshadowed his subsequent amendment in Committee a month later. However, it failed to alert ministers to possible dangers ahead, and the press took little notice.

There is strong evidence that the nonconformity of the south-west had a decided influence on the attitude of its Liberal representatives towards Home Rule. Other Liberal members for the south-west were subject to the same regional nonconformist pressures as Agar-Robartes and Cory. F.D. Acland, the member for Cornwall North-West, showed his concern for the position of Protestant Ulster in his Yeovil speech in April 1912, while Sir George Lambert indicated his lack of interest in Ireland in a speech to his constituents of Devon North a year earlier.[19] The nonconformity of Scotland, Wales and the north of England had a similar effect, though it was less pronounced than in Cornwall.[20] Nonconformity was undoubtedly also a strong element in the reluctance of individual Liberals, like Lloyd George and Sir Joseph Compton-Rickett, to force Protestant Ulster to join Home Rule. Lloyd George's roots in Welsh nonconformity contributed to his lack of active enthusiasm for Irish Catholic nationalism. His awareness of the antipathy of nonconformist Liberal voters for a Catholic dominated Irish Parliament almost certainly affected his calculations on Home Rule. Sir Joseph Compton-Rickett, a prominent Congregationalist and chairman of the nonconformist Liberal members, wrote to *The Times* in October 1912: 'A defeat through the Nationalist vote would be a far less evil than forcing the Bill through, with the certainty of trouble and bad blood for many years to come'.[21]

The influence of nonconformity on the attitudes adopted by Liberal members towards the Irish question should not, however, be exaggerated. It was most powerful in the south-west and the north of England, and probably rather less so in Wales and Scotland where other forces were also operating. There is little evidence that it had much impact on members from other regions. By 1912 nonconformity was probably a stronger force among Liberal voters than among Liberal members, though naturally the parliamentary party took the religious views of its supporters into account.

Nonconformist Liberal members officially welcomed the Bill in May 1912, and the nonconformist *British Weekly* supported Home Rule.[22]

The Government's Ulster policy helped, then, to determine the attitudes of Kemp, Cory and Agar-Robartes – the three most prominent Liberal rebels. The failure to make provision for Ulster forced all three to adopt a more extreme position than they might otherwise have done. Cory actually voted with the Opposition, Kemp spoke out openly against the Bill, and Agar-Robartes moved ultimately from a position of conditional support to one of outright hostility.

The federalists, on the other hand, formed a much larger and less hostile group of critics, for whom Ulster was only an incidental aspect of a far wider problem. They criticised the Bill for not being sufficiently 'federalist' and concentrated their attacks on those features, such as the financial clauses, which would endanger a federal scheme. These were the points emphasised in their Second Reading speeches, and only D.V. Pirie's contribution indicated the strong line on Ulster they subsequently adopted in the debate on the Agar-Robartes' amendment. The federalists did, however, have two reasons for sympathising with the Ulster cause. Firstly, most federalists came from Wales and Scotland, where nonconformity was strong. More important was the consideration that separate treatment for Ulster would strengthen the federalist demand for individual parliaments for all parts of the United Kingdom. Ulster could easily be fitted into a general scheme of Home Rule all round. Captain Pirie was the only federalist to discuss Ulster on Second Reading. He insisted that the Ulster question might have been solved if the Bill had been framed on true federal lines, allowing Ulster separate treatment within a federal system. Pirie added significantly: '. . . and if there were no other solution, then I think Ulster should have the option of standing out, though I do not think she will accept it'.[23] His support for the Bill on Second Reading was definitely qualified, like that of Agar-Robartes. He became progressively more hostile in subsequent speeches, as the Government failed to do anything to meet Ulster's objections.

The overall Liberal response to the carefully developed

Unionist case was hesitant and uninformed. Apart from the dissidents, who were mainly nonconformists or federalists from the Celtic fringe, most Liberals who spoke on First and Second Readings paid little attention to the Ulster question. Many ignored the subject entirely and others ridiculed the Ulster threats as pure bluff. The confused and divided party position on Ulster was faithfully reflected in the *Nation*, the Liberal weekly, which became almost schizophrenic in its comments on Ulster. Lewis Harcourt, the Colonial Secretary, confused matters further by his well-publicised remarks at Rossendale on 4 May. He declared that the 'bombastic threats' of Ulster were founded on nothing more substantial than 'the nightmare of unrealised and unrealisable suspicion'. He dismissed the Ulster question as a mere detail and would not admit that the 'parliamentary mouthings' of the Orange members represented the considered opinion of Ulster. *The Times* condemned Harcourt's folly in speaking of Ulster's attitude with such levity.[24]

3 Agar-Robartes' Amendment for the Exclusion of North-East Ulster, June 1912

The Committee stage of the Bill commenced a month after the Second Reading ended on 9 May. The Cabinet allocated seven days of debate to the first clause of the Home Rule Bill, dealing with the establishment of the Irish Parliament. These included three days devoted to the amendment moved by Agar-Robartes, which was taken on 11, 13 and 18 June. He proposed to exclude the four Ulster counties of Antrim, Armagh, Londonderry and Down, from the jurisdiction of the Irish Parliament. Most biographers and historians have since assumed that this was a significant development, worthy of mention even in the briefest accounts of the 1912-14 Home Rule crisis. Yet rarely have they tried to explain precisely why it was significant.

The amendment was an honest, if politically misguided, attempt by Agar-Robartes to persuade his party leaders to reconsider their Ulster policy. However, it was interpreted by many contemporaries on both sides, and by many historians, as a potential trap. From the Unionist point of view, if they supported it, they could be accused of abandoning the sacred cause of the Union, and betraying their fellow Protestants in the south-west of Ireland. If they opposed it, they would appear to be rejecting the offer of a solution by peaceful means, in favour of a similar result achieved through threats and violence. The Government was also faced with a dilemma, though there is no evidence that they fully recognised it as such. Support for the amendment would imply that their original Bill was faulty on a fundamental point and would obviously create conflict with their Nationalist allies. But if the Government rejected the motion they could be accused of refusing to deal with a problem which might otherwise wreck their entire measure. The Unionists undoubtedly appreciated the significance and the potential tactical pitfalls of the amendment more fully and more rapidly than the Government ever did. It was tactically advantageous to either party that such an amendment should be moved from the enemy camp. The Cabinet's apparent failure to appreciate this, and to ensure that Agar-Robartes' amendment was quietly withdrawn, led some Unionists and subsequent historians to conclude wrongly that a sinister plot was in the making.

Despite the Opposition advantage in having the amendment proposed from the Government benches, they still had to deal with the potential problems it posed. Regardless of its source, the Unionists from the south and west of Ireland inevitably saw the amendment as 'a trap designed to secure an admission that the Northern Unionists were willing to abandon the Unionists in the rest of Ireland to their fate'. Walter Long, who wrote anxiously to Bonar Law from Switzerland on 4 June 1912, shared this view:

I hope the Ulster men will not be caught by the very open trap set for them by Agar-Robartes' amendment. If they are it will mean that for the first time in the history of the H[ome] R[ule] question our Party will be divided. As an Englishman I cannot assent to H.R. in any form, and as one connected by the closest ties with the Provinces of Leinster and Munster I cannot sacrifice my friends there.[25]

Long's views were to have a significant influence on Unionist Irish policy in the long-term, but on this occasion his desire to see the amendment rejected was over-ruled. The Opposition leaders decided to accept Agar-Robartes' amendment. They concluded that the advantages of acceptance outweighed the disadvantage of highlighting the southern Unionist problem. Many Unionists clearly shared Moreton Frewen's view that the Agar-Robartes' amendment '. . . *splits the other fellows*. It is as good a stick as possible with which to beat Redmond. It is full of "good politics".' Walter Long was, therefore, persuaded to support the official party line in the interests of unity.[26]

Unionist support for the amendment was justified in two different ways – on grounds of merit, and tactics. It is important to emphasise that all but one of the British Unionist speakers supported it seriously on its merits, as an attempt to mitigate the evils of Home Rule. Bonar Law declared that this amendment would not remove his opposition to the Bill, but if Home Rule had to come, then this amendment might make it 'less bad' by helping to prevent civil war.[27] This debate, then, marks the significant point at which the *British* Unionists tacitly conceded the principle of Home Rule, by concentrating on Ulster. Several Ulster Unionists already agreed that it was better to salvage part of Ulster from the wreckage, but this was not a view generally shared in Ulster until December 1912.

Only four of the twenty-five Unionist speakers adopted the purely tactical approach of supporting the amendment as a wrecking measure, which might be expected to ruin Home Rule completely. But since Carson's speech was among these four, and was one of the few to receive historical notice, it created the misleading impression that Unionist policy was purely negative and destructive. Carson, Hayes-Fisher, Charles Craig and Walter Guinness argued that Home Rule could never be passed if Ulster was excluded. The Nationalists would reject it, the deplorable finances of the Bill would be reduced to even greater chaos, and the necessary recasting of the Bill would shatter it.[28] The supreme advantage of the wrecking tactic was that it neatly eliminated the difficulty posed by the southern Unionists. It enabled Unionists to deny that they had deserted the southern Unionists, since they supported the amendment only in order to destroy Home Rule altogether. But this wrecking manoeuvre was possibly too clever, as Walter Long had feared before the debate, and it carried its own problems. It threw suspicion on the motives of those Unionists who were attempting to consider the amendment seriously on its merits. Most important, it enabled the government (if only belatedly) to evade some of the fundamental issues by adopting a similar tactical approach.

The first day's debate revealed the Liberals in complete disarray. Speeches from the backbenches suggested that the Government's forces were in retreat or open rebellion and there was no clear guidance from the front bench to rally the wavering supporters. There is no evidence that the Government shared the Opposition's awareness of the potential pitfalls involved in the debate, or that they had even discussed their policy and tactics in advance. The surviving private papers, letters and diaries of leading Liberals do not even mention the Agar-Robartes' amendment before 11 June, and they provide almost no comment on the debate itself in the following week.

The Government scarcely emerged with credit on the first day of the debate, on 11 June. The speeches of Asquith, Birrell and Simon provided little guidance or discipline for their rank and file, and suggested that they were totally unprepared for a discussion of the Ulster problem. Birrell's feeble speech can only be explained by his lack of conviction about the Ulster policy he was supposed to be defending. This was the first time he was forced to deal specifically with the Ulster question in a public speech, but he merely argued that far more evidence was required to prove that Ulster really wanted exclusion. The Prime Minister was even more evasive, and made no attempt to answer the questions of the Opposition or the criticisms of his own supporters. The only argument he advanced for rejecting the amendment was the flat assertion that Ireland could not be split because of the 'fundamental unity of race, temperament and tradition'. The comment of *The Times* on the front bench speeches was partisan, but justified: '. . . we find nothing but embarrassment and the most extraordinary ineptitude and paucity of argument'.[29]

All seven Liberals who spoke from the backbenches, on the other hand, shared some sympathy for the Ulster exclusion amendment. Four of them explicitly supported it, thereby aligning themselves with the Unionists. All seven were Scottish, except for Agar-Robartes. The Cornish member described his amendment as an honest attempt to remove the major storm centre in the path of Home Rule, which would otherwise lead to civil war. He justified his proposal on the grounds that Ireland consisted of two nations, and that the most determined Protestant resistance to Home Rule was concentrated in the four counties specified. Agar-Robartes received unconditional support from three Liberals who were all Scottish and all federalists – D.V. Pirie, Munro-Ferguson and W.H. Cowan. All four voted and spoke in support of the amendment, in direct opposition to their party's official position. D.V. Pirie was particularly hostile in seconding the motion, because he still believed a federal scheme would settle the Ulster question, but had become disillusioned by the Government's 'studied silence' on Home Rule all round. W.H. Cowan argued that the purely temporary exclusion of the four counties was a reasonable price to pay to ensure that Home Rule could be established without armed resistance. Like most Liberals, Cowan assumed that the excluded Ulster counties would eventually choose to join the Dublin Parliament.[30]

Agar-Robartes and the Scottish members who shared his views hoped that the amendment would be considered genuinely on its merits. Though several Liberals thought Agar-Robartes' action naive or misguided, speakers as varied as Birrell and Captain Craig expressed their belief that the proposal was made in good faith. Only Thomas Lough gave way to bitterness in his scathing remarks about his fellow Liberals 'who thrust a proposal upon the floor of the House to give their own party trouble and to give delight to their opponents'. No doubt other Liberals shared Lough's view that the indifference of the dissidents to party interests and tactics approached naivety.[31] Yet their views were consistently held, as well as sincere. Six months later, Agar-Robartes, Pirie, Munro-Ferguson, Jardine and Cowan abstained on Carson's amendment.

Fortunately for the Government, the time-table allowed a brief respite before the debate resumed on 13 June, thus providing an opportunity for a somewhat belated assessment of the situation. The speeches of Carson and Redmond, which opened the second day's debate on 13 June, marked the turning point. They suggested to the Cabinet the most effective tactics to employ, and from that point the Liberal speakers followed a party line which was more clearly prescribed. The Government was able to avoid further humiliation, and to recover its position to some extent, by adopting a tactical approach, where no policy of any kind had existed before. Carson and Hayes-Fisher provided the ammunition for this new departure by the very nature of the wrecking tactics they themselves adopted. The Liberals and Nationalists were able to imitate their methods by arguing that there was no point in considering the amendment constructively on its merits, since the Opposition were deliberately using it as a tactical device to wreck Home Rule.

Redmond developed his argument very cleverly, to allow the Liberal rebels of 11 June a means of escape. He explained that he could understand his Liberal friends giving serious consideration to this proposal if it were put forward as the price of a Home Rule settlement, acceptable to the Ulster Unionists. But since the amendment had now been entirely repudiated by the Ulster members as part of a Home Rule settlement, and was supported 'frankly as a wrecking Amendment' designed to destroy the Bill, no genuine friends of Home Rule could possibly continue to support the amendment.[32] Redmond's speech did not succeed in converting the Liberal dissentients, but may well have ensured that no more Liberals followed Agar-Robartes and Pirie into the Unionist lobby.

Redmond showed his Liberal allies how they could evade the main issue and escape from an otherwise intolerable situation. He provided those Liberals who followed him with a clear line of argument which had been entirely lacking in the first day's debate. Lloyd George repeated the point that the amendment was avowedly supported by Carson to wreck the Bill. It was Ulster's responsibility to make out a serious case for exclusion and the current demand that Ulster should have the right to veto autonomy for the rest of Ireland was intolerable. This line of argument presumably saved Lloyd George from any personal declaration of his views on the

merits of Ulster exclusion. It also enabled Birrell to wind up
the debate more forcefully than he began it, pointing out that
Carson would not allow Home Rule, with or without Ulster.
Consequently it was a pointless exercise to treat the
amendment as if it were a grave Unionist design to reach a
Home Rule settlement.[33]

All the Liberal speakers on 13 and 18 June supported the
official ministerial position, and between them a rather more
coherent Liberal case against Ulster exclusion was at last
formulated. The main emphasis was placed on the tactical
defence, but two other lines of argument were developed
against the amendment. The first was Asquith's point that
Ireland was one indivisible nation, and that Ulster exclusion
was incompatible with the nationality of Ireland. Naturally
Redmond stated this argument strongly on 13 June: 'This idea
of two nations in Ireland is to us revolting and hateful. The
idea of our agreeing to the partition of our nation is
unthinkable'. Most Liberal speakers devoted considerably
more attention to the second line of argument, which
concerned the practical obstacles in the path of Ulster
exclusion. Lloyd George declared that any serious demand for
the partition of Ireland must be put forward as a definite,
formal proposal, giving precise details of its terms, limits and
conditions. Significantly, the Chancellor admitted that he did
not believe it was an impossible feat to find a workable
boundary line; but the four north-east counties were not a
well-defined homogeneous area and the proposal was full of
administrative, financial and geographical difficulties. The
practical problems were underlined by the fact that even the
Ulstermen could not agree as to precisely which sections of
Ulster ought to be excluded. Lloyd George observed that the
amendment proposed the exclusion of only four counties,
whereas Carson demanded six and Charles Craig wanted all
nine.[34]

The Unionists were not impressed by these rather belated
Liberal arguments against some form of Ulster exclusion,
especially as the Government proposed no alternative method
of dealing with the Ulster problem. The Unionists repeatedly
warned the Government that if they rejected Ulster exclusion
and proposed no alternative, then they would either have to

impose their Bill on Ulster by force, or else submit to last-minute negotiations for compromise on Opposition terms. Acceptance of Agar-Robartes' amendment would prevent a humiliating choice between civil war or subsequent capitulation. They rejected Asquith's argument that the onus for making a proposal lay with the Opposition. This was the Government's problem, caused by a Bill which the Liberals introduced and Ulster did not want; it was, therefore, a ministerial responsibility to avoid coercion of Ulster in the name of self-government. Opposition frustration was increased by the Cabinet's continued silence concerning the Second Reading speeches of Churchill and Grey, which had appeared to suggest that they would sympathise with Agar-Robartes' amendment. The two ministers in question incensed the Unionists still further by their conspicuous absence throughout the entire three-day debate on the amendment. The onslaught from the dissident Liberal members on 11 June must have been even more embarrassing for the ministry. W.H. Cowan complained that several Liberals had expected the Government itself to make some proposal for Ulster exclusion; Churchill's remarkable speech had suggested some ministerial intention to offer an olive branch of this nature to the Ulster members. Captain D.V. Pirie condemned the ministry's 'uncertainty, evasiveness, and wilful reticence', and their repeated failure to answer questions about their intentions regarding Ulster.[35]

In the circumstances, Asquith took a most effective step to help restore his credibility in the Agar-Robartes' debate, by putting forward Lloyd George to defend the Government's position on Ulster. Lloyd George broke his public silence on Home Rule for the first time when he spoke on 13 June, in the middle of the second day's debate. Lloyd George and Churchill had been the most forceful advocates of Ulster exclusion in the February 1912 Cabinet. But, unlike Churchill, the Chancellor had seemed to acquiesce in Asquith's decision, and turned aside to other issues which interested him more deeply. Consequently, Lloyd George's personal views on Ulster had never become public knowledge or even rumoured in the press, and his name had not been linked with Churchill and Grey. On the contrary, Lloyd

George had been widely criticised by the Nationalist press for his 'amazing silence' throughout the Home Rule debates and for his failure to mention Ireland in his public speeches outside parliament.[36] The Chancellor's speech on the Agar-Robartes' amendment was his only major contribution to the 1912 Home Rule debate and consequently received all the more attention. It was a clever stroke to co-opt Lloyd George to support Asquith's Ulster policy and to declare that the Cabinet was united on the subject. The implication was that the Cabinet had unanimously agreed that special provision for Ulster was not practicable and that Lloyd George himself shared this view.

Lloyd George's feelings on 13 June must have been very mixed. It is hard to believe that he was entirely happy about delivering a strong speech in defence of a policy which he had emphatically repudiated in the February Cabinet and was to reject again from November 1913 onwards. A careful examination of his speech reveals that he justified the ministerial veto on Ulster exclusion not on principle, but on tactical and technical grounds. Lloyd George did not absolutely oppose the Agar-Robartes' amendment, though he cleverly gave the appearance of doing so. He stated explicitly that, if there was a demand for separate treatment from Ulster, then the Government should give it serious consideration. Though he emphasised the practical difficulties involved in the partition of Ireland, he added significantly that he did not believe they were insuperable.[37] Lloyd George may have salved his conscience further by refraining from voting – a possibility which appears more likely in view of his abstention on Carson's amendment also.

However, the Chancellor's audience was almost certainly unaware of the implications of these subtle innuendoes. His speech disarmed and confused the Government's critics, as was undoubtedly the intention. Previously they had guessed the truth – that the Government's Ulster policy had not been in the least carefully considered and had split the Cabinet. Lloyd George's speech caused them to revise this estimate. The Unionists tended to assume thereafter that the Government had examined the idea of Ulster exclusion, but had been forced to abandon it at Redmond's dictation. They could only interpret the Second Reading hints of Churchill and Grey as a deliberate tactical sham or else as sincere statements which had to be revised at Redmond's demand. This ministerial disparity of views was never satisfactorily explained away, but at least Lloyd George's speech left the Unionists feeling reasonably certain that the Cabinet was now united behind Asquith's Ulster policy. Though *The Times* recognised that the Agar-Robartes' amendment had 'secretly' caused the ministry considerable anxiety, the full extent and true nature of the Cabinet divisions were disguised. The rebels were always thought to be Churchill and Grey, but Lloyd George's name was never linked with theirs.[38] By adopting a tactical approach to the amendment, and with the help of Lloyd George, the Government partially recovered from the fiasco of 11 June, and managed to conceal the full extent of the divisions within the party over Ulster.

The division at the end of the debate on 18 June, however, indicated the influence of the Liberal dissidents. The ministerial majority sank from its potential figure of 114 to the abnormally low 69, with a vote of 320 against 251. Sixty-two Government supporters failed to vote, compared with thirty-five of the Opposition, and five Liberals actually voted with the Unionists. Agar-Robartes and Pirie acted as tellers, while Cowan, Munro-Ferguson and Cory supported them in voting for the amendment, alongside the Opposition. The majority was the smallest so far yielded in the Committee debates, and two-thirds of the unusually high number of ministerial absentees were accounted for by forty-three Liberals. The Unionists were naturally pleased by the division. *The Times*, the *Observer*, and Lord Hugh Cecil claimed that the Government was only saved from defeat by the dead-weight of Nationalist votes. The *Observer* declared that the clear majority of British representatives was opposed to the Government's policy and had practically authorised the resistance of Ulster. *The Times* commented that the debate had brought the Ulster question more clearly before those Liberals whose convictions were not overridden by the whips' orders.[39]

Twenty-three members of each side were paired for the division, but in the absence of a pair-list it is impossible to know which of the forty-three Liberals paired, who failed to obtain pairs, and who deliberately abstained. George Kemp was known to have remained away deliberately and it is probable that several more of those Liberals who were not accounted for did the same. Those twenty-one Liberals who failed to vote with the Government on both the Agar-Robartes and the Carson amendments can be isolated as the most likely to have abstained deliberately on the Ulster exclusion issue. They included Agar-Robartes, Cory, Cowan, Lloyd George, Jardine, Munro-Ferguson and Pirie. At least nine of these twenty-one were nonconformists, five were Scottish, five from the north of England, three were Welsh and five were federalists. The most pronounced common factors were the large number of nonconformists and the even larger number from Scotland and northern England. The Scottish element can be explained in terms of federalism, Presbyterianism and Scottish nationalism, while the influence of nonconformity chiefly accounts for the northern English attitudes.[40]

4 The Public Debate, July – October 1912: Asquith, Bonar Law and Churchill

After the Agar-Robartes' debate, the Government still had six months in which to heed the warnings they were no longer able to ignore. Parliament rose on 2 August, and the major part of the Committee stages of the three Parliament Act measures was postponed until the House reassembled early in October. However, both parties took advantage of the parliamentary recess to stimulate popular support, rather than to reassess their respective positions. The situation was thereby allowed to harden and feelings on both sides were even more inflamed when the Committee stage was resumed.

Asquith took the initiative with a visit to Dublin on 19-20 July – the first British Prime Minister to go there since the Union. He attempted to stir up enthusiasm in the south to rival the hostility in the north. Asquith was given an enthusiastic welcome in Dublin, where he declared that Unionist opposition to Home Rule was 'purely destructive in its objects, anarchic and chaotic in its methods'. The mere suspicion of future oppression was an utterly trivial justification for incitement to civil war: 'I tell you quite frankly I do not believe in the prospect of civil war.' In John Dillon's view, the Prime Minister's visit was 'an unexpectedly brilliant success'.[41]

This Dublin speech was hardly calculated to convince the Unionists that the Prime Minister was taking the Ulster problem any more seriously than he had on 11 April. Accordingly, Asquith's challenge was taken up all the more forcefully at an impressive Unionist demonstration of around 13,000 people at Blenheim on 27 July. Bonar Law, Carson and F.E. Smith were at their most extreme, giving 'full marching orders to lawlessness in Ulster, in terms which will be held to condone any kind of physical outrage . . .'. The Unionist leader's more menacing and irresponsible remarks haunted him for the next two years. He declared that the Government must take the consequences of their flat refusal to consider separate treatment for Ulster:

. . . if an attempt were made without the clearly expressed will of the people of this country, and as part of a corrupt Parliamentary bargain, to deprive these men of their birthright, they would be justified in resisting by all means in their power, including force . . . if the attempt be made under present conditions I can imagine no length of resistance to which Ulster will go in which I shall not be ready to support them . . .

Asquith subsequently charged that he could find 'no parallel in the language of any responsible statesman' for Law's Blenheim threats, which constituted 'a declaration of war against constitutional Government'.[42] Bonar Law's public recklessness in 1912 cannot be justified, particularly as his private statements were far more cautious.

The strongest Liberal reaction to the Blenheim threats came from Churchill. He wrote to *The Times* in an attempt to dam the rising tide of Ulster's passions by emphasising the dangerous consequences of encouraging violence and anarchy.[43] The Blenheim speeches undoubtedly strengthened Churchill's personal view that Ulster should be excluded from the Home Rule Bill, to avert the tragic consequences he feared and condemned. He was no doubt frustrated at being muzzled during the Agar-Robartes' debate in June, and Lloyd George may have had misgivings about his own ambiguous contribution. Both ministers were required by constitutional propriety to suppress their private views, but in this respect Churchill was less reliable and less subtle than Lloyd George. The Blenheim demonstration encouraged Churchill to put pressure on his colleagues and the Nationalists about Ulster exclusion, at first by private manoeuvres, but later by a public bombshell at Dundee.

On 21 August 1912 Churchill sent a significant letter to Lloyd George, revealing that Churchill's views on the Ulster question had not altered in the least since the February Cabinet. The initial Unionist interpretation of his Second Reading speech had been correct:

The time has come when action about Ulster must be settled. We ought to give any Irish county the option of remaining at Westminster for a period of 5 or 10 years, or some variant of this . . . Time has in no way weakened the force of the arguments you used in January [sic], and I am prepared to support you in pressing them . . .

Churchill rightly assumed that Lloyd George's views had not changed since February, despite his speech on the Agar-Robartes' amendment. The Chancellor's reply has not survived, but he confided in another correspondent in August that the Ulster movement was both real and deep and 'we want to leave Ulster out'.[44] Churchill wrote next to Redmond in a futile attempt to settle Ulster exclusion with the Nationalists during the recess. He suggested giving the Protestant counties of Ulster the option of several years' moratorium before joining the Irish Parliament. Pressure was applied with the warning that such an offer should be made soon, and it would come much better from the Nationalists than the Government. Churchill believed the misgivings of the Ulstermen would gradually be overcome once the Irish Parliament was established. The offer would be worth making even if the Unionists refused it, as the English electorate would then know that the Opposition attitude was purely obstructive.[45]

On 12 September Churchill dropped his bombshell in a major speech at Dundee, for which his colleagues were totally unprepared. He publicly proposed the creation of a full scheme of United Kingdom devolution involving ten or twelve separate legislatures. His colleagues were amazed and appalled, even though Churchill emphasised that he spoke only for himself and not for the Government. Not only had the Cabinet long since abandoned federalism for all practical purposes, but the proposal undermined the Government's position on Ulster. Lord Emmott was anxious about Churchill's 'Heptarchy Kite', 'because the form of it gives away the case of Ulster'. If a senior minister could seriously propose ten parliaments for England, then surely Ireland might be allowed two. Bonar Law declared that Churchill's amazing speech virtually offered Ulster separate treatment, and it was certainly widely interpreted as the thin edge of the wedge.[46]

Meanwhile the Blenheim rally was followed up by impressive Unionist celebrations surrounding the signing of the Ulster 'Covenant' between 19-28 September. Nearly half a million Irish people were alleged to have signed the 'solemn Covenant', pledging themselves to use all necessary means to defeat the conspiracy to establish Home Rule. Bonar Law sent a message assuring the Ulster people that they could rely on the support of the whole British Unionist Party, while Balfour and Lansdowne sent messages of sympathy. Carson's speeches reiterated his declarations in the House. Separate treatment for Ulster was not their policy and they merely supported Ulster exclusion because it would make Home Rule impossible. Even the optimistic Liberal press began to express concern. The *Nation* was torn between its former position of ridicule and a dawning recognition that the comedy might turn to tragedy. The *Daily News* and the *Westminster Gazette* also betrayed a growing uneasiness, with admissions that rioting and bloodshed were likely and the Government should be conciliatory to Ulster sentiment. The editor of the Unionist *Morning Post*, H.A. Gwynne, reported gleefully to Law: '. . . the attitude you and the Ulster men have taken up has altogether shaken the Govt. – *vide* the *Westminster*.'[47]

5 The Parliamentary Battle Resumed: Carson's Amendment for Ulster Exclusion

The spirit of Blenheim and Ulster Day was very much in evidence when Parliament re-assembled early in October 1912. The Unionists were spoiling for a fight, and merely biding their time until an appropriate opportunity arose. A closure resolution was passed on 10 October, to ensure that the Home Rule Bill could be forced through the Commons by January 1913. Twenty-seven additional days were allocated for Committee, seven for Report, and two for Third Reading. The Opposition angrily denounced the use of the guillotine as Government tyranny, but the arrangement worked fairly effectively and the Home Rule Bill went steadily through Committee.

The only real excitement of the Committee stage was provided by the stormy scenes during the debate on the Home Rule Finance Resolution. The Unionists seized that opportunity to express their pent-up fury over the Parliament Act, the Government's treatment of Ulster and the final indignity of the guillotine. It was inevitable that the overloaded time-table would provide opportunities for the Opposition to press for divisions when ministerial ranks were thin. The Unionists finally pounced on 11 November, when the division was taken for the Report stage of the Finance Resolution. The Unionists deliberately drafted a wrecking amendment which would destroy Samuel's finance scheme and they organised their supporters to turn up in force unexpectedly early on a Monday. They were summoned by a code telegram urging them to 'Meet me at Marble Arch at four. Susie', and proceeded to pour down to the House in motor cars.

The Government was inevitably defeated on the Unionist wrecking amendment by a majority of 21, since only 131 out of 264 Liberal members were present. A decision was thereby reversed, which four days previously had been upheld in Committee by an overwhelming majority of 121. An emergency Cabinet immediately agreed that an accidental snap defeat did not justify resignation and decided to rescind the adverse vote. This was only achieved after scenes of wild excitement in the House, deliberately planned by the Opposition to sabotage the Government's guillotine time-

table. The House rapidly deteriorated into a state of uproar on
13 November. Liberal speakers were howled down. Pan-
demonium was only ended by adjournment, when an angry
Ulster Unionist hurled the Speaker's copy of the Standing
Orders at Churchill. The offending amendment was finally
reversed, and the Opposition never seriously expected the
Government's resignation. Their manoeuvre aimed for
maximum disruption of the tight Home Rule time-table, and
allowed frustrated Unionists to voice their fury. It also had the
salutary effect of worrying the Prime Minister and temporarily 'awoke him from his lethargic optimism most completely',
as Charles Hobhouse noted.[48]

After the crisis over the snap defeat, the Opposition
relentlessly maintained their pressure on the Government's
time-table throughout the Committee stage. They continually hoped for another snap defeat to lower the ministry's
morale. The *Nation* complained on 7 December that the Tories
were refusing to pair, and 'Liberals are kept chained to the
treadmill. Last week, over ten hours were spent in walking
through the lobbies'. By 12 December, the Committee stage
of the Bill filled 4,000 columns of *Hansard*, though very few
amendments of importance were actually passed. The Bill
finally passed the Committee stage on 12 December, amid
general weariness and a marked decline in parliamentary
attention and attendance.[49]

Asquith had a final opportunity to incorporate special
treatment for Ulster into the Bill at the Report stage during the
first week in January 1913. But there was no advance sign that
he intended to seize this initiative. The Liberal dissidents and
the Ulster Unionists were both determined that the Cabinet
should be made to face the issue squarely. The first move came
from Captain D.V. Pirie, the Scottish federalist whose strong
disapproval of his leader's Ulster policy was now well-
known. He tried unsuccessfully to bring an amendment
before the House in December, proposing that all nine Ulster
counties be excluded from the Bill until a majority of Ulster's
representatives at Westminster petitioned the King in favour
of inclusion. From the Opposition point of view, little was to
be gained from a repeat performance of the Agar-Robartes'
debate. One of the chief arguments used by Asquith to justify

rejection of the Agar–Robartes' motion had been the fact that it had not come from the Ulster Unionists themselves. The Unionists had some justification for calling the Government's bluff and removing one of their favourite debating points by taking the initiative from Pirie.

The Ulster Unionist Council considered the question during Carson's visit to Belfast in December 1912. By mid-December they had decided to put down their own amendment at the Report stage, excluding the entire province of Ulster from the Bill, and supported by the whole Unionist party. This amendment was placed on the Order paper on 28 December, in the names of Carson, Sir John Lonsdale, and Captain Craig. The aims which inspired the amendment were undoubtedly partially tactical, though probably less so than the Government believed. The Unionists detested Home Rule whether Ulster was excluded or not. Naturally, therefore, they would like to see the Bill abandoned altogether. A tactical approach was also necessary to reassure the Unionists of the south and west, who dreaded being abandoned in the Catholic section of a partitioned Ireland. This was the first formal demand for Ulster exclusion from the Unionist side, and the southern Unionists were alarmed by the Opposition's increasing concentration on the plight of the Ulster Protestants. The southern Unionists would only acquiesce in the amendment when it was presented to them as a tactical device, rather than a breach of faith.[50]

But the Unionists did not primarily move the amendment as a wrecking tactic, for they must have anticipated the Government rejection of a nine-county exclusion proposal. Naturally, Carson continued to hope that Home Rule would be abandoned, but as the months passed this had become increasingly unlikely. Obviously, therefore, it was wise to consider the consequences of the anticipated passage of Home Rule and to try to make the best of an unwelcome situation. If Ulster could not be used to wreck Home Rule, then at least Ulster herself should not be wrecked by Home Rule. Therefore the motion was chiefly intended to be treated as a serious discussion of the principle of exclusion. This amendment effectively marked the tacit concession of the principle of Home Rule by *both* groups of Unionists as a result of concentrating on Ulster. Carson probably held out little hope that the debate would induce the ministry to change its official policy at this stage. But he wanted to warn the Government that the Report stage was their last chance to avert civil war by incorporating Ulster exclusion into the Bill. The debate also enabled the Unionists to emphasise that the alternative to exclusion was the employment of coercion to force Ulster into Home Rule. The Irish Unionists sought an 'earnest and deliberate consideration of this proposal', underlining that the Government alone must bear the heavy responsibility for the disastrous consequences of its rejection.[51]

The Cabinet met on 31 December to decide how to deal with Carson's amendment. The Prime Minister's opinion was again decisive, as in that other critical Cabinet meeting of 6 February 1912. Tactical considerations received priority, as Pease noted in his diary:

We decided to stick to policy – of no concession now to those who admittedly pursued a hostile attitude to bill, even if concessions could be given – but it was recognised that any now would be fatal to the financial and other proposals of this Bill and we must proceed with it. Churchill and George blew off steam.

John Burns' diary provides another clue: 'Cabinet . . . re Ulster: proceed as before despite the doubts and fears of the Dromios. P.M. stiff and solid about it.' Charles Hobhouse's diary adds more significant information. He noted Asquith's expressed conviction that it was 'merely a wrecking or embarrassing amendment', which should automatically be refused. But just as the matter was nearly settled, Hobhouse himself objected that this was a very significant step for Carson and the Ulster Unionists to take:

. . . they were right in saying the responsibility would be ours if serious disturbances broke out later in Ulster which could be attributed to our refusal to exclude Ulster; moreover I was certain that we had no means of coercing Ulster, for the troops were not to be relied on, even if we wished to coerce . . . Ll. George and Churchill took up the running and advised no banging of the door against Ulster, Ll. G. particularly strongly . . .[52]

Several points of significance emerge from these three diary entries. The Prime Minister remained 'stiff and solid' in his stubborn determination to maintain his original policy towards Ulster. Moreover, Lloyd George and Churchill, the two 'Dromios', resisted Asquith's decision just as energetically as they had done in February. It had been obvious in the intervening period that Churchill's opposition to Asquith's policy had not diminished in the least, but Lloyd George had been less vocal about his views. These diary extracts confirm that Lloyd George had never been reconciled to the official Ulster policy, despite his general silence on the subject and his speech of qualified support on the Agar-Robartes' amendment. The Chief Secretary had also shown his concern by writing the previous day to ask for Sir David Harrel's advice. The reply must have alarmed Birrell, for Harrel had changed his mind quite sharply since the previous February. He now seriously wondered whether it would not be advisable to give the Ulstermen what they asked for. The exclusion of Ulster might involve administrative complications, but it would give Home Rule for the rest of Ireland a far better chance of ultimate success. This letter seems to have influenced Birrell's contribution to the Cabinet discussion, for he emphasised the powerful racial and religious abhorrence of the Ulster Protestants towards a Dublin Parliament.[53]

It is also important to examine the only reason given for maintaining the original Ulster policy. It was argued that concessions at this late stage would destroy the practical machinery of the Bill. This was Asquith's chief argument against the amendment in his speech during the debate: '. . . there is not a single effective or operative Clause in the Bill which, if Ulster were excluded from its operation, would not become practically unworkable and unmeaning'. The objections raised by George Cave and D.V. Pirie would appear justified. Cave pointed out that, if there were indeed grave reasons for excluding Ulster, they should be considered on their merits, 'and if the effect is to destroy or alter the form of this particular Bill for Heaven's sake withdraw it and bring in another'.[54] Considerable re-drafting would obviously have been necessary to allow for Ulster exclusion, but Lloyd George had not considered this an impossibility in his Agar-Robartes' speech. Moreover, Asquith himself evidently did not find this objection quite so overwhelming when negotiations for an agreed settlement became necessary in 1914. In any case, if he really believed from the start, as he later claimed, that Ulster exclusion might have to be finally conceded, then it was shortsighted to draft a Bill which could not accommodate it.[55]

A whole day was allocated for discussion of Carson's amendment on 1 January 1913. The debate covered much well-worn ground and only a few points deserve mention. Most supporters of the amendment argued from general principle. Carson alone made out a case for nine-county exclusion on its merits. He argued that it was more sensible to have a larger mixed community, than to create a smaller, homogeneous stronghold of Unionism. Several other speakers implied that the principle of Ulster exclusion might be admissable under certain circumstances, though some form other than nine-county exclusion would be necessary. The most damaging of these, from the Government perspective, was naturally the only Liberal, Captain Pirie, who revived his abortive December amendment. This proposed the acceptance of Carson's amendment, providing that the nine counties could be included in Home Rule if the majority of Ulster's representatives petitioned the King to that end. Bonar Law suggested instead an amendment whereby 'any county in Ulster might be given power to decide whether or not it should come into the new Parliament or remain in the British Parliament'. More significantly, the Unionist leader added that he might vote for such a motion.[56]

Asquithian optimism was a major feature of the debate on the Liberal side. The only important statements of the ministerial position were made by Asquith and Churchill, ably supported by Redmond. The remaining five Liberal speakers were all backbenchers, four of whom rehearsed the familiar arguments and contributed little. The Prime Minister continued to reject Carson's view of the possible consequences if Home Rule was forced on Ulster and refused to speculate on contingent policies relating to a hypothetical eventuality. Austen Chamberlain complained that Asquith 'declined to do anything to avert the crisis, under the conviction that, after all, the clouds may pass away, and that Ulster will become reconciled'. As usual, severe criticism came from Captain Pirie on the Government's back benches: 'This Bill represents a very short-sighted policy . . . Statesmanship demands something different'.[57]

By agreeing to wind up the debate, Churchill played the role so ably performed by Lloyd George in the Agar-Robartes' debate. It was another excellent manoeuvre to disguise the extent of the Cabinet divisions over Ulster, especially in view of Churchill's public statements and his opposition to the Cabinet decision taken the previous day. His tactics were essentially the same as Lloyd George's on the earlier occasion. Churchill put forward a purely technical argument based on a literal interpretation of the amendment. His speech was chiefly confined to a narrow examination of the impracticability of nine-county exclusion. Since the debate was in part intended as a discussion of the principle of exclusion, this approach was hardly constructive, but it did allow Churchill to avoid expressing his private opinion. He was careful not to oppose the general principle of Ulster exclusion, and to add that there were many variants of this amendment which might command his support.[58]

The amendment was rejected by 294 to 197, indicating poor attendance on both sides. Seventy-seven Liberals failed to vote, including Captain Pirie, while Sir Clifford Cory voted as usual with the Opposition. These figures compared unfavourably with only forty-eight abstentions and hostile votes on the Agar-Robartes' division. The Liberal critics were not as vocal in the January debate, since it was much briefer, and the Government had its backbenchers under more effective control. This did not mean that the doubts and fears of June 1912 had disappeared, but rather that they were expressed in abstentions. Of the seventy-seven who failed to vote on Carson's amendment, twenty-six were nonconformists, thirty were federalists, thirty were strongly connected with the north of England, fourteen with Scotland and nine with Wales. The non-voters included the four members primarily responsible for the Agar-Robartes' amendment – W.H. Cowan, Munro-Ferguson, D.V. Pirie, and Agar-Robartes himself. Three of these four were Scottish federalists and three were nonconformists. George Kemp's retirement had, by this time, removed one ardent Liberal opponent of Home Rule from the scene and Cory showed his feelings more actively by voting in the Opposition lobby. It is impossible to know which of the remaining seventy-three Liberal non-voters deliberately abstained, particularly in the absence of a pair list. The most likely dissidents were to be found amongst those who also abstained previously on the Agar-Robartes' amendment, examined above. The most outstanding of these double non-voters on Ulster exclusion was Lloyd George, whose example was not followed on this occasion by Churchill.[59]

If Asquith was seriously worried by these Liberal absten-tions, or by fears of the possible consequences of his Ulster policy, he no doubt took comfort in the far greater state of disarray in the ranks of the Opposition. The long drawn-out Unionist schism over tariff reform had reached a crisis at the end of 1912. The Opposition differences were unexpectedly settled in mid-January 1913, however, so that the tariff reform controversy no longer provided a welcome diversion from the Home Rule debate.

6 The First Circuit Concluded

The Report stage of the Irish Bill was completed by 13 January, in an unusually depleted and apathetic House. Flagging interest revived slightly for the two-day Third Reading debate on 15 and 16 January, when the Ulster question again dominated proceedings. Questions and counter-questions were exchanged, but the replies were evasive. F.E. Smith challenged the Government to place their cards on the table: 'Will you on any terms consent to the exclusion of Ulster? If so, what are those terms?' The Chief Secretary merely threw the ball back into the Opposition court. The demand for nine-county exclusion was an 'arrogant' claim, intended to destroy Home Rule. In the absence of any practicable proposal from Ulster, Birrell argued that the Bill held the field. He supported the Prime Minister's position that the responsibility for making detailed proposals lay with the Unionists. This verbal sparring established that the Government had no intention of relenting over Ulster, at the eleventh hour, while they still held the political initiative. Asquith preferred to maintain his stand on the whole Bill, and to take the massive gamble that the Ulster Unionists would accept the measure in the last resort. The Unionists indulged in a final attack on the ministry's blindness, false optimism and shortsightedness. Balfour was 'shocked at the utter want of comprehension of the Ulster case'. F.E. Smith declared that 'shifty, groundless, and irresponsible hopefulness, exercised at other people's expense, is a political cowardice and a public danger'. Bonar Law again accused the ministry of drifting: 'They have put their head in the sand, and refused to look at the facts'.[60]

The Liberal dissidents also returned to the attack on Third Reading. Agar-Robartes was adamant that 'unless you solve the Ulster question, the Bill is foredoomed to failure, and therefore I am obliged to give my vote against it'. Like the Unionists, he believed 'optimism must be running riot' if the Government believed this measure would reconcile Ireland. Unless the four north-east counties of Ulster were allowed to contract out, the Government was bound to apply coercion to enforce the measure: 'How are they going to deal with Ulster ? Are they going to emulate the example of Oliver Cromwell and turn Belfast into another Drogheda ?' If, on the other hand, the four counties were excluded, and the Bill fulfilled all the ministerial promises, then in a few years those counties would be anxious to join the rest of Ireland. The Cornish rebel attacked the ministry for rejecting his own amendment, on the grounds that it was not moved by the Ulster Unionists, and yet subsequently rejecting also a similar amendment moved by Carson. Moreover, though the ministry constantly asked for Ulster's proposals, Agar-Robartes suggested that only Churchill had taken the question of four-county exclusion at all seriously, when he flew his kite at Dundee.[61]

Captain Pirie's position was more qualified and in this respect more accurately reflected the opinions of the majority of the Liberal critics. They were prepared to vote for the Third Reading, treating it as a vote of principle on the question of Irish self-government. But they were not satisfied with its treatment of Ulster. Pirie criticised the Prime Minister's evasive, 'happy-go-lucky' approach to the issue of Ulster exclusion. Pirie was concerned for the Protestant minority and believed Ulster must be converted rather than dragooned. Despite much idle talk about a search for settlement, Pirie thought the Prime Minister had made little effort to discover points of agreement and had evaded crucial questions on the Ulster issue.[62]

The results of the Third Reading division suggest that most of the Liberal critics followed Pirie's example. The Bill passed by a majority of 110 – 367 to 257. The ministerialist vote was almost identical to that on Second Reading, reflecting great credit on the whips' efforts at the end of such an arduous session. The number of Liberals who failed to vote with the Government (including those paired and those voting with the Opposition) had risen only from ten to thirteen since Second Reading. Of the thirteen who failed to vote with the Government, at least four were ill, abroad or otherwise engaged, while Agar-Robartes and Cory voted with the Unionists as expected. The Scottish federalist, W.H. Cowan, was probably the only member of the remaining seven who deliberately abstained, given his strong views on Ulster, Scottish Home Rule, and federalism. The Liberals were delighted with the Third Reading results which indicated a British majority of about forty, excluding the Irish votes. The announcement of the figures was received in the Commons with great enthusiasm, reflecting the renewed confidence in the party in January 1913. This mood of optimism was understandable, so long as it did not conceal the very real problems and divisions which had appeared during the first parliamentary Home Rule circuit.

Several conclusions emerge from this examination of the debates on the Ulster problem in 1912. The Government argued throughout the session that the responsibility for proposing a solution to the Ulster question lay with the Unionists. This contention was always rather weak, since the Liberals introduced the Home Rule Bill, and it was essentially their problem to deal with basic deficiencies in the measure. But the argument collapsed altogether after Carson introduced his Ulster exclusion amendment. The Opposition's mixed motives should not obscure their actual support for two different Ulster exclusion amendments and the more detailed suggestion put forward by Bonar Law on 1 January. On the other hand, when F.E. Smith asked specifically, on Third Reading, on what terms the Government would consent to the exclusion of Ulster, the question was evaded. Asquith tried to justify his failure to produce a proposal for Ulster on the grounds that separate treatment for Ulster would not reconcile the Opposition to Home Rule. Yet the Unionists had every right to argue that they detested Home Rule, but if it was to be imposed regardless of their views, then they preferred to exclude Unionist Ulster as the lesser evil. The official Government position was in many ways at least as negative and intransigent as that of the Unionists. They consistently evaded the repeated questions put to them about the way they intended to deal with Ulster.

The Cabinet and the Parliamentary Party were far from united in support of this negative position. Asquith skilfully managed to disguise the full extent of the criticism, by delegating Lloyd George and Churchill to support the official Ulster policy at key points in the parliamentary debate. Birrell was careful to conceal his private misgivings. Even so there was considerable public speculation about Cabinet divisions over Ulster and Churchill and Grey were thought to favour special treatment for Ulster. The first parliamentary circuit had also revealed that a number of Liberal members sympathised with the views of Agar-Robartes and D.V. Pirie, which corresponded fairly closely with the attitude of many English Unionists.

The Government's insistence that a detailed proposal on Ulster must come first from the Unionists was unnecessary as well as unrealistic. So long as the ministry could maintain its own majority on the issue, it could force through an amendment making special provision for Ulster, providing this was done by January 1913. The agreement of the Unionists would have provided an unexpected bonus, but it was not absolutely vital. The first parliamentary circuit was the crucial one, when alterations could be inserted by the Government to meet the Ulster case. The Parliament Act allowed Asquith to impose a solution to the Ulster question during the first circuit, without either the cooperation or the agreement of the Unionists. The debate in the 1912 session determined the final form of the Bill. If an amendment to conciliate the Ulster Protestants was not inserted at Committee or Report stages in 1912, it could never be adopted at all except by Opposition consent. The Unionists reiterated these points throughout the 1912 debates, together with the ominous warning that such consent on an Ulster compromise was highly unlikely in 1913 or 1914.

A strong case can be argued that Asquith would have been wise to follow the advice of Churchill, Lloyd George, Agar-Robartes and Pirie. The Government might well have improved their position by seizing the initiative and making a definite proposal to deal with the Ulster problem during the 1912 session. Certainly, ministerial acceptance of the amendments moved by Agar-Robartes and Carson would have been most unwise on tactical and practical grounds. However, the Government could have substituted their own official amendment. The actual details of the scheme would have presented major problems, but these would have been less formidable than in 1913-14, when agreement with the Opposition was required and feeling on both sides had hardened. Possibly 'Home Rule within Home Rule' would have provided a more flexible and reasonable starting-point, from the Liberal viewpoint, than the proposals made by Agar-Robartes or Pirie. Some form of administrative autonomy would thereby be granted to part of Ulster and this could later be extended to embrace Ulster exclusion, if necessary. Considerable re-drafting would have been involved, including a complete revision of the financial provisions, which might not have been entirely a bad thing. But, as Lloyd George suggested during the Agar-Robartes' debate, amending the Bill to provide for Ulster might be very difficult, but it was not impossible. In any case, if Asquith's gamble failed and he found it necessary to negotiate terms with the Unionists in 1914, as was in fact the case, a major revision would still be necessary, but in the worst circumstances and under acute time pressure.

It is a pity that the Government did not examine the arguments in favour of special treatment for Ulster more carefully in 1911, before the Bill was ever introduced. Any scheme would have been criticised from some quarters, but the principle would have won some support from members of both parties. At the same time it would have undermined Ulster's case against the Bill and deprived the Ulster Unionists of much popular support in Britain. Having missed the first and best opportunity, it would undoubtedly have required considerable courage and initiative to incorporate special terms for Ulster into the Bill at a later stage in the first circuit. But the longer they delayed in making concessions over Ulster, the harder it became to reverse the original decision. It had always been true that any amendment to exclude part of Ulster would be an admission that the original Bill was far from perfect. That admission became increasingly difficult to make as time passed and Liberal leaders publicly committed themselves more and more deeply to the defence of the initial decision. Asquith's pride was involved, as well as his habitual preference for the status quo, which had influenced his Ulster policy from the start.

Instead of taking a courageous initiative in the 1912 session, the Prime Minister kept his head in the sand. Admittedly this course could be justified. Asquith preferred to avoid pressing Redmond for concessions at an early stage, since this would have caused anxiety about Redmond's uneasy cooperation during the next two circuits. The two debates on Ulster exclusion at least served the purpose of dropping a hint to the Nationalists, without in the least committing the Government. But by rejecting both amendments, and suggesting no alternative, the Government placed itself in a weakened and vulnerable position. They were thereby committing themselves ever more deeply to the Ulster policy of February 1912, which had never been thoroughly examined. The emphasis which the Government placed on the need for a Unionist proposal suggests a lack of appreciation of the implications of the Parliament Act in the first circuit. The tactical advantages of a Government initiative before January 1913 appear to have been more fully recognised by the Opposition. By failing to put down a Government amendment on Ulster, Asquith was making some doubtful assumptions and running dangerous risks. If the threats of rebellion proved to be more than bluff, then he was taking the risk that Ulster exclusion would ultimately have to be agreed on terms acceptable to the Opposition. Even more alarming was the risk that an agreed settlement over Ulster would prove to be impossible. After January 1913, Asquith had lost the tactical advantage he possessed during the first parliamentary circuit, and had no plans for dealing with the distinct possibility of a full-scale rebellion in Protestant Ulster.

IV
FROM DEADLOCK TO REASSESSMENT: MOUNTING PRESSURE FROM THE ULSTER CAMPAIGN, 1913

The situation was one of political deadlock at the end of the first parliamentary circuit. The Prime Minister had refused to compromise over Ulster while he still retained the political advantage and could dictate the terms. From January 1913 Asquith had to gamble on his assumption that the whole Bill could be pushed through without serious resistance from Ulster. Much depended on the accuracy of his initial estimate of the Ulster situation, and the extent to which this situation altered in the eighteen months before the Bill would pass for the third time. Meanwhile, the Cabinet marked time while the Home Rule Bill ran its course through the Lords and then through its second parliamentary circuit. Its rejection by the Lords was as inevitable as its acceptance in unaltered form during the second passage through the Commons. The time to consider negotiation was not reached until the end of the 1913 session, and only then because the Government was subjected to mounting pressure from three directions. First, the crisis reunited the diverse supporters of Home Rule all round, in a general demand for a compromise settlement. Second, the Unionists organised a noisy campaign for a general election on Home Rule and tried very hard to persuade the King to intervene on their behalf. Most important of all, the Ulster situation deteriorated so rapidly that the Cabinet was at last induced to examine it more closely and take it more seriously. The combined pressures reduced the Government's complacency by the autumn of 1913 and persuaded ministers that they needed to play for time or for terms.

1 Home Rule in Parliament, 1913
The Home Rule Bill was debated in the Lords from 27 to 30 January and rejected on Second Reading – 'as short a shrift as was given to the Bill of 1893', in the words of the *Nation*.

Crewe, Haldane and Morley were the chief speakers for the Government, in a situation aptly described by Haldane: 'I felt full of conviction, and charged as hard as I could against the Stone Wall of Unionist Peers, who listened in gloomy silence. The House was crammed full – but I felt it was like trying to upset a mountain'. The Upper House shorn of its veto power seemed to John Burns like 'a picturesque ruin in motion', and Herbert Samuel found the debate '. . . deadly dull. They remind me of mummies in a tomb discussing the affairs of the live people up above'.[1] The Lords' debate covered ground already very well trodden in the Lower House, but one interesting feature was noted by several observers. Many peers on both sides were no longer prepared to defend the old form of government in Ireland, though they were by no means agreed on the nature or extent of the change required. Morley commented that Home Rule 'has made strides since '93', for there was now a 'sulky conviction that the thing is bound to come'.[2] Conciliatory speeches were made by Unionist peers such as Grey, Curzon and St. Aldwyn, while even Irish Unionists like Dunraven recognised the need for change.

The overwhelming rejection of the Bill in the Lords by 326 to 69 did not demoralise the Liberals, partly because of its inevitability and also because the Parliament Act had encouraged complacency. Richard Holt noted that although Home Rule and Welsh Disestablishment had been rejected by enormous majorities in the Lords, '. . . things are different now and we have only to wait patiently and loyally for another 12 or 15 months to secure our objects'.[3] In any case, many Liberals felt that the defeat in the Lords was counterbalanced by their narrow by-election gain of the Londonderry seat from the Unionists on 30 January. This was an important moral victory for Home Rule, since the Unionist representatives for Ulster were now outnumbered by seventeen to sixteen, thus weakening the argument that Ulster contained a Protestant and Unionist majority.

The short session of 1913 lasted from 10 March until 15 August and provided a lull before the storm that was to follow. The withdrawal of the Franchise and Registration Bill in January 1913, after it became too closely entangled with the suffragette campaign, was a serious blow to the Government's prestige, since it was one of the three major measures proceeding under the Parliament Act. New legislation was confined to the minimum and parliamentary attention was again concentrated on the Home Rule and Welsh Church Bills. Important Liberal proposals for settling labour disputes, for reform of the educational system and the Upper House, and even Lloyd George's land scheme, had all to be postponed. Inevitably, the 1913 session was a tedious and abridged version of its predecessor. John Burns found the Commons disillusioned and depressed, lacking in interest and enthusiasm, while Ilbert feared that 'a kind of dry rot has set in among the Liberal rank and file'.[4]

This depression in the Liberal ranks was also partly due to the Marconi scandal, which provided the main excitement of the session. Lloyd George, Rufus Isaacs and Lord Murray of Elibank had unwisely taken out shares in the American Marconi Company, despite the fact that the English parent company had a contract with the British Government. Though the ministers' dealings were misguided rather than criminal, they provoked intensive investigations which reached a climax between February and June 1913. The Marconi affair was a depressing business for the Cabinet, and lowered the morale of their backbenchers, while the ministry's prestige in the country sank. Marconi had one side-effect which did not displease all Liberals. As Ilbert put it: 'L.G. has lost his halo. The sober and religious people who were his strongest support have lost their confidence in him . . .'[5]

By-election results also contributed to the air of gloom and disenchantment among Liberals, which reached a peak in June 1913. The loss of Newmarket on 16 May and the increased Unionist majority at Altrincham on 28 May had a demoralising effect on the party, though in fact a statistical analysis of all by-elections from January to June 1913 reveals a slight improvement in Liberal performance. On the whole, however, by-elections were not considered to have any direct bearing on Home Rule prospects. It was widely believed among politicians that the electorate was utterly apathetic about Home Rule. A report from Joseph Pease's Rotherham constituency noted 'a complete apathy with regard to Home Rule. Among all the workmen here I have heard no one mention the fireworks of Sir Edward Carson . . . There is more interest in the land question'. Many Liberals shared Charles Masterman's view that by-elections were fought chiefly on issues other than Home Rule: social questions like Insurance and the land scheme were 'the only things that count'.[6]

The second Home Rule circuit did little to alleviate the general air of gloom. The Parliament Act specified that Bills must be introduced in the last two circuits in precisely the same form they left the Commons the first time. Committee and Report stages were accordingly dispensed with, since Commons' amendments were not allowed. Although the Parliament Act authorised the Commons to 'suggest' amendments to the Lords, Asquith insisted that any such 'suggestions' must not destroy the identity of the Bill. The idea of a 'suggestion' stage was abandoned in 1913, since the Opposition condemned the procedure as futile and fatuous. The Unionists were well aware of the difficulties involved in trying to 'oppose' legislation in a session where the passage of the two major Bills was a foregone conclusion and hostile amendments were not allowed. Carson denounced the proceedings as 'sham and hypocrisy', contrasting the parliamentary 'farce' with the stern reality of events in Ireland. Bonar Law commented sourly that they could debate the Bill, but were not allowed to alter a single line.[7]

The only stages of the Home Rule Bill which were actually debated were the Second Reading on 9 and 10 June, and the Third Reading on 7 July. The debates were no more than a formality, carried out in a thin House, and lacking inspiration. The Third Reading was the fifth time the general principle of the Bill had been discussed. It was scarcely surprising that for a whole hour on Third Reading nobody sat on the Opposition front benches and only six members on their back benches. Ministerial whipping was efficient on both divisions, maintaining a good majority. The Second Reading was passed by 368 to 270, despite a full Opposition turnout, and the Third by 352 to 243. These results compared very favourably with those in the first circuit, especially in view of the reduction in

Government numbers due to by-election losses. Only three Liberal dissentients can be isolated from these division lists. From now on, Agar-Robartes joined Sir Clifford Cory in voting consistently with the Opposition against Home Rule on all the major divisions. Captain D.V. Pirie abstained on both divisions, which was scarcely surprising and clearly deliberate in view of his statements in the previous circuit.

The two debates followed their familiar course. The main new feature was the increasing Unionist emphasis on the demand that Home Rule be submitted to the electorate. The usual charges were laid against the ministry. Asquith was blamed for failing to take any initiative in seeking a compromise settlement. Balfour and Bonar Law warned that time was running out, and the Government was 'drifting without any fixed plan towards an inevitable disaster'. Asquith and Birrell merely responded, as usual, that they were prepared to consider any reasonable suggestion for Ulster consistent with the principle of the Bill. [8]

On the Third Reading a significant new note was sounded from the Liberal backbenches. Edward Hemmerde's warning to the Government was very different from those they were accustomed to hearing from Agar-Robartes and Pirie: 'I hope there will be no wavering on the part of the Government, and no attempt at compromise. I believe they have gone to the very limits of compromise'. [9] Asquith might have taken comfort from Hemmerde's wholehearted support, but he may rather have interpreted this speech as a potential new problem. The Prime Minister had now moved so far in the one direction, that to retreat or change tack would increasingly alienate die-hard supporters like Hemmerde. Both parties had their die-hards and their compromisers at opposite ends of the spectrum of opinion on Ulster and feelings hardened as the crisis developed. In the Liberal camp the compromise group led by Agar-Robartes, Pirie, Churchill and Lloyd George had been forced to articulate its views first, in criticism of the official policy. This group would obviously have been very much larger if Ulster exclusion had been Asquith's policy from the start. A majority of members supported Government policy for reasons of party discipline and custom, or from lack of strong private views. As it was, the official party policy was Home Rule for a united Ireland and the rank and file had been supporting this policy through two arduous parliamentary sessions. Hemmerde's speech was the first important sign that any compromise move might provoke criticism from a 'die-hard' Liberal group, which interpreted concessions to Ulster as humiliating retreats.

The Home Rule Bill was rapidly rejected in the Lords for the second time on 14 and 15 July, but by this date the Government was steadily regaining confidence, after reaching the depths of depression in June. A session in which little had been achieved ended on 15 August. A six months' recess gave members a much-needed rest, but it also allowed the various extra-parliamentary pressures on the Cabinet to reach a climax.

2 Pressures towards Compromise: (i) The King and the Campaign for Settlement by Consent

Three forces outside parliament were, meanwhile, driving the Government to recognise the critical nature of the situation and take appropriate action. Among these forces was a campaign for settlement by consent, which gathered strength from various quarters outside the official party leadership. The backbone of this campaign lay in the Home Rule all round movement, which temporarily recovered a rather tenuous unity and purpose in the autumn of 1913 and the spring of 1914.[10] The federalist movement had been quiescent during the first two Home Rule circuits, and many former supporters had deserted the cause once they realised that the Irish Bill paid only lip service to Home Rule all round. Despite disillusionment, however, a hard core of federalists welcomed the opportunity to resume their 1910–12 campaign, which the Irish deadlock appeared to offer. Ulster exclusion was rejected as a method of compromise during the first two parliamentary circuits, and United Kingdom devolution still seemed to offer a potential alternative, with some appeal to men of peace on all sides.

Up to the middle of 1913, the most active leaders of this movement for settlement were a group of Unionist federalists led by Lords Hythe, Dunraven and Grey. They wrote articles, addressed meetings, appealed privately to the Unionist leaders, and pressed strongly during the Irish debates in the Lords for a non-party conference to discuss a federal settlement. William O'Brien, the Independent Irish National-ist, also contributed to the conciliation movement through letters to *The Times* and the party leaders, and by appeals for conference and compromise in all his parliamentary speeches on Home Rule. From summer 1913 the campaign for settlement by conference gained momentum from an additional source. The new development was the revival of Liberal enthusiasm for a federal solution, with O'Brien providing the connecting link between the Liberal and Unionist branches of the movement. The leaders of the Liberal campaign for federalism via conference were Loreburn in the Lords and Murray Macdonald and Arthur Ponsonby in the Commons.

Murray Macdonald, the Scottish federalist, had been ominously quiet throughout the first two Home Rule circuits, but in June 1913 he criticised the Government's Home Rule policy in an anonymous pamphlet on *The Constitutional Crisis*. He condemned the Government for approaching the Irish problem in a piecemeal, haphazard way, acting as the party needs of the moment dictated, and appealed instead for a national and federal solution, before it was too late. Arthur Ponsonby, another Scottish Liberal member, entirely shared Macdonald's views on the need for an all-party settlement on the lines of United Kingdom devolution, and criticised the Government for drifting.[11]

From the middle of 1913, the suggestion was frequently made that the King should call the proposed conference, and George V did not discourage the movement for settlement. Murray Macdonald's pamphlet impressed the King, and Arthur Ponsonby evidently decided to press the advantage through his brother Fritz, who had recently replaced Lord Knollys as the King's second private secretary. Arthur Ponsonby introduced Macdonald to his brother, who proceeded to use his influence to promote the idea that the King might call a non-party conference to discuss settlement. The efforts of Macdonald and the two Ponsonbys no doubt helped the King to reach the point where, by early August, he felt the only possible solution was an agreed settlement between the party leaders, possibly based on the idea of general devolution. The King expressed this view to Asquith in August and to Lansdowne in September, suggesting that an all-party conference might end the existing deadlock. Both party leaders were discouraging, convinced that formal conferences would achieve nothing without an agreed basis for negotiation.[12]

Meanwhile, the movement for settlement by conference received significant support from a more influential Liberal quarter. Lord Loreburn, the former Lord Chancellor and chairman of the 1911 Home Rule Cabinet committee, had always been sympathetic to United Kingdom devolution, but felt that his new position of independence allowed him to speak more freely. During the Home Rule debate in the Lords in July 1913, Loreburn joined Dunraven and Grey in appealing for a settlement by consent along federal lines. The King was much impressed by Loreburn's observations, as also was William O'Brien, who lost no time in enrolling a new supporter. In August 1913, O'Brien met and corresponded with Loreburn, who promised to do all he could 'from the point of view of an independent man who wishes for a peaceful settlement'. Loreburn hoped to bring about a conference by appealing to the British Unionists' sense of public duty and by influencing public opinion in the direction of 'moderation and good sense'.[13]

Loreburn finally ventilated his ideas through a well-publicised letter to *The Times* on 11 September 1913. He suggested 'a Conference or direct communication between the leaders' in an attempt to reach a common agreement, since all parties stood to lose by fighting out the Irish quarrel to the bitter end. For a letter which aroused a storm of controversy, it was exceptionally mild and vague. It did not specifically suggest United Kingdom devolution as a basis for the proposed settlement, though this was implied. Nowhere was any form of Ulster exclusion even mentioned, since Loreburn disliked the idea, though historians have mistakenly tended to assume that this was what his letter proposed.

Loreburn's letter provoked stronger reactions than it deserved. As Birrell explained: 'Everyone thought it originated from the Cabinet: instead of being the output of an always disgruntled ex-colleague'. Ministers were indignant, since not one of them had been consulted. The Opposition leaders were suspicious of a 'conference trap' and Carson publicly refused 'to be led into the spider's parlour !'[14] The Nationalist leaders were deeply shocked, interpreting the letter as 'a flag of fear' prompted by the Cabinet. They thought it was a premature ministerial move towards compromise, which would only stiffen Ulster's resistance.[15] In fact, as Morley pointed out: 'Loreburn's intervention was well meant, but for untying the knot, it is moonshine.' Realists in both parties shared Lansdowne's view that 'Loreburn does not seem to me to help us much so far as materials for a compromise are concerned.'[16] Lord Loreburn's letter had less actual effect than some contemporaries and historians have assumed from the storm of debate it aroused. Loreburn's initiative was not alone responsible for the opening of negotiations between the leaders, which were inevitable anyway, but it helped to create an atmosphere which allowed conversations to begin sooner than might otherwise have been the case. In particular the famous letter made the King more than ever insistent on the merits of a settlement by consent. After talking to the King in mid-September, Lord Curzon commented that the King was disposed to take advantage of the 'new situation' created by the appearance of Loreburn's letter, by renewing his suggestions of conference.[17]

The discussion of Loreburn's letter concentrated on his proposal for an all-party conference and paid little attention to his hints about Home Rule all round. This was justified, because by 1913 the devolution debate was almost dead. By late autumn 1913, the federalist leaders of the compromise movement had again failed to persuade party leaders to adopt United Kingdom devolution as a basis for settlement. The party leaders did not discard the federalist alternative altogether, however, since it provided a supremely useful tactical cover for initiating or disguising the discussion of the more delicate matter of Ulster exclusion.[18] The movement for settlement by consent had been more successful in promoting interest in the general idea of a conference or conversations between the leaders. The campaign had proved particularly effective in increasing the pressure on the King to intervene to promote such a compromise.

3 Pressures Towards Compromise: (ii) The Unionist Campaign for Dissolution and Royal Intervention

Meanwhile, far greater pressure was being applied from another direction. The Unionists mounted a powerful campaign demanding an appeal to the people before the Home Rule Bill passed the Commons for the third time. Unionist arguments began with the familiar claims that Home Rule had not been submitted to the electorate in the 1910 elections and that the Parliament Act had left the Constitution in abeyance until the House of Lords was reformed. Consequently, they contended that additional powers must be granted to the electorate or the King (or both) to check the actions of the Commons while the Lords' veto power was in commission. The King was heavily involved, because some Unionists urged him to use the royal prerogative of changing his ministers and advising a dissolution, while others even encouraged the use of the royal veto against the Home Rule Bill. Most Unionists sought a general election as a means of wrecking Home Rule, with the implicit assumption of a Unionist victory at the polls.

The main emphasis of the campaign was placed on the demand for a general election. Professor A.V. Dicey and Lord Selborne also advocated a referendum on Home Rule, but this was generally seen only as a second option in case the Government rejected the dissolution proposal. Law and Lansdowne quickly abandoned the alternative idea that the King might veto the Home Rule Bill, since this was strongly opposed by most Unionists. St. Loe Strachey, in particular, waged a furious campaign in the *Spectator* against the exercise of the royal veto, which might easily humiliate the Unionists and injure the monarchy.[19]

Unionist advocates of an early dissolution included Bonar Law, Lord Lansdowne, Lord Selborne, Professor A.V. Dicey and St. Loe Strachey, editor of the *Spectator*. The campaign had the advantages of support from the official party leadership, combined with Dicey's intellectual authority, and the publicity provided by *The Times* and the *Spectator*. The Unionist leaders made the demand for a dissolution the focal point of their speeches during the 1913 parliamentary circuit of the Home Rule Bill. It was clear, however, that they placed more weight on the results of a direct appeal to the King. Bonar Law had already horrified George V in May and September 1912 with the argument that it was the King's duty to dismiss his Liberal ministers and appoint others who would allow the Home Rule question to be decided at a general election. On 31 July 1913, Law and Lansdowne stated their case for dissolution even more forcefully in a lengthy memorandum to the King. This document repeated the contention that the King had a constitutional responsibility to take urgent steps to dissolve parliament on the Home Rule question before the 1914 session began. It suggested that the King should address a memorandum to the Prime Minister, indicating that his ministers ought to save him from an impossible situation, by submitting their Bill to the people.[20]

The King was extremely worried by the increasing volume of conflicting advice, warning and near-blackmail, especially as the royal prerogative of advising a dissolution had become the subject of heated controversy in *The Times*. George V felt his responsibility acutely and responded by seeking the advice of many leading politicians from both parties, who were invited to stay at Balmoral during the months of August, September and October 1913. As Sir Almeric Fitzroy commented:

The King's perfect constitutional propriety has never been in question: if Lord Lansdowne and Mr. Bonar Law have sought to draw him, they met with no encouragement for the doctrines put forward by certain Unionist publicists. On the other hand, it would be equally wrong to assume that he takes his orders from the Prime Minister.

Lord Crewe visited Balmoral early in September and described the King's state of mind vividly to Asquith. George V was convinced that the passage of the Bill would mean civil war in Ireland, while its failure would make the government of the rest of Ireland impossible. He found no consolation in the doctrine that he should merely take his ministers' advice, because he was oppressed by his moral obligation to do all in his power to prevent a collision.[21] The King adopted the course suggested by Law and Lansdowne, presenting the Prime Minister with two formidable memoranda on 11 August and 22 September. These recapitulated the Unionist arguments in favour of a dissolution, outlining the difficulties of the King's own position and asking for a reasoned ministerial response.[22]

The Prime Minister replied in three lengthy written statements in September, using logical, simple arguments. Asquith stated that the royal veto on legislation had not been exercised for two hundred years and the principle was firmly established that the monarch should accept his ministers' advice. Though the King retained theoretical powers to change his ministers, the authority of the Crown had been undermined when that prerogative had last been exercised in 1834. If the King intervened on one side by dismissing ministers who had a parliamentary majority, the Crown would inevitably become 'the football of contending factions' in the ensuing election. Finally, Asquith argued that the Parliament Act had not in any way increased the sovereign's constitutional responsibilities and that an early dissolution would offer no solution to the Irish question. If the Government won the election, the Ulster Unionists had stated that it would not alter their resistance to Home Rule, and if the ministry was defeated, little would be proved about public attitudes to Home Rule, since the election would be fought on numerous other controversial issues.[23]

By early October 1913, the Prime Minister considered that the question of an early dissolution was closed. Asquith had taken great pains to answer all the King's queries and was no doubt relieved to learn from Birrell at Balmoral that his 'efforts have had a bracing effect and got rid of some dangerous matter'.[24] Lord Esher informed Balfour on 8 October that there was no chance of a general election or referendum on Home Rule, and Balfour recognised that the King feared compromising the Crown if he forced an early dissolution. Even Bonar Law admitted that if they succeeded in forcing an election: '. . . we are not certain of winning, and even if we do win, there will be I think the certainty of lawlessness in Ireland on the other side . . .'.[25]

Thus, by the autumn of 1913, most Unionists recognised that they had failed in their primary aim of forcing an early dissolution before the Home Rule Bill passed. They had, however, been considerably more successful in achieving their secondary goal of urging the King to intervene to prevent trouble in Ulster. Though George V wisely refused to take the extreme step of precipitating a general election, the Unionist campaign made him view his responsibilities even more seriously than he might otherwise have done. He might have no technical obligation to intervene, but he felt a keen moral duty to prevent the consequences of Asquith's Home Rule policy, if pursued to its logical conclusion. The increasing certainty that the Government would not allow an early dissolution, which would in any case probably solve nothing, clarified matters and increased the pressure for compromise negotiations. As Unionists slowly accepted that the Ulster dilemma would not be solved by an early general election, they were forced to consider 'what is the next best course to pursue'.[26]

4 Pressures towards Compromise: (iii) the Ulster Campaign

One of the most powerful forces driving the Government in the direction of compromise was the campaign in Ulster. The foundations were being laid in the first half of the year for the rapid expansion in the strength of the movement which took place after June. By the end of 1913, the Government's attitude was transformed; they were obliged to recognise the Ulster movement as a new and independent factor in their calculations. Obvious problems existed in estimating the significance and gravity of the Ulster movement. The Unionists encouraged a wide dissemination of information through the press, and the Chief Secretary had at his disposal the reports of the Royal Irish Constabulary. Caution had to be exercised in using both sources, which were subject to bias and exaggeration, but Birrell took caution to extreme lengths in selecting the information to be passed on to the Cabinet.

Press reports alone might have been expected to alarm the Cabinet sufficiently to demand a thorough examination. The organisation and recruiting of the Ulster Volunteer Force received considerable publicity throughout 1913. The U.V.F. relied heavily on retired British army officers, including Lieutenant-General Sir George Richardson, who assumed command in September and re-organised it on a regimental basis. These officers had the encouragement of men with such distinguished military reputations as Lord Roberts. When Lord Willoughby de Broke formed the 'British League for the Support of Ulster and the Union' in March 1913, he obtained the support of 100 peers and 120 members of parliament and boasted a membership of 10,000 a year later. In June, Carson headed the Irish Unionist members on a tour of British towns, to encourage British support for the Ulster cause. From the autumn of 1913, pressure was increased in Britain by the massive agitation organised by Lord Milner and Leopold Amery in support of Willoughby de Broke. They employed agents all over England, enrolling men and obtaining signatures and money for the British Covenant supporting the Ulster resistance movement.

The main efforts of the 1913 campaign in Ulster were concentrated in the second half of the year, during the parliamentary recess. Public gatherings were held throughout Ulster on 12 July, the largest taking place at Craigavon, where 18,000 people marched in procession. The Ulster Unionist Council formally organised itself into a 'Provisional Government' on 24 September, consisting of a Central Authority of seventy-six members, a Military Council and four Committees to deal with specific matters. Special services were held throughout Ulster to commemorate 'Ulster Day' on 28 September, while Carson toured the province for two weeks, inspecting the U.V.F. and addressing meetings. Carson informed Bonar Law on 20 September that everything in Ulster was progressing splendidly and enthusiasm was growing instead of declining, indicating that the press reports were fairly accurate.[27] Carson's tour ended on 4 October with a meeting of 20,000 people at Armagh, at which 4,300 Volunteers paraded. During his tour he had inspected 22,000 men on parade in six counties.

Most of this was common knowledge, since it was so widely reported in the newspapers. The Chief Secretary also had access to the more detailed information provided in the monthly police reports from Ulster. These survive in the form of the condensed *Intelligence Notes*, drawn up at the end of each year to summarise the police reports. The statistics provided in the *Intelligence Notes* on the growth of the Ulster Volunteer Force and the accumulation of arms were particularly significant. The U.V.F. consisted of men who had signed the Covenant and were prepared to enrol and train for military service in the campaign against Home Rule. Numbers were reported as 41,000 in April 1913, rising to 56,651 by September 1913, and up to 76,757 by November. Information concerning the accumulation of arms was more difficult to obtain up to the middle of 1913, consisting mainly of scattered reports and rumours of arms shipments. More precise figures were provided from October 1913, when it was reported that 10,000 rifles were ready for issue to the U.V.F. at short notice. Police observation revealed that about 4,000 modern rifles were imported from Birmingham and distributed throughout Ulster during October and November 1913, by three large Belfast arms dealers under contract to prominent Unionist leaders. Police returns estimated that a total of 17,051 arms of all descriptions were in the possession of the Ulster Unionists in December 1913, rising to 24,879 by March 1914. This increase took place despite the Government Proclamations issued on 4 December 1913, prohibiting the importation of arms and ammunition into Ireland and also forbidding their carriage along the coast. The urgency of the situation was further underlined by the decision of the more extreme Nationalists to create an armed force of their own. The 'National Volunteers' were established at a meeting in Dublin on 25 November 1913 and 4,000 men enrolled immediately.[28]

The Chief Secretary viewed the reports from the Royal Irish Constabulary with some caution. Methods of police investigation were rudimentary and scarcely amounted to a sophisticated espionage system. Moreover, the political neutrality of the R.I.C. was questionable. Birrell informed the Prime Minister in 1913 that the police reports were obviously prejudiced: 'If there were to be a *big row*, we cannot rely upon the R.I.C.', since many were hand in glove with the Ulster Covenanters, and resignations were 'pouring in'.[29] Consequently, Birrell allowed 'a liberal discount' for bias when interpreting the police reports, so that the condensed information provided in the *Intelligence Reports* may well have under-estimated the gravity of the situation.

The Irish Secretary had to decide how these reports should be interpreted, and how much of this information should be circulated to his colleagues. Birrell had long been uncertain and ambivalent about the situation in Ulster, torn by his loyalties to Asquith and the Nationalists, between what he wished to believe and what he feared to be the true situation. His vacillation was encouraged by the conflicting advice he continued to receive from the two highly respected Protestant civil servants, whose opinion he valued greatly. Sir James Dougherty, Birrell's Under-Secretary, held firmly to his conviction that 'this Ulster outcry is largely a game of bluff' and the fanatical 'fire eaters' were in a small minority. But Sir David Harrel, Under-Secretary from 1895 to 1902, had gradually swung round to the opposite view and believed that Dougherty 'greatly underestimated' the strength and danger of the Ulster movement.[30] Birrell instinctively inclined towards Harrel's gloomy forebodings, but was reluctant to admit their truth, or act on them, especially as he had already acquiesced in a Cabinet policy based on Dougherty's assumptions.

The Chief Secretary skirted the problem by providing the Cabinet with minimal information on the Ulster situation until November 1913. The police reports circulated to the Cabinet in February and October 1912 and April and October 1913, provided no basis for any kind of complete picture. Apart from the obvious difficulty presented by the bias and the elementary espionage techniques of the police, the random and localised nature of the brief extracts was confusing to the uninitiated. Enthusiastic recruiting for the U.V.F. in Antrim, for instance, might be offset by apathy in Tyrone, as in the October 1913 report. Eye-witness accounts of various local demonstrations were largely meaningless to ministers not acquainted with the local parishes of Ulster and merely added to the impressionistic material so readily available in the press.

135

A careful synopsis of all the local material, complete with statistical tables indicating the situation in all nine Ulster counties and showing the monthly acceleration in drilling, recruiting and arms accumulation, would have been far more helpful.

The King intervened in March 1913 in an attempt to break Birrell's silence. George V had been alarmed to receive a lengthy, anonymous document from a magistrate in Ulster who claimed to know the leading Ulster Unionists well. The writer alleged that there were '100,000 able-bodied Orangemen, nearly all armed with revolvers, prepared to follow their leaders to any length in resistance to Home Rule'. The King was sufficiently worried to request the Irish Secretary's views on the document. Birrell delegated the task of preparing a reply to his Under Secretary, who justifiably feared that 'the Chief will think it too optimistic'. Despite this difference of opinion, however, Birrell relied heavily on Dougherty's draft in compiling the memorandum for the King and Cabinet on 15 April. With the Chief Secretary's mind in a continual see-saw of indecision over Ulster, it was undoubtedly easier to pass on Dougherty's more consistent and sanguine opinions. The result was a muddled document which mainly argued that the anonymous memorandum grossly exaggerated the extent of Ulster's military preparations. This was contradicted by the more anxious tone of the conclusion, which admitted the dangers of the situation and was obviously Birrell's attempt to balance Dougherty's optimism.[31] It was scarcely a document to inspire confidence or to enlighten the King and Cabinet on the Ulster campaign.

This demonstrated Birrell's preference for adopting a neutral, central position and his reluctance to draw any firm conclusions from the available information to guide his colleagues. He generally refrained even from hinting at his private misgivings over the official Ulster policy, no doubt assuming that Churchill and Lloyd George were in a better position to act as critics. The Cabinet only received the doubtful benefit of a written commentary from Birrell on the Ulster question on two occasions. This was the first and they had to wait more than another year for the second. It was clearly unwise and potentially dangerous for Birrell to conceal the extent of his personal misgivings from his colleagues, when he had access to the police reports and ministers relied on him to transmit the information. By keeping the Cabinet ill-informed and circulating a memorandum which he evidently judged to be over-sanguine, Birrell was reinforcing the arguments for maintaining the status quo. He was effectively minimising the gravity of the Ulster movement to a degree which involved partial abdication of his own responsibility.

It was not until October 1913 that a few ministers complained about the inadequacy of Cabinet information on the 'goings-on' in Ulster.[32] This had the desired effect. Detailed reports and statistics based on the *Intelligence Notes* summarised above were finally circulated to the Cabinet more frequently. Only in November and December 1913 did the Government at last receive tabulated information confirming the acceleration in the growth of the U.V.F. and the escalation in the importation of arms and ammunition to Ulster.[33] It is surprising that ministers did not complain earlier, particularly as the copious press coverage of the Ulster movement should have alerted them to the limitations of the information supplied by Birrell. There is not even any evidence that the police reports from Ulster were ever discussed in Cabinet before autumn 1913. The Government as a whole can therefore be criticised for preoccupation with their own departmental affairs, but Birrell and Asquith were mainly to blame for evading full Cabinet examination of the Ulster question for so long. The Irish Secretary provided too little information and minimised the danger of the situation. This apparent lack of concern helped to justify the policy to which the Government had become increasingly committed in 1913, and the Prime Minister failed to press for a more adequate analysis of the Ulster problem.

Although the true extent of the danger was not revealed to the Cabinet until November 1913, Birrell had recognised since August that the force of the evidence would not allow him to remain on the fence much longer. From the middle of the year, the Chief Secretary became increasingly convinced that the Ulster movement was a grave threat to the prospects of Home Rule. However, he experienced considerable difficulty in persuading the Prime Minister that this was the case. As early as 24 July 1913, Birrell admitted the seriousness of the Ulster situation in an interview with the King, whose anxiety had been increased by the steady stream of Unionist warnings and the Prime Minister's silence. The Chief Secretary commented later that, since he himself believed in the real possibility of riots, bloodshed and religious strife in north-east Ulster, it was not easy to check the King's 'torrent of hearsay'. The King subsequently informed Lord Curzon that 'Mr. Birrell was the only minister who seemed to have grasped the extreme danger of the situation in Ireland – that the others had scoffed at the idea of Civil War or been indifferent to it'.[34] Birrell's royal audience of 24 July 1913 is particularly significant because the Chief Secretary made the first clear admission, since his August 1911 letter to Churchill, that he was prepared to accept Ulster exclusion. The King subsequently described Birrell's suggestion to Asquith:

[Birrell] seemed to think that perhaps an arrangement could be made for Ulster to 'contract out' of the Home Rule Bill, say for 10 years, with the right to come under the Irish Parliament, if so desired, after a referendum by her people, at the end of that period.

However, the Chief Secretary was careful to keep within safe limits by urging that it was the duty of the Opposition to make the first move by coming forward with a practical proposal to this effect. When the King argued that Redmond would never agree, Birrell answered that 'he would have to agree', and could 'easily be squeezed' by the threat of an early dissolution.[35] Birrell's proposal was based upon the same principle as the suggestion made to Churchill two years earlier.

By the end of August 1913, the Chief Secretary at last concluded that he must impress upon Asquith the full gravity of the situation and try to persuade him that Ulster exclusion might be a practicable solution. Birrell warned the Prime Minister on 30 August that police reports showed they were heading for 'a *shindy* of large proportions', which would involve a massive military operation by the army. This prospect forced the Government to face a crucial policy question; did they have a duty to announce their '*willingness* to consider the *exclusion* from the Bill of some portions of

Ulster'? As usual, however, Birrell could see both sides of the Ulster question all too clearly and proceeded to weaken his case by emphasising the strength of the opposition to Ulster exclusion in both Irish camps. The Irish Secretary's hopelessly mixed feelings and conflicting loyalties were illustrated vividly in the ambivalence of this letter. It swung from the belief that they should 'steer right on' to the anxious fear that four county exclusion ought to be offered before shooting Protestants. Asquith's non-committal reply increased Birrell's concern, prompting him to send a second futile appeal a week later.[36]

Birrell's gentle persuasion clearly had very little influence on the Prime Minister, for obvious reasons. From 1911, the Chief Secretary had recognised reluctantly that some form of Ulster exclusion might prove to be the only practical solution. But even at this late stage, when Birrell's anxieties about Ulster were intense, his loyalty to the Nationalists prevented him making a strong, unqualified proposal of Ulster exclusion. The Chief Secretary's ambivalent position, combined with the distractions of his wife's terminal illness and the Larkin affair, meant that when he finally urged Ulster exclusion on Asquith, his appeal lacked force and consistency; it was hedged around with qualifications which gave Asquith ample excuse for ignoring it. Tentative suggestions from the Chief Secretary left Asquith untouched, particularly when neither minister was personally enthusiastic about the course of action proposed. A far stronger initiative was needed to force Asquith's hand, but Birrell was unable to provide this in autumn 1913, for reasons of temperament and circumstance.

The Prime Minister responded very slowly to the appeals of Birrell and the King. Although Asquith admitted to George V on 11 August that he was prepared to consider any practical Unionist plan of temporary Ulster exclusion, his comments suggested that he considered this scarcely necessary:

The P.M. regarded the whole situation with almost frivolous optimism. He admitted there would be trouble in Ulster but he hoped it would soon evaporate. He thought it would have died away long ago had it not been for Carson.

In response to Birrell's anxious appeal of 30 August, the Prime

Minister reiterated the official policy, as if to strengthen the Chief Secretary's resistance to temptation. They could not withdraw the Bill, but any proposal from the right quarter for separate treatment of the four counties must receive full consideration as a possible amendment.[37] Little progress was being made so long as Asquith continued to insist that the proposal must come from the Unionists and might be incorporated by agreement into the existing Bill. After an interview with the Prime Minister early in September, Murray Macdonald commented: 'I had hoped for nothing from the interview; but the result is even more unsatisfactory than I had anticipated. The optimism of the P.M. regarding the prospects in Ulster is staggering'.[38]

But although Asquith frequently made light of the situation, and minimised the significance of the police reports for the King's benefit, even he gradually began to take the Ulster movement more seriously. The Prime Minister wrote a long memorandum on the Irish problem for the King in mid-September 1913. The inconsistencies in the document betrayed the influence of Birrell's ambivalent views, and Asquith's admissions about Ulster's resistance to Home Rule were insignificant:

. . . the genuine apprehensions of a large majority of the Protestants, the incitements of responsible leaders, and the hopes of British sympathy and support, are likely to encourage forcible resistance (wherever it can be tried); there is the certainty of tumult and riot, and more than the possibility of bloodshed . . .[39]

By mid-September 1913, then, both Asquith and Birrell were belatedly coming to recognise the dangerous nature of the Ulster situation and to examine the alternative policies available.

From April 1912 to the summer of 1913, the party leaders on both sides generally maintained extreme positions, for and against the Home Rule Bill. The Liberals sought to push through their original Bill for the whole of Ireland, while the Unionists aimed to promote an early dissolution to turn the Liberals out, wreck Home Rule and prevent civil war in Ulster. By the autumn of 1913, however, a combination of pressures was gradually forcing both parties to start thinking instead about possible escape routes from the logical consequences of their politics of intransigence.

V
SECRET MEETINGS AND SHIFTING GROUND: TOWARDS ULSTER EXCLUSION, SEPTEMBER – NOVEMBER 1913

Haldane confided in Lord Esher '. . . that it is difficult to get the Prime Minister to make any preparations in advance of a difficulty; that the bent of Mr. Asquith's mind is towards a solution *ad hoc*; and that he is always inclined to optimistic views in face of a complicated situation.' (Esher to George V, 29 Sept. 1913, Esher, *Journals*, III, 140).

The Government had two possible ways to deal with the Ulster problem in autumn 1913. They could press forward with their avowed policy of giving Home Rule to the whole of Ireland, regardless of the consequences, and make preparations to deal firmly with any resistance from north-east Ulster. This was still the official policy of the Government, represented publicly mainly by Birrell and Asquith. Alternatively, they could introduce some form of Ulster exclusion to meet the Ulster Unionist grievances.

Irrevocable policy decisions had been taken in the first parliamentary session, which severely limited the Government's alternatives thereafter. The Government might have been wiser to provide special terms for Ulster, either in the original Bill of April 1912, or as an amendment during the first Parliamentary circuit. The ministry would thereby have retained the initiative, instead of becoming dependent on the doubtful goodwill of the Opposition for an agreed settlement. If Lloyd George, Churchill, Birrell and Grey were justified in believing that the most effective strategy was to include provision for Ulster in the original Bill, then the best opportunity had already disappeared by January 1913. From the autumn of 1913, when the Cabinet as a whole finally began to recognise the gravity of the Ulster situation, they had to work from a weak, defensive position. They could not alter their Bill without the agreement of the Opposition and any compromise proposals would be regarded as an admission of the fundamental weakness of the Bill. Moreover, with the passage of time the Unionists would raise their terms for settlement. They had also committed themselves very deeply and would only retreat at a high price.

From September 1913, then, the Liberals were at a disadvantage. The Prime Minister attempted to keep his options open for as long as possible. He negotiated for the most favourable terms, while keeping both sides guessing as to whether he would ultimately insist on the original Bill. This finely balanced tight-rope walk depended on the Government being able to claim that they could and would use the army to enforce their Bill for the whole of Ireland. Some element of choice did still exist between September 1913 and March 1914, but it was gradually reduced by the pressures for compromise acting on King and Cabinet.

The Government was also pushed further in the direction of an Ulster compromise by the change in the balance of power within the Cabinet on Irish policy. This was largely a response to the belated recognition of the gravity of the Ulster situation. Between September and November 1913, ministerial support for Ulster exclusion increased noticeably. This important shift in opinion was accompanied by the effective displacement of Birrell by Lloyd George, as Asquith's second-in-command directing Home Rule policy. The weak and uncertain partnership of Birrell and Asquith, based on the maintenance of the 1912 Bill, was replaced by the more forceful, but frequently discordant, leadership of Lloyd George and Asquith. The Chancellor influenced Cabinet policy intermittently but powerfully in the direction of an Ulster exclusion compromise, enthusiastically supported by the more persistent but less responsible First Lord.

From autumn 1913, Asquith was increasingly forced towards a compromise based on some form of Ulster exclusion. He retained, however, the advantage of determining the timing and the final terms of any settlement. Asquith and Redmond were agreed that, if concessions had to be made, they should be postponed until the last possible moment. This would prevent the Opposition raising their demands once they had a firm Government offer. Moreover, the faint hope always existed that if concessions were postponed indefinitely, they might never have to be offered at all.

Thus the meetings which took place between Asquith and

Bonar Law on 14 October, 6 November and 10 December 1913, and the subsequent meetings with Carson, served several purposes. There is no evidence that the Prime Minister discussed his motives, even with his more trusted colleagues, but his probable intentions can be deduced through an analysis of his actions and statements. It seems likely that Asquith never intended that the discussions with the Opposition leaders should lead to an early settlement. After January 1913, his party had the most to gain from a last-minute agreement, so that Asquith could easily justify a policy of playing for time. Continued negotiations would allow him to avoid for as long as possible the choice between increasingly unattractive alternatives. Time was also needed to win Redmond's grudging agreement to any compromise, by showing him that minimal concessions would not satisfy the Opposition. While negotiations continued, Asquith would also be able to reassure the public that the Government was dealing with the situation, and he could ask the Unionist leaders not to encourage the Ulster agitation. The earlier conversations between the leaders admittedly served a more positive purpose, since they were partially exploratory on both sides. Each party needed to discover the minimum terms the other might be prepared to accept and the extent of the concessions they might make for the sake of a settlement.

The negotiations between the party leaders from September 1913 to January 1914 were disconnected, desultory and largely futile. Terms appeared to be offered, only to be later withdrawn; 'concessions' were offered which were known to be unacceptable; Bonar Law and Carson were alternatively encouraged and discouraged. The 'conversations' were a prolonged tactical manoeuvre, which partially disguised the awkward fact that the Prime Minister was not at all sure where the final destination lay. However, Asquith and Lloyd George were masters of this kind of political game. Their frequently adroit management encouraged the baffled Opposition, and subsequent historians, to mistake makeshift tactics for grand strategy. The 'conversations' between the leaders have, therefore, received greater prominence in the Home Rule struggle from 1911-14 than they deserve. They have also been made to appear more purposeful and logical than they probably were. This analysis of the last months in which ministers had any freedom to manoeuvre will examine the Cabinet's discussions and divisions behind the scenes, and attempt to explore the significance of the negotiations which apparently led nowhere.

1 Churchill, Lloyd George and Ulster Exclusion, September – October 1913

In September and October 1913, when the King consulted leading politicians of both parties at Balmoral, Asquith and Birrell were still nominally directing the ministry's 'policy of drift'.[1] They had been reluctant to admit the gravity of the Ulster situation and failed to alert their colleagues to the need for a revised policy to meet the danger. The result was a confused and divided Cabinet. Birrell confided in Asquith that the King was naturally bewildered by seeing so many people separately, 'each with a stand of his own, . . . Winston, Grey, Harcourt, myself – none quite the same'. Birrell failed to synthesise these views, suggesting that it rested with the Prime Minister to reduce his colleagues 'to a harmonious whole'.[2] But the views expressed by Asquith were drawn largely from Birrell's witty and discursive letters, inconclusive and scattered with qualifications though they were. There is little evidence that Asquith was thinking independently at this stage and, lacking a clear lead from Birrell, the Prime Minister seemed incapable of taking a strong initiative.

During September, Asquith admitted to Churchill that he was prepared to consider proposals for temporary Ulster exclusion, but still insisted that 'the important thing is to emphasize the dangers of rejection, when the ship is just reaching port'.[3] The First Lord was impatient and used his visit to Balmoral in mid-September to full effect, providing Asquith with an edited version of his discussions. On 17 September, Churchill had a 'confidential, personal and informal' conversation with Bonar Law during a game of golf. The Unionist leader suggested a secret meeting 'between one or two on each side', as a preliminary to a wider conference between the British party leaders. Churchill understood that Law was prepared to consider Ulster exclusion as a basis for

the secret talks, though Bonar Law emphasised 'the impossibility of our considering leaving Ulster out unless there should
be a large measure of consent to it among the loyalists in the
South and West'. Churchill confided in Bonar Law that he had
'no doubt that the Nationalists could be made to agree to the
exclusion of Ulster'.[4]

Churchill admitted to Asquith that this remarkable
conversation had restored his former enthusiasm for a
compromise. Churchill had always wished to see Ulster
provided for, as Asquith well knew; but Carson's recent
.behaviour had a 'stiffening effect' on him, since he strongly
resented attempts to overthrow the Government by threatening civil war before the Bill even passed. However, Churchill
now believed that Asquith should write to Bonar Law,
suggesting that they have a talk. A significant ambivalence in
Churchill's attitude to the Ulster problem was revealed here.
Churchill confided to the Prime Minister: 'I wish it were
possible to do two things:- (1) treat these Ulstermen fairly and
(2) give them a lesson. But I am afraid No. (1) will get in the
way of No. (2)'. Churchill could be the strongest ministerial
advocate of Ulster exclusion, but also the keenest to use firm
methods to control the illegal preparations of the Ulstermen,
who were not 'playing the game' by the First Lord's rules.
Asquith replied that the suggested consultations would have
only 'provisional value' without Redmond and Carson, but
Churchill assured Bonar Law that he would do his best to
promote discussions. Churchill continued his diplomatic
endeavours at Balmoral by informing Balfour that he had
always favoured Ulster exclusion and that 'many of his most
important colleagues agreed with him'.[5]

Churchill learnt even more about the views of the Unionist
leaders from F.E. Smith, while participating in military
manoeuvres in Northampton on 24–25 September. Smith had
just returned from Ulster, where he was closely in Carson's
confidence. Smith evidently had few scruples about disclosing
the confidential opinions of his colleagues, to the King, to
Churchill and to Lloyd George. F.E. Smith revealed that he,
Bonar Law, Balfour and Carson held surprisingly similar
views. Bonar Law had '. . . long thought that if it were
possible to leave Ulster as she is, and have some form of Home

Rule for the rest of Ireland, that is on the whole the only way out'. F.E. Smith himself thought the Irish Unionists would ultimately be persuaded to agree to Ulster exclusion, and Balfour was gloomily resigned to the possibility that 'the separation of Ulster from Ireland may be the least calamitous of all the calamitous policies which still remain open to us'. Ulster exclusion was preferable to the existing policy of 'letting things drift to a catastrophe'.[6]

The British Unionist leaders believed that Carson held the key to the situation. Carson was far more moderate and realistic in private than his public statements ever suggested, as a frank letter to Bonar Law revealed on 20 September:

. . . on the whole things are shaping towards a desire to settle on the terms of leaving 'Ulster' out. A difficulty arises as to defining Ulster and my own view is that the whole of Ulster should be excluded but the minimum would be the 6 Plantation counties and for that a good case could be made. The South and West would present a difficulty and it might be that *I* could not agree to their abandonment though I feel certain it would be the best settlement if Home Rule is inevitable . . . I have such a horror of what may happen if the Bill is passed as it stands and the mischief it will do to the whole empire that I am fully conscious of the duty there is to try and come to some terms.

Three weeks later, Carson confided in Lansdowne that if separate treatment were offered to Ulster, he doubted if he would feel justified in asking men to go on preparing for resistance, by which they could obtain no more than was already offered them.[7]

The most uncompromising Unionist was Lord Lansdowne. He was leader of the party in the Upper House and was regarded as a legitimate spokesman for the southern Unionists. He remained isolated in Perthshire, extremely worried by the apparently conciliatory attitudes of his colleagues, even, it seemed, of Carson and Balfour. Lansdowne criticised Carson for too readily assuming that Home Rule might be inevitable and rebuked Balfour for giving up hope of an early dissolution. Some form of Ulster exclusion should only be considered if the worst came to the worst.[8] Fritz Ponsonby reported from Balmoral on 6 October that 'Lansdowne was most uncompromising. He wouldn't hear of any conference and refused to give an inch. Bonar Law was much more inclined to listen to reason'. Lord Curzon was amongst those who shared Lansdowne's views in September, leaving their colleagues pessimistic about prospects of a settlement. As Lord Selborne remarked: 'If Lansdowne and Curzon are against contracting Belfast out, upon *what* can anyone "confer".'[9]

At the yeomanry manoeuvres, F.E. Smith gave the King and Churchill a selective impression of his colleagues' opinions, dwelling on the more conciliatory statements of Carson and Bonar Law, without their qualifications or Lansdowne's even stronger reservations. Among other things, the King learnt that 'Carson would be quite ready to agree to leaving Ulster out, and was sure a satisfactory solution could be thus arrived at'. Lansdowne was convinced that F.E. Smith's indiscretions had led the King and Stamfordham into 'a kind of fool's paradise', in which Lansdowne and Curzon were the only obstruction to a reasonable settlement. Both Lansdowne and Law wrote to Stamfordham, attempting to correct the 'misunderstanding', but to little avail.[10]

Law and Lansdowne would have been even more worried had they known of F.E. Smith's conversations with Churchill at the manoeuvres, and his subsequent correspondence with Lloyd George. Smith sent a letter to the Chancellor on 26 September, marked 'secret and confidential', describing: 'long and interesting talks with the King and with Winston. The basis W[inston] and I discussed was (1) Exclusion of Ulster with facilities for later adherence (2) Acceptance of an agreed Bill by the Unionists for the rest of Ireland'. Neither Churchill nor F.E. Smith had the least authority to consider the matter so specifically, but Smith was the more indiscreet. He discussed a plan whereby the Unionists conceded a great deal and he also committed it to paper in his letter to Lloyd George. As additional bait for the Chancellor, F.E. Smith suggested that a conference should be held to cover other issues such as land reform, as well as Ireland. Smith knew only too well that in 1910 Lloyd George and Churchill had shared his ambitious ideas for a national coalition to solve all the outstanding problems. Smith probably also had some idea that the Chancellor was again thinking along these lines in the autumn of 1913 and that the inclusion of land reform would have special appeal. Lloyd George's reply indicated that F.E. Smith had indeed touched a sympathetic cord: 'You know how anxious I have been for years to work with you and a few others on your side. I have always realised that our differences have been very artificial and do not reach the "realities".'[11]

Lloyd George showed Smith's letter to the Prime Minister and Churchill. No record exists of the meeting, though it is significant that Birrell was not invited. Lloyd George then sounded out the Unionists indirectly through the editor of the *Glasgow Herald*, F. Harcourt Kitchin. On 29 September, Lloyd George and Kitchin 'discussed the political situation with all the cards on the table', and Kitchin promptly passed the information on to Bonar Law, as was obviously intended. Lloyd George mentioned the Ulster exclusion proposal originally discussed by Churchill and F.E. Smith, but emphasised that the first move must come from the Opposition. He suggested that, if the Unionist leaders would bring forward an Ulster exclusion amendment in the Lords, the Government would then be able to enter a conference to discuss terms.[12] Law and Lansdowne, however, had no intention of taking any such initiative and believed the Ulster situation would eventually force the Government to approach the Unionists. Bonar Law commented to Lansdowne that it would be extremely foolish 'to give the enemy the idea that we were not only ready but anxious for a settlement on those lines'. He was willing to try to obtain a settlement by consent, but was not prepared to give away their case in advance. Meanwhile, as Bonar Law observed to Balfour, there was nothing further to be done, and they must wait for the next move from the enemy.[13]

Lloyd George was probably not surprised that the Unionists refused to make a formal compromise offer, though this had to be more definitely established. Meanwhile, he turned his attention to the Nationalist leaders, since their agreement to a compromise over Ulster would be necessary, whatever form the negotiations took. The day after his discussion with the editor of the *Glasgow Herald*, Lloyd George assumed the Chief Secretary's role once more, and, on Asquith's authority, had a careful talk with his Nationalist friend T.P. O'Connor. The Chancellor gave a version of the truth which suited his purpose. He claimed that the Tories would go into conference provided the Liberals consented to Ulster exclusion by plebiscite. In fact, only F.E. Smith had made any such suggestion and the formal Opposition position was that no preliminary conditions should bind any discussions. The gloss did place the necessary pressure on the Nationalists. Lloyd George also vastly understated his own part in pressing for Ulster exclusion, giving the impression that he considered the proposal 'out of date' and that only Churchill favoured it. The most favourable interpretation of Lloyd George's motives is that he wanted to retain his own freedom of manoeuvre and was acting the part of the neutral arbiter. Lloyd George also warned T.P. O'Connor that Churchill might speak in favour of Ulster exclusion at Dundee, while again implying strongly that he disapproved of this development. After consulting Dillon, T.P. O'Connor sent Lloyd George a memorandum pointing out the absolute impossibility of the Nationalists supporting Ulster exclusion.[14]

On 7 October O'Connor wrote to Churchill in an attempt to persuade Churchill to moderate the speech he was due to make the following day at Dundee. He argued that his friends in Ireland were irreconcilably hostile to the mutilation of their country, that the time was not yet ripe for a conference and that feeling among the Liberal rank and file was hardening against concession. Where T.P. O'Connor wrote to discourage Churchill, F.E. Smith urged him on. After suggesting points for Churchill's speech, Smith applied heavier pressure: 'I think you will agree that I have played up well. I hope you will do the same now . . . I have run no small risks and incurred considerable censure'. Lansdowne would have deplored the post-script: '*Carson is most reasonable*. I think he would be glad to meet you'.[15] Churchill's Dundee speech on 8 October satisfied Smith rather than O'Connor. Churchill declared that the Unionists appeared now to be claiming only special treatment for north-east Ulster, instead of their earlier attempt to block Home Rule for the rest of Ireland. The Government could not ignore the new claim for special treatment, if put forward sincerely. A settlement by agreement would offer advantages far beyond anything currently in sight. The Government's Home Rule Bill held the field, '. . . but our Bill is not unalterable, and the procedure of the Parliament Act renders far-reaching alterations possible. But only upon one condition – there must be agreement'.[16]

Unionist reactions to the speech varied from F.E. Smith's gratified approval to James Campbell's flat condemnation on behalf of the southern Unionists. Lord Curzon thought the party leaders should make a rapid and conciliatory response to Churchill's offer, before this golden opportunity passed by and they drifted to disaster. It was wrong that 'secondary' men like F.E. Smith should speak for the party in halting and noncommittal tones in an emergency of this kind. Curzon had clearly become more conciliatory since late September – a particularly significant change, because Curzon was a useful barometer of Unionist party opinion. The Nationalist reactions were more uniformly hostile. John Dillon assured a *Daily Chronicle* correspondent that 'the whole idea of lopping off part of Ireland is quite unworkable, and so grotesque that I am sure the Government will never dream of it'. Redmond at Limerick condemned Churchill's suggestion of Ulster exclusion as 'totally impracticable'.[17]

Having attempted to influence the public and the Opposition, Churchill turned his attention next to his own colleagues. Their reactions to his speech were clearly mixed. The *Nation* commented that Churchill's speech 'was not a Cabinet deliverance, though it does not follow that the Cabinet disapproves it'; according to Massingham, its tone was close to the real mood of the governing minds of Liberalism. Even Morley, while protesting that the Dundee speech did not represent the views of the Cabinet, reluctantly admitted that Asquith 'professed not to find much that was "faulty" in Winston's speech'. Probably Asquith found it useful to fly an Ulster exclusion kite from a ministerial source known to be 'independent'. On 14 October, a week after his controversial speech, the First Lord forced the issue further with an appeal to the Cabinet:

. . . not to close the door to a temporary exclusion of the homogeneous anti national part of Ulster, and [thought] if we could avert a crisis by exempting

151

Ulster for 5 years we ought to do it *but only* 'if Carson and the Tory party would accept the compromise and agree not to repeal it'.[18]

Lloyd George thought this proposal was premature, in view of the hostility or apathy of many of their colleagues. He passed a note across the Cabinet table to Churchill: 'I was sorry you made the offer before you and I had an opportunity of talking them round. I fear it has made the position more difficult. I hope that is not so. But I fear it'. Consequently, Churchill was far more cautious when he spoke next at Manchester, on 19 October. He welcomed every 'fair and honourable proposal' compatible with the unity of Ireland and the establishment of an Irish Parliament. The Unionist Chief Whip commented acidly to Bonar Law: 'I understand Winston's platitudes to mean that he has had his say and leaves the next step for Asquith'.[19]

2 Asquith's Meetings with Bonar Law, October – November 1913

Meanwhile, the Prime Minister was engaged in his own secret manoeuvres, almost entirely independently of his colleagues. The pressure from Churchill, Lloyd George and the King, combined with the growing volume of alarming information from Ulster, at last induced Asquith to explore the problem further. He met Bonar Law to discuss the Irish situation on 14 October and 6 November, though the Cabinet was not informed of these secret talks until 11 November.

On 8 October, the day of Churchill's Dundee speech, Asquith wrote a cool letter to Bonar Law, expressing willingness to participate in 'an informal conversation of a strictly confidential character between yourself and myself'. The Prime Minister indicated that a conference between the party leaders was out of the question under existing circumstances and carefully phrased the invitation to place the responsibility for initiating talks on Bonar Law. Asquith had visited the King at Balmoral from 6 to 9 October and George V was given the credit for persuading his Prime Minister to extend the invitation.[20] However, the offer was almost certainly the culmination of the activities of Lloyd George and

Churchill in the preceding three weeks. Asquith had not actively discouraged their discussions with F.E. Smith and had profited from the information Churchill obtained at Balmoral. Moreover, Lloyd George had undoubtedly consulted the Prime Minister before sounding out the Unionists through the editor of the *Glasgow Herald*. Consequently, Asquith knew he could not expect a formal initiative from the Unionists, despite their willingness to discuss the situation, so he finally compromised with his own carefully structured invitation. The fact that this letter was sent on the day of Churchill's Dundee speech was probably less of a coincidence than it was made to appear.

Though the Prime Minister was fairly well informed of his two colleagues' activities, they probably had no precise knowledge of the use he intended to make of their preparatory moves. Asquith appears to have kept his own counsel and certainly assured Bonar Law on 14 October that 'not a soul knew' of their meeting. The Prime Minister's secrecy contrasted markedly with Bonar Law's reaction to the invitation. The Unionist leader discussed the guidelines for the meeting at length with Lansdowne and Balfour, who in turn corresponded with Carson, Curzon and Steel-Maitland. Bonar Law had recently seen Curzon, Robert Cecil and Walter Long, and thought all of them would welcome a settlement. Lansdowne and Balfour were alarmed about the forthcoming meeting. When he discovered that Bonar Law might be willing to compromise over the geographical boundaries of Ulster, Lansdowne replied firmly that complete exclusion of the whole province must be their aim.[21] Lansdowne confided to Carson that he regarded the meeting with profound mistrust. He feared that the Government would offer terms which would appear reasonable to the British public, but would be unacceptable to the Unionists, 'and then throw upon us the odium of having obstructed a settlement'. Balfour, in turn, was dismayed to learn that Bonar Law intended to explain the difficulties which the Unionists faced in carrying out some form of Ulster exclusion. Balfour warned his successor: 'I rather hope you will not make your very candid admissions to Asquith unless you can extract from him equally candid admissions as to the weakness of his *own*

153

political position !'[22]

Bonar Law failed to heed Balfour's warning when he met Asquith at Cherkley on 14 October 1913. This was no doubt partly due to Law's nervousness and inexperience, but was also encouraged by the Prime Minister's ability to appear equally frank, while divulging little and minimising the extent of his own problems. In particular, Asquith insisted that the Government was by no means absolutely dependent on the Nationalists, rather the reverse, since the Nationalists were powerless without the support of the Liberal Party: 'If he or the Government decided on any course which commanded the support of their own party the Nationalists would have no choice but to accept it'. Having discussed the mutual difficulties of reaching an arrangement, both leaders agreed that some efforts were worthwhile to avoid the dangers ahead. Asquith emerged as the more skilful negotiator, drawing from Bonar Law a series of frank admissions, which were barely mentioned in Law's account of the conversation. Bonar Law's most significant admission was that 'he was clearly in favour of an option of inclusion', rather than permanent exclusion. He also expressed willingness to throw the southern Unionists 'to the wolves', unless there was a general outcry led by Lansdowne, but insisted that the concurrence of his colleagues was essential. The Unionist leader managed at least to avoid committing himself as to the geographical area to be excluded, while Asquith made it plain that he had in mind only the four north-east counties. The Prime Minister promised that, after reflection, he would communicate with Bonar Law again. This first conversation had been exploratory, but Asquith had obtained the more useful information.[23]

Asquith discussed the meeting only with the King and Lord Crewe, and though he sent Bonar Law a brief note promising some comments and suggestions, none were forthcoming. Asquith's speech at Ladybank on 25 October did little to clarify the situation. He admitted that settlement by consent was desirable and invited an 'interchange of views and suggestions, free, frank, and without prejudice'.[24] The King expressed the hope that Bonar Law would meet the Prime Minister's overtures half-way, and the Unionist leader dutifully promised not to 'close the door' against agreement by consent. Bonar Law accordingly declared at Newcastle on 29 October that the Opposition would consider carefully any proposals the Prime Minister might make, with a real desire to find a solution.[25]

The Prime Minister wrote to Bonar Law the day after the Newcastle speech, suggesting that time might be saved by a second conversation, rather than written communications. The two leaders met for the second time at Cherkley on 6 November, but neither gave much encouragement to the other, both emphasising the growth of opposition to settlement among their rank and file. Bonar Law stated that he had to contend with the development of a die-hard movement against compromise, as well as Carsonism. The Prime Minister conceded that he might be able to carry his own Cabinet and party with him, but he could not answer for that and still less for the Nationalists. This comment on the Nationalists contradicted Asquith's statement at their previous meeting. It was also weakened by his subsequent acknowledgement that Redmond realised this was his last chance and he must choose between a compromise or nothing. Asquith further stipulated that he was no more a plenipotentiary than Bonar Law and was 'not even a bearer of proposals'. This was only too true, of course, since the Prime Minister had so far apparently only mentioned these discussions to Lord Crewe.[26]

After this unpromising start, and with these reservations in mind, they proceeded to discuss 'hypothetical' methods of excluding part of Ulster. When Bonar Law commented that Carson would initially demand the whole province, Asquith replied that it was impossible, and asked what attitude Carson would take towards the exclusion of the four Protestant counties only. Bonar Law answered guardedly, that he did not know Carson's 'real mind', and thought '. . . the very minimum which they would accept would be the six Plantation Counties'. Bonar Law gained the impression that Asquith tacitly agreed to the six-county definition of Ulster, but Asquith's account merely noted that Bonar Law was disposed to insist on Tyrone and Fermanagh. In view of later developments it is important that Bonar Law specifically rejected both 'Home Rule within Home Rule' and the automatic inclusion of Ulster at the end of a certain term of years. He insisted that the excluded area must have the option of voting by plebiscite for or against inclusion, after the expiration of a prescribed period. Bonar Law suggested that this exclusion period ought to be at least ten years, five being too short, but Asquith brushed that problem aside as 'a matter of detail' which could be considered later. When they discussed the government of the excluded area, Bonar Law insisted that legislation must remain with the Imperial Parliament and Asquith made light of the administrative and financial difficulties involved. The Prime Minister finally emphasised that if a settlement was reached, the Unionists must try to induce the Lords to pass an agreed Bill, and must give it a fair trial after its passage.[27]

The two leaders placed different interpretations on this second conversation, causing subsequent bitterness and misunderstanding. When they parted, Asquith's recollection was that he promised only to report the substance of their conversation at the next Cabinet. Bonar Law understood the Prime Minister to make a more explicit commitment: 'I shall definitely make this proposal to my Cabinet on Tuesday and I think I can carry my Cabinet and my own Party with me'. The Unionist leader informed Walter Long that Asquith 'told me definitely that he would propose to the Cabinet the exclusion of part of Ulster, either the four or the six Counties – probably the six'. Bonar Law also told Balfour that Asquith 'really means to try to force a settlement' on those lines.[28] This news had a mixed reception. Balfour was affected by Law's optimism. The conversation seemed to indicate a courageous attempt by Asquith to cut his way out of the 'current mess', and Balfour thought their party might support a compromise to avert rebellion in Ulster. Walter Long, on the other hand, fully shared Lansdowne's alarm at the prospect of compromise. Long warned Law that they ran grave risks of smashing their party if they came to any arrangement with the Government. Most of their supporters would believe their leaders had betrayed them and sacrificed their loyalist friends in south-west Ireland.[29]

Bonar Law expected to learn the result of the Cabinet discussion from the Prime Minister within a few days.

However, ten days after the meeting, the Unionist leader told Balfour that he had heard nothing from Asquith: '. . . it remains to be seen whether he will show the courage and statesmanship which were indicated'. In fact, on 12 November, Asquith did inform the Cabinet of his second conversation with Bonar Law, but emphasised that he had not in any way committed himself or them.[30] The Cabinet had an even more important discussion of the Ulster problem the following day, but the results were not conveyed to the Unionists.

Robert Blake has argued that Bonar Law believed Asquith had broken his word, while Roy Jenkins has defended the Prime Minister against this charge.[31] In any case, Bonar Law was somewhat naive to assume that Asquith would make a firm Ulster exclusion proposal at the next Cabinet. The Unionist leader's bitterness increased in retrospect because he believed that Asquith had misled him about the fundamental purpose of these meetings. Bonar Law understood that the aim was to attempt to reach a definite preliminary agreement about an Ulster compromise. The Prime Minister's motives can only be deduced from the evidence. It seems unlikely that he intended to make any precise commitment to the Unionists at this early stage. He was far more concerned to use these first two meetings to discover what the Opposition might be prepared to accept and undoubtedly learned a good deal more from this second conversation. Asquith may also have talked in terms of a proposal he evidently considered 'hypothetical', in order to gain the information required for effective bargaining at a later stage.

3 Ministerial Divisions over Ulster Exclusion

The Ulster problem had received scant attention in the Cabinet since the crucial meeting of February 1912 and many ministers gave it little thought. Birrell and Asquith had made little attempt to educate their colleagues about Irish realities until October–November 1913, when Lloyd George and Churchill demanded more information and an appropriate policy change. Asquith's enigmatic silence and Birrell's troubled indecision meant that their colleagues were given little clear direction. Ministers had to draw their own conclusions from Birrell's noncommital memoranda, from Churchill's remarks and from press coverage of events in Ulster. The result was a curious mixture of views and assumptions, based too often on superficial knowledge. The distractions created by the Marconi scandal, industrial disputes, naval policy and the suffragette campaign further explain the ministry's neglect and indecision over Ulster.

By the autumn of 1913 the increasing gravity of the Ulster situation forced ministers to devote more time and attention to the problem. Even so, surprisingly few formal Cabinet meetings were held to discuss the Ulster question in this critical period. Asquith preferred confidential talks with a few selected ministers, mainly Lloyd George, Crewe, Churchill, Grey and Birrell. No Cabinets met during the busy days of the various Balmoral conversations in September. The first Cabinet meeting since July was held on 14 October, when Asquith at last informed his colleagues of his communications with the King, but said nothing of his meeting with Bonar Law that same day. A general discussion took place on the Ulster question, and Morley commented that ministers had reached no decision: 'The disposition has been not to define their attitude or for the moment unnecessarily to limit freedom of opinion within their ranks either in council or on the platform'.[32] Consequently, numerous public speeches were delivered during the next few weeks, including Churchill's address at Manchester, Asquith's at Ladybank on 25 October and Grey's at Berwick the following day. The Ulster situation was again discussed at formal Cabinet meetings on 12, 13 and 24 November and by a select group of ministers at a dinner given by Lloyd George on 12 November. The views expressed at these important Cabinets in October and November, combined with statements made in private correspondence and public speeches, provide the first reasonably comprehensive picture of ministers' attitudes and divisions over the Ulster question. An analysis of these views will show how the balance of opinion in the Cabinet was shifting towards a policy of Ulster exclusion.

The Cabinet was badly divided on the subject of Ulster. At the two extremes were those who sought to maintain the status quo of the 1912 Bill, involving Home Rule for a united Ireland, and those who favoured some form of Ulster exclusion. When the subject was last discussed in Cabinet, as long ago as February 1912, Crewe and Loreburn had been the ministers most strongly opposed to Ulster exclusion. By October 1913 Crewe and Asquith were revising their views and Loreburn had resigned. The firmest opponents of Ulster exclusion in 1913-14 were McKenna, Runciman, Harcourt and Samuel, followed rather half-heartedly by Burns. The views of Lloyd George, Churchill, Birrell and Asquith have already been considered at length. Further analysis is now required to define the positions taken by McKenna, Runciman, Harcourt, Burns and Samuel on the one side and by Haldane, Morley, Crewe and Grey, who were moving towards the other.

The group of ministerial 'die-hards', who supported the 1912 Home Rule Bill all the way, were dominated by McKenna and Runciman. It is significant that these two ministers were equally opposed to Churchill in the Cabinet controversy over the naval estimates. Unfortunately, the Cabinet row over naval policy, lasting from October 1913 to February 1914, coincided with the escalating crisis in Ulster, inflaming tempers and diverting ministers once again from Irish problems. As First Lord of the Admiralty, Churchill demanded an increased naval budget for 1914–15, to double the number of dreadnoughts to be built in 1914. Churchill's 'big navy' policy offended the traditional Gladstonian pacifist element in the Cabinet, and infuriated the Chancellor, who was expected to finance the militaristic expansion. Thus, friction over naval policy also threatened the close collaboration on Irish policy between Churchill and Lloyd George.

Churchill's chief critic over the naval estimates was Reginald McKenna, the Home Secretary, who had been most reluctantly obliged to make way for Churchill at the Admiralty in 1911. The suspicion arises that the strength of McKenna's opposition to Ulster exclusion was partially inspired by resentment against its most enthusiastic advocate. Certainly the two issues were strongly connected by the end of 1913, as Sir George Riddell noted in December: 'The Navy estimates and the Ulster question are causing serious differences in the Cabinet. There is, no doubt, strong opposition to Winston on both. I saw McKenna today. He has been working up the case for reducing the estimates, and is strong against concessions to Ulster'. Churchill's Dundee speech alarmed McKenna, as he revealed to his friend and ally, Walter Runciman, on 12 October:

We know that the exclusion of Ulster is absolutely impossible in practice, and that to attempt it is to kill Home Rule. Carson knows it too, and it is merely playing into his hands to talk about it as a feasible solution. I remember that the suggestion was emphatically vetoed in the Cabinet a year ago. Has anything unexpected happened since ?

This last question showed how far a minister like McKenna could become immersed in his own departmental problems, including the suffragettes and Welsh Disestablishment. It was also sadly typical of most ministers' ignorance of developments in Ireland, until emergencies forced the sister isle again upon their attention. However, unlike Haldane and Morley, the Home Secretary did not revise his opinions when the Irish Office enlightened him about events in Ulster, in October and November 1913. McKenna was delighted that Redmond vetoed Ulster exclusion so forcefully at Newcastle on 14 November and remarked to Riddell: 'That shuts the door'.[33]

Walter Runciman shared McKenna's commitment to Gladstonian Home Rule for the whole of Ireland and his dislike of Ulster exclusion, though he recognised from 1912 that the Ulster movement was 'an awkward and serious affair'. Runciman remained convinced that Ulster exclusion was '. . . absolutely unworkable, for to cut out the four counties would make it impossible for any form of Irish Government to succeed on a national basis'. On 17 October he delivered an outspoken attack at Batley on Churchill's Dundee offer. He declared that it was impossible to abandon their principles or to cut Ulster out of the Bill, so they must pass the Home Rule Bill into law as it stood. Ten days later, Runciman assured Herbert Gladstone that they would not 'show the white feather – no matter however persuasively Bob Reid [Loreburn] may write or Carson declaim !'[34]

Lewis Harcourt shared the conviction of McKenna and Runciman that Ulster exclusion was out of the question.

Harcourt refused to believe there might be serious trouble in Ulster and irritated the King at Balmoral in September 1913 by his obstinate reiteration of his opposition to Ulster exclusion. Two months later, Harcourt declared at Bradford that 'no accommodation or agreement could be approached on a basis of the abandonment of their policy'. At the Cabinet on 13 November he commented that: 'To pass H.R. with Ulster excluded would be impossible. Liberals would have none of it'.[35] But Harcourt was far too busy at the Colonial Office to have much time to interfere in Irish affairs.

John Burns, the ineffectual President of the Local Government Board, agreed with Harcourt's judgment in the November Cabinet that Ulster exclusion was impossible. Burns supported the existing Bill in public speeches, arguing that civil war would not take place and that Ireland must remain united. In the privacy of his diary, Burns subsequently noted that he would have preferred a more determined attempt to carry out their original policy, instead of a compromise.[36] His attitude may have been influenced by his dislike of Lloyd George; but, by this time, few of his colleagues would have been much impressed by Burns' support, whatever his motives.

After the defection of Asquith and Crewe, the anti-exclusion lobby in the Cabinet was substantially weakened and all the more dependent on the support of Samuel, Haldane and Morley. Of these, Herbert Samuel proved to be their only fairly reliable ally. He shared their dislike of Ulster exclusion, especially as he had invested far more time and effort in the existing Bill than any of them. If Ulster was excluded, Samuel believed that his carefully-constructed financial scheme would be wrecked. He was convinced that it would be impossible to devise a workable plan to replace it 'based upon a fiscal separation between Ulster and the rest of Ireland'. It would be even more difficult to accomplish such a feat as part of a last-minute compromise. Alarmed by news of Churchill's Dundee speech, Samuel wrote to Asquith on 10 October:

The total exclusion of N.E. Ulster is open to such grave disadvantages – both in the injury it would do to the idea of Irish nationality, and in the difficulty it presents in providing for the proper government of that district itself – that it seems better to submit even to further complications of the Home Rule machinery than to adopt that counsel of despair.[37]

Samuel proceeded to formulate these 'further complications', which were submitted to the Cabinet in two drafts in November and December. The basic proposal was that those Ulster representatives who desired differential treatment should constitute a third House of the Irish Parliament called the 'Ulster House' to sit in Belfast. Bills passed by the Irish Parliament would not operate in Ulster without the assent of the Ulster House.[38] Samuel's colleagues rejected the plan unanimously, evidently horrified at the prospect of a combination of Samuel's complicated Ulster scheme with his even more elaborate fiscal provisions. The only aspect of the plan which was later temporarily revived was the legislative veto. Despite his personal views, Samuel was subsequently prepared to abide by the majority decision and cooperate in devising plans in 1914 for Ulster exclusion.

Lord Haldane had initially supported Lloyd George's proposal for Ulster exclusion in February 1912, but once the Government's policy was established Haldane supported it whole-heartedly. On 4 October 1913, Harcourt told the Prime Minister that 'Haldane is against any concessions on Home Rule and anxious to send a select army into Ulster *at once*'. Haldane firmly believed that the Government should adhere rigidly to their policy. He urged the Cabinet to take very strong precautions against trouble in Ulster, in the belief that bloodshed could be avoided by good management and firm military control.[39] These were strong words from the former War Minister and they appear to have been fairly widely known. Lloyd George probably calculated that Haldane was the most formidable opponent of his Ulster exclusion scheme and invited him to the select dinner party to discuss the problem on 12 November. Lloyd George apparently succeeded in converting Haldane, who made no attempt to resist the Chancellor's Ulster exclusion proposal either then or at the Cabinet next day. Haldane's opposition was probably directed not so much against the policy of Ulster exclusion *per se*, as against the Asquithian tendency to drift. He was prepared to support either the policy of full Home Rule, or Ulster exclusion, provided it was firmly conducted. Haldane probably appreciated the advantages of a clear compromise policy under Lloyd George's direction.

Lord Morley's views on the Ulster question are harder to define, especially as his abilities and insight were declining rapidly with old age. Even so, Morley was still highly respected on the strength of his past career as writer and politician and his comments on the Irish problem carried considerable weight. He had been one of the most committed Home Rulers ever since 1885 and he had been Irish Secretary when the two Gladstonian Bills were debated. Morley's attitude to Ulster exclusion was not unlike Birrell's, since they were influenced by some of the same conflicting forces. Asquith later told Redmond that Morley had been one of the two most vehement opponents of Ulster exclusion in February 1912, whereas he had become one of its leading supporters by November 1913. Morley's *volte face* was probably more fitful and inconsistent than Asquith's remark suggests. Like Birrell, Morley wanted to grant Home Rule to a united Ireland. As a Gladstonian Liberal, however, he was sensitive to the charge that such a policy ignored minority rights and might involve the use of coercion. Up to October 1913, Morley tended to emphasise the difficulties of Ulster exclusion and to oppose talk of compromise. After Churchill's Dundee speech, he expressed the fear that a split in the Liberal Party was inevitable if Ulster exclusion gained popularity.[40]

Morley gradually modified his views towards the end of 1913 as his dread of bloodshed increased. After the Cabinet discussed Lloyd George's exclusion proposal on 13 November, Morley wrote to Carnegie that the danger of bloody collision in Ireland 'is a good deal more possible than people think'. It would ruin British sympathies for Home Rule, leave 'Hell-fire' behind in Ireland and start Home Rule in a savagely divided country. By December, Morley was convinced that Ulster was in deadly earnest and that attempts must be made at conciliation. But he was inclined to vacillate and showed an irritating tendency to criticise all the proposals for conciliation subsequently put forward by his colleagues. Thus Lord Esher commented in January 1914:

Morley is himself very undecided and has no clear insight or opinion, at one moment overwhelmed with dismay at the prospect of armed conflict, at another using language of menace towards 'rebels'. This attitude of mind is characteristic of the whole Government.[41]

Up to October 1913, then, the ministerial forces seemed weighted fairly heavily against the Ulster exclusion plans of Lloyd George and Churchill. The majority of the Cabinet, through ignorance, indifference or genuine principle, preferred to retain the 1912 Home Rule Bill intact. Asquith's attitudes and uncertainties were widely shared by his colleagues. Samuel, Haldane and Morley ultimately admitted the need to compromise, but not until November 1913, and they were scarcely the most vocal, convincing or enthusiastic of converts. A great deal depended on whether Asquith, Crewe and Grey, who held the centre position between the two extreme groups, were ready and able to help swing the balance in favour of a compromise solution.

Crewe and Asquith appear to have followed similar paths since February 1912, uncertain about the effectiveness of their existing policy, but equally uncertain that Ulster exclusion would solve their problems. Crewe shared Asquith's cool commitment to Home Rule as a long-standing debt of honour and a practical necessity — a view influenced by his experience as Lord-Lieutenant from 1892-5. Crewe was also on more intimate terms with Asquith than most colleagues. Throughout the summer and early autumn of 1913, Crewe echoed the indecision of Asquith and Birrell. When Crewe saw the King in August, Fritz Ponsonby reported that Crewe had no suggestions to offer; he admitted there would probably be civil war but saw no way out of it. At the end of October, Crewe conceded cautiously, in a private letter, that '. . . the prospect, which some of us have always foreseen, of some sort of coming to terms . . . seems less remote than it yet has'. However, though he admitted the need for a compromise, he was critical and not particularly helpful at the Cabinet on 13 November.[42] Like so many of his colleagues, Crewe saw the problems of every course of action and recommended none, though he was prepared to support whatever line Asquith ultimately adopted.

Sir Edward Grey was more constructive. He had, in any

case, been closer to the position held by Lloyd George and Churchill ever since February 1912. Grey was generally admired in the Cabinet for his clear judgment, his integrity and his sense of responsibility. His reputation stood so high that his intermittent comments on the Irish problem were particularly influential. Like his fellow Liberal Imperialist, Haldane, Sir Edward Grey's approach to Home Rule was pragmatic and rational. He had always been far more acutely aware of the significance of the Ulster issue than most of his colleagues. As early as 1901 he had commented that the Ulster difficulty was the greatest obstacle in the path of Home Rule and whatever policy was next adopted must avoid that pitfall. Grey's well-publicised Second Reading speech on the Home Rule Bill in 1912 indicated that he was uneasy about the policy adopted in the February Cabinet and prepared to consider alternative methods of dealing with Ulster. Grey's fears increased by the autumn of 1913, as news from Ulster confirmed his stand. In his Berwick speech, on 27 October 1913, Grey proposed 'Home Rule within Home Rule' as the most effective form of settlement by consent. He explained that this would involve a form of administrative devolution for the Protestant Ulster counties, to allay their fears that matters such as education, land and the police would be administered unfairly.[43] Home Rule within Home Rule had much to recommend it, as many Liberals and Nationalists recognised its advantages. It has already been argued that it might have been the safest way to introduce provision for Ulster into the original Bill in 1912, since it did not violate the principle of a united Ireland. In the course of 1913 Dillon, T.P. O'Connor and Redmond each showed willingness to accept it as a limited compromise which did not offend their national aspirations.

Despite its advantages, Grey was not prepared to press hard for Home Rule within Home Rule if his colleagues appeared to prefer Ulster exclusion. In his Berwick speech he dismissed four county exclusion as 'not a very hopeful or a very practical solution'. The following day, however, Grey told Churchill that he was afraid he might have gone too far in opposing exclusion and had not intended to 'rule it out or shut the door'.[44] At the dinner on 12 November Grey let Lloyd George sweep aside his reference to Home Rule within Home Rule and he appears to have said nothing about it at the full Cabinet next day. Lloyd George was probably correct in assuming that he could rely on Grey's support for a temporary Ulster exclusion scheme if necessary. Like Haldane, Grey's main concern was to ensure that some firm and unified policy for Ulster should be adopted rapidly. He would not allow his personal preference for Home Rule within Home Rule to impede the adoption of an alternative plan which would achieve the same goal. Probably Grey realised that, by autumn 1913, Home Rule within Home Rule was not likely to satisfy the Unionists, whereas in 1912 it could have been incorporated into the Bill without the need for Opposition agreement. Certainly, the Unionists totally rejected the idea by November 1913, as Bonar Law emphasised when he met Asquith for the second time. It is all the more surprising, then, that the Prime Minister formally proposed Home Rule within Home Rule to Bonar Law on 23 December 1913. By then it was too late to be anything other than a tactical manoeuvre.

Clearly, in October 1913 Churchill and Lloyd George had a difficult task in persuading their colleagues that some form of Ulster exclusion must be conceded. Probably those ministers who proved most influential in swinging the balance of Cabinet opinion towards Lloyd George's position by November were precisely those colleagues he invited to his secret dinner party – Asquith, Crewe, Grey and Haldane. No doubt Lloyd George exaggerated when he informed Redmond on 25 November that Grey, Haldane and Churchill would join him in resigning, if no offer was made to Ulster very soon. But the threat was indicative of the change of mood of the influential centre group in the Cabinet. But the mixed motives of those who ultimately supported exclusion, and the continued hostility of McKenna's group, meant that Lloyd George was never able to seize the initiative as firmly and consistently as Haldane and Grey had hoped.

4 Lloyd George's Ulster Exclusion Initiative, November 1913

Lloyd George timed his intervention carefully, to take

advantage of this shift of opinion within the Cabinet towards Ulster exclusion. Government morale was at a low ebb early in November 1913. The Cabinet discussion of 12 November indicated that ministers were depressed by the Ulster situation. They thought the loss of votes at two by-elections the previous week had been influenced more than usual by the Irish question. Asquith attributed the reduced Liberal poll at Reading and Linlithgow largely to 'Ulsteria'.[45] It was a good psychological moment for Lloyd George to seize the initiative on the Ulster question, whereas Churchill's overtures in October had been premature. By the time the Chancellor intervened, Birrell had at last provided detailed reports indicating the increasing gravity of the Ulster crisis and Birrell's own reputation had sunk very low. Moreover, the Cabinet also learnt for the first time on 12 November that Asquith had met the Unionist leader, who might be prepared to accept some form of Ulster exclusion.

Lloyd George presented his Ulster exclusion proposal to a carefully selected group of his colleagues, invited to dinner at 11 Downing Street after the Cabinet on 12 November. He invited only Asquith, Crewe, Grey and Haldane. These were the four ministers he judged capable of swinging the Cabinet more decisively towards Ulster exclusion. The Irish Secretary was not invited. The Ulster problem was the chief item on the agenda, though the discussion also covered the date of the next election, education and the financial situation. The Prime Minister 'raised question of Ulster but offered no suggestion as to outlet' and Lloyd George swept aside Grey's attempt to discuss Home Rule within Home Rule. Instead, the Chancellor proposed a scheme intended to:

. . . knock all moral props from under Carson's rebellion, and either make it impossible for Ulster to take up arms, or if they did, put us in a strong position with British public opinion when we came to suppress it. Therefore suggested temporary exclusion of Ulster with an automatic inclusion at the end of the term . . . This scheme met with general approval – no objections raised to it.

The Prime Minister 'expressed satisfaction' after the dinner party, while Grey and Haldane described it as the best discussion they ever had as a Cabinet.[46]

After winning the support of the inner circle, Lloyd George drove home his advantage when the full Cabinet resumed next day. Samuel's intricate scheme was rejected and Grey did not even attempt to propose Home Rule within Home Rule after his experience the previous evening. The way was clear for the Chancellor to present his exclusion scheme for the second time in two days. He added the further information that the Ulster Protestant counties should be automatically included after a definite term of five or six years. Lloyd George argued that his plan had two powerful advantages. Firstly, immediate, violent resistance to a change which would not affect Ulster for several years would be premature and ridiculous. Secondly, two British general elections in the intervening period would give the electorate and the Imperial Parliament ample opportunity to reconsider the automatic inclusion of Ulster. The proposal 'met with a good deal of support' and Lloyd George passed a note to Churchill across the table commenting: 'It's going quite well I think'. Asquith later confided to Redmond that Churchill and Morley were the chief enthusiasts; but, as has already been established, Asquith, Crewe, Haldane, Grey, and Birrell, also gave varying degrees of support. It was finally agreed that the Prime Minister should discuss the exclusion proposal with Redmond the following Monday.[47]

Later that day Samuel wrote a memorandum criticising Lloyd George's suggestion that two general elections would postpone the decision about the fate of the Ulster counties. If the ultimate decision effectively lay with the Imperial Parliament, Samuel argued that pressure from the Ulster Protestants would be maintained. The Ulster question would continue to plague British politics and would dominate the next election, so that exclusion would almost certainly become permanent. Samuel suggested instead that the issue should be settled 'by plebiscites in the area in question at intervals of years'. This would at least take the problem out of British politics and give some hope of ultimate inclusion.[48] Samuel's proposal was remarkable for its similarity to the suggestion made by Bonar Law on 6 November at the second meeting with the Prime Minister. This suggests that the two parties were closer to an agreement at this stage than Asquith was prepared to admit, at least on the method of exclusion if not its geographical limits. The basis for further discussion between the party leaders existed, but if he recognised this the Prime Minister reserved the knowledge for later use. He did not encourage Cabinet discussion of Bonar Law's proposal. No attempt was made to hammer out a compromise between the Lloyd George scheme and the terms acceptable to Bonar Law, though Samuel's memorandum suggested this was not impossible. The Unionist leader had some reason to resent Asquith's minimal efforts to push forward towards an early settlement.

Lloyd George's secret dinner party on 12 November, and the Cabinet which followed next day, marked the effective displacement of Birrell by Lloyd George as the Government's chief representative in the Irish negotiations. The Chief Secretary had been excluded from the Chancellor's dinner party and contributed little to the full Cabinet discussion. He merely repeated the essential problem – that Ulster would resist but the exclusion of any part of the province was universally opposed by all sections of Irish opinion.[49] Birrell's inability to take a constructive initiative to resolve the Ulster dilemma was exposed more vividly than usual at this juncture.

Ever since 1911, Birrell had appreciated that Ulster exclusion might become a practical necessity. He had even suggested that course privately to Churchill in 1911 and again to Asquith and the King two years later. Birrell disliked the expedient and he also knew that if he was personally responsible for its adoption, the Nationalists would regard it as a deep betrayal of trust. Thus, when the Cabinet majority appeared to favour the Lloyd George scheme, Birrell felt obliged yet again to act as the Nationalists' spokesman and plead their case against it. He must have realised that the ministry's weakness and indecision were increased by his own ambivalence on the Ulster question, especially as he was distracted by labour troubles in Ireland and by his wife's illness. Moreover, Birrell probably felt that if Ulster exclusion had to be forced on the Nationalists, then it was better that it should be imposed by a minister with no prior commitment to the Irish leaders. Birrell naturally shrank from the ordeal of wringing humiliating concessions from his Irish friends. He may also have recognised that if Ulster exclusion was necessary, then Lloyd George was better equipped to gain full Cabinet support and to handle the delicate negotiations with the Nationalists.

Therefore, immediately after the crucial Cabinet of 13 November, the Chief Secretary sent a letter of resignation to the Prime Minister, couched in the strongest terms: 'I feel *convinced* that in the real *interests* of peace and party – I ought at the earliest possible date to be relieved of my present office, which all of a sudden has become extraordinarily distasteful to me'.[50] But this *cri de coeur* was over-ruled. Birrell was retained as a reluctant hostage to the Government's doubtful good faith in maintaining its 1912 Home Rule position. The Chief Secretary continued to control the Irish administration from Dublin Castle and to help Asquith keep his options open by making public speeches in support of the official policy. Birrell played an increasingly reluctant and nominal role in subsequent negotiations over Ulster with both Nationalists and Unionists, leaving the initiative entirely with Lloyd George and Asquith.

5. Sounding Out the Nationalists

The Prime Minister had told Bonar Law on 6 November that Birrell would sound out the Nationalists, but a week later Asquith decided that he would himself discuss the Lloyd George scheme with Redmond. Denis Gwynn has provided a masterly analysis of Redmond's situation, showing that he was angry and resentful because he believed compromise was already inevitable. Redmond knew, however, that he would damage British support if he appeared unreasonable. His speech at Newcastle on 14 November accordingly combined all the traditional Nationalist objections to Ulster exclusion with the cautious admission that: 'I shut no door to a settlement by consent, but . . . we will not be intimidated or bullied into a betrayal of our trust'. Lloyd George remarked that Redmond must naturally put his claims high, and Lord Edmund Talbot interpreted the speech 'as being preparatory to a climb down'.[51]

The Prime Minister met the Nationalist leader for an hour

on 17 November 1913, for their first discussion together of the Ulster question. The techniques of persuasion required that Asquith emphasise the gravity of the situation in Ulster and the King's desire for compromise, and that he should exaggerate Bonar Law's intransigence. Asquith briefly described his second conversation with Bonar Law, claiming wrongly that the Unionist leader demanded 'the total and permanent exclusion of Ulster from the Bill'. Bonar Law's actual proposal for optional inclusion by plebiscite was much closer to the Lloyd George plan than Redmond was permitted to know. The Nationalist leader might be expected to concede more, if he imagined the Unionist terms to be higher. Asquith cleverly prepared the ground for the Lloyd George scheme, painting a gloomy picture of escalating military preparations in Ulster. Against this background, Lloyd George's 'modified proposal' of 13 November appeared a reasonable means of preventing a 'baptism of blood'. Asquith hinted that the exclusion scheme might be used as a purely tactical manoeuvre, designed to show that the Government was reasonable, but never to be implemented because it would be rejected by the Opposition. Thus the plan was presented as very moderate, possibly a mere hypothetical expedient and unlikely to be carried. Redmond was finally reassured by the information that the Prime Minister did not 'approve of this suggestion, and stated that he told the Cabinet that, in his opinion, 20 or 30 Liberal members would vote against such a proposal'.[52]

Redmond must have suspected that Asquith was overstating the case to prepare for a compromise. The Nationalist leader was too shrewd and experienced not to be unaware of this common tactic. He replied at the interview that 'if put forward at the last moment by B. Law as the price of an agreed settlement, he might look at it. Otherwise he couldn't entertain it for a moment'. It would split his party and at the outside they could only abstain from voting against it. A week later Redmond sent Asquith a lengthy memorandum providing a forceful justification of his position. He argued that the magnitude of the Ulster peril had been considerably exaggerated and that any exclusion offer from the Government would be interpreted as proof of the effectiveness of the

Orange threats. Redmond insisted that compromise proposals should not be discussed until the passage of the Bill was certain, by which time Bonar Law might be forced by his own difficulties into taking the initiative. The Prime Minister read out Redmond's letter to the Cabinet on 24 November, when it was discussed at considerable length. The Cabinet decided to make no commitment and Asquith wrote to Redmond on 26 November that no offer would be made to Bonar Law at this stage. However, the Prime Minister took care to leave himself freedom to manoeuvre: 'We must, of course, keep our hands free, when the critical stage of the Bill is ultimately reached' to close with any reasonable proposal ensuring Home Rule by consent.[53]

Meanwhile, Lloyd George in turn was engaged in squeezing information from Dillon and putting additional pressure on Redmond. The Chancellor interviewed Dillon on 17 November, shortly after the Prime Minister's meeting with Redmond. Whereas Redmond's response to the Lloyd George scheme had been a flat refusal, Dillon's attitude was more friendly. Lloyd George understood that Dillon was 'more favourably inclined to this scheme' than to Home Rule within Home Rule, which he had earlier supported. If it were Dillon's decision, Lloyd George concluded that he could obtain the assent of the Nationalists. But, like Redmond, Dillon was emphatic that the scheme should only be put forward at the last moment, when the Irish leaders might be able to carry it in Ireland, accompanied by the Home Rule Act. Lloyd George agreed that it would be 'highly undesirable to commit ourselves at this stage to this proposal'. Instead, he thought Asquith should announce, early in the 1914 session, that he intended to move a series of proposals dealing with the Ulster problem at the 'suggestion' stage. This would make it very difficult for the Unionists to 'indulge in rowdyism' until the nature of the proposals was subsequently revealed.[54]

Lloyd George's last admission was very significant. It suggests that Lloyd George intended all along to allow his scheme to be apparently forgotten during the winter, while the Unionists were confused by Asquith's sham manoeuvres and the Nationalists were being pressed in the required direction. Lloyd George's plan would suddenly be produced again at the appropriate moment in the 1914 parliamentary time-table as if it were the natural outcome of the intervening negotiations.

The success of his interview with Dillon may well have encouraged Lloyd George to put maximum pressure on Redmond immediately, in the hope that sledge-hammer techniques would succeed where Asquith's curiously devious methods had failed. Lloyd George interviewed Redmond on 25 November and reassured him that it would be a 'fatally wrong step in tactics' for the Government to make any proposals at the present. However, some offer must be made when the time came to suppress the Ulster movement and Lloyd George used powerful arguments in favour of his own proposal. He also informed Redmond that 'it had the approval of the Cabinet generally' and that: '. . . under certain circumstances, if no offer were made, Sir Edward Grey, Lord Haldane, Mr. Winston Churchill – and, inferentially, I gathered, himself – might resign, which would mean a general débâcle, which would be a very serious thing for Home Rule . . . .'[55]

How far this extraordinary interview had Asquith's blessing is not known and Redmond must have noticed inconsistencies in the statements of the two ministers. Lloyd George was justified in claiming general Cabinet approval for his scheme but the Prime Minister had preferred to play down that point. It is also unlikely that Grey, Haldane and Churchill knew precisely how they fitted into the Chancellor's plans, though the implications regarding their views were broadly true. Lloyd George's comments most certainly did not have the Chief Secretary's blessing. Birrell was clearly shocked when he met Redmond two days later and learnt about the interview. In his anger and his concern to reassure his friend, and undo some of the damage, Birrell over-reacted by discounting most of the Chancellor's statements. The Irish Secretary claimed that the Cabinet 'had never even considered' the adoption of Lloyd George's proposal, and that 'he knew for a fact that there was very strong and bitter opposition to it amongst members of the Cabinet'. It was ridiculous to suppose that it could lead to any settlement by agreement.[56]

The Nationalist leader must have felt angry, confused and

deceived after receiving such conflicting accounts of Cabinet policy, within ten days, from the three ministers most directly concerned with Ireland. Birrell's comments came closer, in some respects, to the viewpoint Asquith conveyed in circuitous fashion on 17 November; but Lloyd George reflected the total situation more accurately, if too brutally. The Chancellor no doubt over-emphasised his colleagues' united support for his scheme, while Birrell gave an exaggerated impression of the size and importance of the group of ministers who were bitterly opposed. The Chief Secretary may have been justified in claiming that the full Cabinet had not considered the immediate or formal adoption of the plan, but the inner circle from which he was now excluded had advanced further in this direction than he knew.

The contradictory accounts of Cabinet policy which Redmond received illustrated the divergent viewpoints within the ministry and the damage which could be caused when no clear collective policy was imposed. More of the senior ministers, including Grey, Crewe, Haldane and Morley, had moved in the direction sought by Lloyd George and Churchill. A united, collective policy might have been possible at this stage had there been any decisive direction from the top. Instead, Asquith kept his plans to himself. He allowed Lloyd George to take the initiative, but he also refused to accept the resignation of the Chief Secretary who now represented an almost impossible policy. The extent of the collaboration between Asquith and Lloyd George from September 1913 is not clear; for the most part, the Prime Minister seemed to approve the Chancellor's activities. Birrell was left with the doubtful title of Irish Secretary, while Lloyd George assumed real control of Home Rule policy. The Prime Minister appears to have made no attempt to mediate between the two ministers or to coordinate their views. Consequently the combined effect of their three interviews with Redmond was more harmful than constructive. It was scarcely surprising that rumours of Cabinet dissensions over Ulster policy abounded.

By November 1913 the Prime Minister's secret conversations with Bonar Law had served their main purpose. They provided Asquith with the information to help him formulate his ultimate negotiating position. Independently of these secret meetings, ministerial differences over Ulster became clearer and the balance of Cabinet opinion swung gradually towards exclusion. Lloyd George's secret dinner party of 12 November, and the Cabinet meeting the following day, marked an important watershed in the Government's Irish policy. The Chancellor took advantage of the shift in opinion within the ministry to advocate his own exclusion scheme, which received considerable support. At the same time, Birrell was effectively displaced by Lloyd George as Asquith's chief lieutenant in dealing with the Irish crisis.

VI

THE DRIFT TO CATASTROPHE
NOVEMBER 1913 – MARCH 1914

'I believe your Aged Squiff to be a double-dealing, dishonest man.
He is delaying on purpose to wear us down' (F.S. Oliver to Milner, 25
January 1914, Milner Papers, box 195).

'. . . matters would now drift to a catastrophe' (Curzon to Bonar
Law, 15 December 1913, B.L.P. 31/1/32.)

1 Playing for Time: The Cabinet Policy of 'Wait and See'

The Prime Minister was clearly determined to keep his
options open for as long as possible. It was not inconceivable
that something might yet turn up to remove the necessity for
excluding Ulster. The Nationalist insistence that concessions
should be reserved until the last possible moment coincided
with Asquith's interests and reinforced his natural inclination
to postpone unpleasant decisions. He also wanted to play for
time, as he needed to convince the Nationalists gradually that
concessions were crucial, to counteract the effect of the
unfortunate opening negotiations with Redmond.

A shroud of secrecy surrounds the plans and the intentions
of the Prime Minister at this stage. It was not in his
temperament to reveal his aims or his motives to his
colleagues, as Bonar Law did so freely. Asquith kept his own
counsel, committing little to paper which might in any way
incriminate him, or elucidate the working of his mind.
Consequently he has eluded historians just as he frustrated the
press and infuriated the Opposition. More evidence survives
about Lloyd George's plans, probably because these were
more precisely formulated and the Chancellor lacked his
chief's addiction to secrecy. But it is not at all clear how far the
two men cooperated in these months, particularly as Asquith
was generally careful not to reveal his reactions to Lloyd
George's ideas.

It is probably safe to suggest that Lloyd George believed his November exclusion scheme would be the best ultimate solution and that it would be all the more effective if it were placed in cold storage until the 1914 parliamentary session. It is more difficult to know whether Asquith shared this view. It seems likely that he did, since he eventually acted upon it and his negotiations during the next few months prepared for it very effectively. The Prime Minister was probably working on the assumption that Lloyd George's plan might have to be the final negotiating position, though he was prepared to consider any better alternative if one presented itself. The conversations with the Unionist leader had almost certainly served their primary purpose, from Asquith's point of view, after the first two meetings. By that time he had as much information as he was likely to obtain about the Unionist position from Bonar Law's perspective. Subsequent meetings with Carson might provide useful information about Ulster Unionist attitudes but, for the most part, further negotiations were designed chiefly to confuse and delay.

After the second meeting with the Prime Minister Bonar Law had initially expected an early response, but by mid-November he was more suspicious of Asquith's intentions. As Robert Blake put it: 'A black fog seemed to have settled upon the deliberations of the Liberal leaders and all through November little could be discovered except dubious gossip and distorted rumour'. H.A. Gwynne, editor of the *Morning Post*, commented in mid-November that 'Asquith is refusing to do anything but keep his own counsel, and wishes to keep the matter undecided till Parliament meets'. Ten days later, Bonar Law heard rumours that the Cabinet had decided to make no overtures to the Opposition and on newspaper evidence the Unionist leader was not surprised. He told Lansdowne that they could do nothing more until Asquith made the next move, since they had expressed their readiness to exchange views.[1]

These impressions were confirmed by a long conversation between Churchill and Austen Chamberlain on board the Admiralty yacht, *Enchantress*, on 27 November. Churchill stated emphatically that the Cabinet had never excluded the possibility of separate treatment for Ulster. Though Red-

mond naturally hated it, the Government was not absolutely
bound to the Nationalists and the Irish were not indispensable.
Churchill 'pressed a little' for the Lloyd George plan, which
was dismissed by Chamberlain, along with Home Rule within
Home Rule. Chamberlain insisted that the only basis for
conversations was the course urged by Bonar Law on 6
November, giving the excluded counties the option of
inclusion by plebiscite in five or ten years. Churchill argued
that if the Unionists would concede automatic inclusion after a
fixed term, the Government might be able to offer more
favourable terms on the boundary question as a *quid pro quo*.
When Churchill said that Asquith could make no further
advances at present, particularly as time was on the ministry's
side, Chamberlain condemned this as a dangerous gamble
with bloodshed. The conversation convinced Chamberlain,
however, that Churchill, Lloyd George, Grey and Asquith
genuinely wanted a settlement:

. . . but that as to the means they have no clear ideas and that the hot and cold
fits succeed one another pretty quickly; that A[squith] means to 'wait and
see' and will not give his 'casting vote' till the last moment.[2]

This analysis was probably fairly accurate. The Cabinet of 24
November had agreed that no offer should be made to Bonar
Law at that stage, though further discussions were not entirely
precluded.

Asquith's uncompromising Leeds speech on 27 November
surprised friend and foe alike. The Prime Minister stated that
he would close no door to a 'reasonable and honourable way of
peace', but he saw no immediate prospect of a settlement. He
claimed that the Cabinet was united behind the Home Rule
Bill, and meant to 'see this thing through' without any
surrender of principle and without submitting the issue to a
fresh election. The Opposition press interpreted this speech as
a repudiation of Asquith's Ladybank overture and 'a storm of
reproaches was forthwith launched from half-a-dozen plat-
forms'.[3] Bonar Law replied to the Leeds speech in an equally
uncompromising and far more impassioned outburst in
Dublin the next day. He believed Asquith's remarks indicated
that the attempts to find a compromise settlement had
collapsed, because Redmond had given his orders, or Asquith

was 'determined to wait and see'. Chamberlain felt particularly bitter. He had talked freely to Churchill about Ireland on the very day of the Leeds speech, but received no hint that Asquith was meanwhile engaged in slamming the door in their faces: 'It is difficult now to think that the Ladybank offer was made in good faith and impossible to believe that he means business. He has blown conciliation to the winds . . . '[4]

Asquith's motives in making his Leeds speech are impossible to fathom. It may have been an error of judgment, or a diversionary tactic intended to confuse his opponents still further. His colleagues were bewildered by the 'stiffness of Asquith's attitude at Leeds', and attempted to repair the damage. Early in December, Haldane and Grey poured oil on troubled waters in their speeches at Birmingham and Bradford, insisting that the door opened at Ladybank had not been closed. When he appreciated the unhappy reactions of his colleagues, the Prime Minister responded with a more conciliatory speech at Manchester on 5 December, but this failed to satisfy Churchill and Morley.[5] They had both urged Asquith to resume negotiations with Bonar Law, but without success. They discussed their anxiety over this delay when they dined with Chamberlain and F.E. Smith on 8 December 1913. Morley and Churchill indicated that Dillon and Redmond would not actively oppose negotiations, though they might sulk a little. The two ministers asked Chamberlain to write Morley a formal letter, to be shown to Asquith, emphasising the urgency of a rapid settlement. Chamberlain obliged with a letter warning that if the talks did not offer prospects of success by Christmas, then revolution and civil war would replace settlement.[6]

2 Secret Meetings Continued: Asquith and Bonar Law, 10 December 1913

Unknown to his colleagues the Prime Minister had already approached Bonar Law again on 3 December, suggesting a further talk. It was not surprising that the Unionist leader found the situation 'very funny' and hardly knew what to make of it.[7] Asquith probably suggested this further meeting partly in order to placate his anxious colleagues and the King.

He may also have sought to soften the effects of his Leeds offensive, which had provoked stronger reactions than he had intended. The predominant motive, however, was probably to play for time. It was vital to prevent a deteriorating situation from collapsing into chaos before the Lloyd George scheme could be presented to parliament in the 1914 session.

Some leading Unionists entertained profound misgivings about this third meeting, fearing that Bonar Law was allowing himself to be manipulated by Asquith. They felt that Bonar Law had revealed far too much to the more experienced politician at the first two meetings and should refuse to participate in Asquith's 'Fabian policy' any further. Lord Edmund Talbot, the Unionist Chief Whip, believed that Asquith intended to keep Bonar Law busy until 1914 discussing unacceptable 'offers', and expected the Unionists to keep Ulster quiet while these futile negotiations proceeded. These Unionists probably underestimated their new leader and Lord Crewe's comments were more astute: 'Bonar Law has shown a good deal of capacity . . . He gives the effect of being free from vanity or any self-seeking, and thus gets himself respected'.[8] If Bonar Law had been too naive previously, he had learnt his lesson and adopted the 'stiff upper lip' recommended by his colleagues at the third meeting.

Probably neither leader hoped for much from their talk on 10 December. But its futility exceeded Bonar Law's expectations to such an extent that he could not understand why Asquith bothered to see him at all. Each leader found the other less hopeful than at their last meeting. Both agreed that the Ulster difficulty still remained at the root of the matter. The Prime Minister then explained that the Cabinet favoured the Lloyd George scheme, with automatic inclusion at the end of a definite period. Bonar Law predictably rejected this as hopeless, arguing as Samuel had done, that the agitation in Ulster would continue during the excluded period.[9]

At this stage Asquith began to prepare the ground for creating his smoke-screen. Though in 1914 he reverted to the Lloyd George plan as his fundamental negotiating base, he informed Bonar Law at this third meeting that 'he did not think this a feasible plan'. The Prime Minister had thus led both Redmond and Bonar Law to believe that he personally did not approve of the Lloyd George exclusion scheme. This made his subsequent advocacy of Home Rule within Home Rule appear more plausible, as an alternative. Asquith suggested to Bonar Law that Ulster could easily be given practically complete autonomy within the Irish Parliament. He implied that Home Rule within Home Rule and the Lloyd George plan were considered equally admissible by the Cabinet. In fact Grey's proposal had made no impression on the select inner Cabinet at Lloyd George's dinner and Grey had mentioned it only half-heartedly at the full Cabinet on 24 November. Since Bonar Law had rejected Home Rule within Home Rule at their second meeting, it was no surprise that he again pronounced it 'quite useless', since Ulster wanted to remain under the British Parliament.

The Prime Minister's response provided some insight into his intentions. He agreed that Home Rule within Home Rule probably would not satisfy Ulster. He argued, however, that it would appear reasonable to people in Britain, so that Ulster's resistance would forfeit British sympathy if the Unionists rejected the plan. Bonar Law insisted that his proposal on 6 November for optional inclusion by plebiscite after a prescribed term was the only possible basis for agreement; anything else might increase the Government's tactical advantage in terms of public appeal, but could not lead to a settlement. Neither leader seriously examined the proposals of the other and the detailed questions involved in each scheme were not considered. The only explanation Bonar Law could subsequently give for the meeting was that Asquith was 'in a funk about the whole position and thought that meeting me might keep the thing open at least'. The Unionist leader saw no chance of a settlement. He believed Asquith 'is simply at sea and does not in the least know what to do', and meanwhile intended to drift.[10]

Bonar Law's colleagues became restless and suspicious as a consequence of this third meeting. Lansdowne analysed the Prime Minister's 'desultory and tentative' statements at all three meetings, concluding that 'nothing like a firm proposal, or even a clear indication of Mr. Asquith's own views, has been put forward'. Balfour was convinced that 'the Government think they will get into least trouble by letting things slide', using Home Rule within Home Rule to mitigate British public hostility.[11] Walter Long feared that the Prime Minister '. . . is congratulating himself over the fact that he has so far succeeded in his object, namely, procrastination and, to some extent, deception of the Opposition'. Many Unionists shared Lord Milner's belief that Asquith was 'only playing with the idea of negotiations to gain time', and would move when he judged it best for his own tactical advantage. They pressed their leader to demand a definite written statement of Asquith's proposals, if talks were to continue.[12]

The Unionist leaders had considerable justification for their fears. They guessed the Prime Minister's general strategy fairly accurately, but they were wrong on one vital point. Asquith had successfully led them to assume that Home Rule within Home Rule would be his ultimate negotiating position. The Unionists also underestimated their own leader. Bonar Law's tactics required patience to counter Asquith's policy. He was alive to the danger that the Prime Minister might be playing a game with them, but he believed this was more than counterbalanced by Asquith's 'funk about the resistance of Ulster'. Like many Unionists, Bonar Law was convinced that Asquith would do almost anything to avoid coercing Ulster and would 'not face that when it comes to the point'.[13]

3 Asquith's 'Suggestions' and Sir Edward Carson

As usual, the Prime Minister's colleagues were not in agreement about his Ulster policy. Lord Crewe gave full support to the delaying tactics, and told Walter Long on 14 December that 'we have no offer of any kind to make and don't intend to suggest one'. But as Lansdowne discovered, 'Morley and W. Churchill are evidently much more in earnest, or much more alive to the danger of delay than Asquith'.[14] On 10 December, Morley regretfully informed Chamberlain that the third meeting had failed, suggesting that a new line of approach was advisable, since Carson held the keys to the whole situation. Chamberlain agreed that Carson ought to meet the Prime Minister and Morley showed Chamberlain's letter to Asquith.[15] This intervention provided the opportunity to open new talks and the Prime Minister immediately wrote to Carson proposing an interview. Asquith probably seized the chance as much because it permitted further weeks of procrastination as for the information it might yield. Lansdowne and Law found the sudden transfer of the Prime Minister's attention from Law to Carson 'a little strange'. They both agreed, however, that it might be useful for Asquith to discuss Ulster's attitude with Carson, since the main problem was to satisfy Ulster.[16]

Asquith met Sir Edward Carson for the first of two informal discussions on 16 December 1913. He was well acquainted with the Ulster Unionist leader and felt instinctively more relaxed with a barrister colleague than with a Canadian businessman. The Prime Minister found Carson 'on the whole less pessimistic' than Bonar Law, though Carson naturally emphasised his difficulties in going beyond the position of his Ulster supporters. Carson expressed his sincere anxiety for a permanent settlement which would not be followed by incessant agitation from both sides in Ulster and would not lead to ultimate separation. He suggested that specified Ulster counties should be excluded until the Imperial Parliament decided otherwise.[17] This proposal bore an obvious resemblance to the Lloyd George scheme, since the latter implied that the intervention of two elections would allow the Imperial Parliament to decide the ultimate fate of the excluded counties.

The Prime Minister did not follow up the suggestion, or attempt to reconcile it with the Lloyd George scheme, any more than he had pursued Bonar Law's proposal of optional inclusion by plebiscite. Instead, Asquith suddenly produced a hybrid plan of his own, which was not only more limited than the proposals of Lloyd George, Carson, and Bonar Law, but bore little relation to any of them. Two days after their meeting, Asquith promised to send Carson 'a few rough suggestions' before they met again, and these were forwarded on 23 December. A covering letter explained that the Nationalist leaders knew nothing of them and Asquith had only discussed them with one or two of his colleagues — probably Crewe and Simon. The Prime Minister stated that he had no authority to make proposals at this stage. His *Suggestions* aimed rather at 'opening up the field for practical discussion, and inviting counter suggestions to be made upon the same terms and in the same spirit'.[18]

The *Suggestions* which Asquith sent to Carson were a curious cross between Grey's Home Rule within Home Rule and Samuel's legislative veto for the Ulster members. The basic proposal was that an undefined area, termed 'statutory Ulster', should be granted special administrative and legislative rights. This involved a limited form of Home Rule within Home Rule, giving 'statutory Ulster' control over the local government board, education and local patronage, under Westminster's supervision. In the legislative sphere, a majority of the Ulster members in the Irish Parliament could appeal to the Imperial Parliament against legislation for their area concerning education, religion, land tenure, or tax increases.

Carson consulted Bonar Law before sending the Prime Minister a flat rejection on 27 December. Carson stated that it would be useless for either Bonar Law or himself to submit the *Suggestions* to their respective colleagues, because 'however guarded, the basis is the inclusion of Ulster in the Irish Parliament'. Lansdowne commented that they were no more than 'a clumsy attempt to carry out Grey's ideas of giving Ulster Home Rule within Home Rule', which Bonar Law had already ruled out. The Unionist leader himself remarked that 'Asquith's suggestions are utterly fantastic and have no sense in them at all . . .'.[19]

The Prime Minister must have anticipated this rejection for he cannot seriously have intended the *Suggestions* to form the basis for a settlement at this stage. The meetings with Bonar Law and Carson had clearly shown him what the Unionists might be prepared to accept. Bonar Law had rejected Home Rule within Home Rule as 'quite useless' at their meetings on 6 November and 10 December. Even with the addition of the legislative veto, the proposals were far more limited than Bonar Law or Carson had indicated they were willing to concede, especially as the Ulster Protestants were to be represented at Dublin. Moreover, the *Suggestions* could not even be expected to hold much appeal for Asquith's own colleagues, though they might welcome the 'offer' as a tactical move to strengthen their position. In November, the Cabinet had rejected Samuel's legislative veto proposal and shown little interest in Grey's Home Rule within Home Rule – the two components of the 'new' scheme. The only group which might conceivably acquiesce in the *Suggestions* was the Nationalists; Redmond and Dillon were prepared to support Home Rule within Home Rule and O'Brien advocated the Ulster legislative veto.

The purpose of the unexpected *Suggestions*, then, was probably two-fold. Asquith knew that he could not hope to prolong talks with the Unionist leaders for many more weeks, unless he made some sort of offer. By deliberately making an offer which he knew the Unionists must reject, he could hope to confuse the Opposition as to his real intentions and gain further time. Secondly, the *Suggestions* formed the overture to a more positive attempt to negotiate with the Nationalists. The clumsy approaches to the Irish leaders in November, based on the Lloyd George scheme, had failed abysmally. The *Suggestions* could be produced at a later stage to demonstrate that Asquith had actually made an offer based on concessions he believed the Nationalists could accept. It could then be argued that further concessions were required, since the Unionists flatly rejected the offer. A similar advantage would be gained if the British public was informed of the *Suggestions*.

The Prime Minister's next move was to invite Carson to a second meeting on 2 January 1914, despite the Ulster Unionist leader's conclusive rejection of the *Suggestions*. Asquith's intentions were soon clear. He sought to place on the Unionists the responsibility for rejecting his 'carefully considered suggestions' and to use these as a lever to induce the Opposition to formulate detailed counter-proposals in writing. The Prime Minister expressed his disappointment with the terms of Carson's letter. He had hoped that his *Suggestions* for 'veiled exclusion' would be dealt with in a less summary fashion, or that some alternative proposal might have been made, since he professed to have offered 'substantial concessions'. The tactical significance of Asquith's *Suggestions* was underlined when he asked Carson how he could expect 'to have British sympathy on his side, if he challenged Civil War in resistance to such a proposal ?' The Prime Minister built up to his final request that:

. . . [Carson] should at least present in black and white some suggested method by which 'unveiled' exclusion could be put into effect without mutilating the Home Rule scheme as a whole, and hopelessly offending Nationalist sentiment.

Carson agreed to consider this request, but made no promises.[20]

Carson adopted the formula suggested by Bonar Law in his reply to the Prime Minister. He stated firmly that, until the principle of Ulster exclusion had been agreed, it was pointless to formulate detailed proposals for the administration of the excluded area. The Prime Minister tried once more to press Carson to commit himself to some definite Ulster exclusion proposal, as a *quid pro quo* for the *Suggestions*. Asquith wrote that the position would be clarified if the two Unionist leaders would explain precisely what form of 'naked exclusion' they had in mind, as they rejected his own *Suggestions*. Since Asquith already knew the preferences of the two Unionists, his request implied a desire for tactical advantage, rather than information. Carson therefore terminated the communications with a terse statement; by Ulster exclusion he meant that he had always wanted Ulster to remain under the Imperial Parliament, giving the Dublin assembly no powers within the excluded area.[21]

The Unionist leaders were led to assume that when the Government eventually made formal proposals they would be on the narrow lines of Home Rule within Home Rule, rather than some form of 'naked' Ulster exclusion such as the Lloyd George scheme. They concluded that Asquith intended to publicise his limited *Suggestions* at an appropriate time to improve his position in Britain and 'advertise his own reasonableness, and the bigotry of the Unionist Party'.[22] Bonar Law was due to speak at Bristol on 15 January, and since he knew how intensely his supporters disliked the idea of 'secret' negotiations, he felt it was vital to announce that they had failed. After consulting Asquith, Bonar Law announced at Bristol that talks had taken place between the leaders, so far without result, and he entertained no hope of a successful outcome. This speech suited the Prime Minister's purposes, since it carried the implication that the Opposition were responsible for terminating negotiations. This was only partly true, but the King interpreted the Bristol speech in this sense and Bonar Law incurred the royal displeasure.[23]

4 The Naval Crisis and Ulster: Lloyd George versus Churchill, January 1914

The Prime Minister did not inform the Cabinet about the talks with Carson and the *Suggestions* he had presented to the Unionists until 22 January 1914. Asquith kept his own counsel throughout the Irish negotiations to a far greater degree than his opposite number. Crewe, Haldane, Grey, Morley and Simon knew something of the developments, though probably not a great deal. The Prime Minister no doubt postponed discussing the Irish situation because the Cabinet crisis over the naval estimates reached its climax in January 1914. Lloyd George and Churchill were the keenest ministerial advocates of Ulster exclusion, but they were also the chief protagonists in the battle over the navy. McKenna and Runciman were among the bitterest enemies of Churchill's 'big navy' policy, so that Lloyd George was aligned with the firmest opponents of Ulster exclusion. The naval crisis had reached such proportions by January 1914 that there was some danger of Churchill or Lloyd George resigning and precipitating the Government's collapse. The situation was further complicated by suspicions that Churchill was looking for an excuse to return to the Unionist Party. Asquith sought to avoid increasing the areas of conflict by maintaining his accustomed reticence on the equally explosive question of Ireland.

Lloyd George, McKenna, Runciman and Simon insisted that they would only agree to finance two capital ships and by mid-January Churchill threatened to resign if he did not get four. Lloyd George feared the 'Navy tangle' would involve the 'smash' of the ministry and became convinced that Churchill was 'only waiting to choose between Home Rule or Navy before he quits a sinking ship'. Lloyd George, Simon, Runciman, McKenna and Trevelyan believed that Churchill should be allowed to resign. Runciman positively gloated that '. . . all looks set fair for a united Liberal party minus . . . this brilliant unreliable Churchill who has been a guest in our party for eight and a half years'.[24] The significance of the naval crisis, in terms of the Irish question, was revealed by C.P. Scott's comment, on 15 January, that Lloyd George and Simon were:

> . . . strongly of opinion that Churchill was only waiting for a favourable opportunity to leave the party and Simon thought that if he resigned on Home Rule and the coercion of Ulster it might be more damaging . . .

Runciman agreed with Trevelyan's view that it was vastly preferable 'that Winston should leave as a protest against economy than against the suppression of an Ulster rebellion'. Trevelyan was anxious that Churchill 'should be got rid of at once', before he had chance to organise a parliamentary following over the Ulster question, where he might do more harm.[25]

On 21 January, Lloyd George actually challenged Churchill directly, in the Prime Minister's presence. The Chancellor alleged that it was useless to make concessions on the naval estimates, because Churchill would resign over the Irish question if he did not resign over the navy. Churchill, in confusion, disclaimed any such intention, while refusing to commit himself in advance. The Prime Minister no doubt disliked this incident intensely and expressed full confidence in Churchill, but Lloyd George believed he had increased Churchill's difficulties in taking the course predicted.[26] Lloyd George's own motives were not above suspicion either. Haldane considered the campaign against arms growth an excellent issue, which Lloyd George might seize, to 'break away from the Government and to take the lead of the Radical and Labour Party' and possibly escape from a bad budget.[27]

However, the attack was concentrated mainly on the First Lord and his aggressive intentions. Simon circulated a memorandum to the Cabinet on 29 January, representing the views of McKenna, Runciman, Hobhouse, Beauchamp and McKinnon Wood. They claimed that Churchill's naval expansion would harm causes to which they were pledged and expose the Government to serious parliamentary attack from left-wing Liberals and Labour members; meanwhile 'Ulstermen who profess that our defeat is the only protection against "civil war" will hardly resist the temptation offered'. The letter concluded, a little smugly, that 'our single desire is to promote absolute unity under your leadership, with the view of giving Home Rule the best possible chance'.[28] Despite the numerical superiority of his ministerial opponents, Churchill emerged the victor. At the Cabinet on 29 January, Lloyd George made a final futile effort to withstand Churchill's demands, while the Prime Minister appealed 'for unity in face of peril of great interests', especially Home Rule.[29] By 11 February the First Lord secured his four capital ships, conceding only a conditional promise of reductions for 1915.

Lloyd George appeared to have abandoned the fight by February, much to the disgust of his fellow pacifists and 'economists'. McKenna, Simon and Hobhouse consequently wrote to inform the Chancellor that they could no longer follow his lead in the Cabinet and McKenna even accused Lloyd George of having become 'Churchill's man'.[30] In one significant respect, Lloyd George's interests conflicted with those of his fellow 'economists'. McKenna and Runciman, especially, were irreconcilably opposed to Churchill on both the naval estimates and the Ulster question, but Lloyd George did not share their view that the Home Rule cause would best be served by Churchill's resignation. However alienated the Chancellor and the First Lord had become during their struggle over the naval estimates, in the last resort Lloyd George was probably prepared to compromise over the navy to retain Churchill's support over Ulster.

5 Asquith's Allies and the 'Suggestions', January – February 1914

The crisis over the navy had reached critical proportions when Asquith informed his colleagues about the breakdown of the Ulster negotiations and the *Suggestions* made to Carson, in the Cabinet of 22 January. The Prime Minister was probably not unduly disturbed that his colleagues were distracted from the Irish talks by more pressing matters. Those ministers who were normally the most concerned about Ulster were the most heavily engaged in the naval imbroglio, enabling Asquith to pass lightly over the termination of the Irish negotiations. He emphasised Carson's 'flat refusal' of his *Suggestions*, which were represented as not only reasonable, but even generous. The Cabinet remained largely ignorant of the character and context of the talks with Carson and Bonar Law, within which Carson's ultimate response appeared less unhelpful. Asquith informed the King of the 'general opinion' within the Cabinet that his own *Suggestions* went to the extreme limits of generosity.[31] This statement is hard to accept at face value. The opponents of Ulster exclusion, such as McKenna and Runciman, may well have considered the *Suggestions* excessively generous, but the advocates of exclusion were unlikely to share their view.

Lloyd George and Churchill, admittedly, urged that parliament and the country should be informed of Asquith's *Suggestions* as soon as possible. But this was clearly intended as a tactical move to demonstrate the Government's willingness to make apparently reasonable offers to Ulster. Notes passed across the Cabinet table between Churchill and Lloyd George indicated that they had by no means abandoned the Chancellor's exclusion scheme in favour of the Prime Minister's hybrid plan. For the moment, however, they appreciated the publicity value of announcing Asquith's *Suggestions* when parliament opened. These might temporarily appease British and Nationalist opinion, and undermine the Unionist case for supporting an Ulster rebellion, until the time came to surprise the Opposition with the Lloyd George exclusion scheme.[32]

Some ministers were probably too preoccupied with other matters, or too ignorant of the detailed development of the Irish negotiations, to question the value of publicising a scheme which had been totally rejected by the Opposition. Other ministers acquiesced precisely because they saw the tactical advantages of the situation. The King, however, sought a solution, and detected the false note in the Prime Minister's proposal. Since Ulster would never agree to send representatives to a Dublin Parliament, the King pointed out firmly on 26 January: '. . . the danger of laying before Parliament and the Country, your proposed concessions if they are to be your last word, as you run the risk of closing the negotiations which in my opinion would be disastrous'.[33] The

King's protest did not deter the Prime Minister, who had probably never intended his *Suggestions* to be the last word and did not propose to lose their tactical benefits.

The Prime Minister's next step was to communicate his *Suggestions* to the Irish leaders, to put pressure on the Nationalists by demonstrating that 'reasonable' offers would not satisfy the Unionists. Asquith met Redmond at 10 Downing Street on 2 February in the presence of a silent Birrell. Redmond had heard nothing at all from the Government since the end of November 1913 and was gravely concerned that the growing National Volunteer movement in the south would precipitate violence before a Home Rule settlement was reached. Asquith followed the technique of his previous interview with Redmond on 17 November, maximising his own problems and minimising the extent of the concessions so far contemplated by the Cabinet.

The Prime Minister first informed Redmond of the interviews with Bonar Law and Carson, emphasising their refusal to accept anything short of the total exclusion of Ulster. Asquith twisted the truth when he claimed that he and his colleagues 'were all firmly opposed to the exclusion of Ulster, or any part of Ulster, even temporarily'. Asquith confided in Venetia Stanley that he 'developed the situation with such art as I could muster, until the psychological moment arrived for discharging my bomb'. The Prime Minister outlined his *Suggestions* for Home Rule within Home Rule, combined with an Ulster legislative veto, assuring Redmond that they were 'only his own personal idea, and had not been submitted to the Cabinet or accepted by them'. This statement was as misleading as Asquith's failure to mention that the *Suggestions* had already been rejected by Carson and Bonar Law. Indeed, by stating that 'no offer' had been made to the Unionists, he implied that they had not seen the *Suggestions*. The Prime Minister explained that such an offer would deprive the Ulster Unionist case of all moral force in the event of its anticipated rejection. Asquith commented to Venetia Stanley that Redmond 'shivered visibly' when his bomb was delivered, and was considerably perturbed, but 'the general effect was salutary'. As the Prime Minister informed the Cabinet next day, Redmond considered the *Suggestions* 'offensive to Nationalism, but the P.M. formed the view he would accept them later on, with protest'.[34]

At this stage Asquith had not decided whether to make use of the *Suggestions* during the parliamentary session, as a further device to gain time, and to try to show the Nationalists that they constituted a genuine offer. Nor was he sure whether it would be advisable to announce the *Suggestions*, if at all, during the Address debate, when parliament opened on 10 February. Redmond's reaction helped Asquith to reach a decision. The Nationalist leader sent a detailed reply to the Prime Minister on 4 February, arguing forcefully that no definite concessions of any sort should be proposed in the Address debate. The Nationalists would be placed in an impossible parliamentary position in deciding how to vote at such an early stage in the final circuit. Redmond 'might be forced into closing the door on proposals which, if they came at a later stage in the struggle, and under other circumstances, I might be in a position to consider in a different spirit'. Since Asquith expected the Opposition to reject the *Suggestions*, they would simply provide an opportunity for destructive criticism by the Unionists, tending to demoralise both Liberals and Nationalists before the formal debate commenced. The Nationalist leaders privately hoped that concessions would only be announced at the 'suggestion' stage, after the Home Rule Bill had passed the formal Committee stage. Redmond could then say he disliked the alterations, but accepted them as the price of Home Rule.[35]

6 Parliamentary Battle Resumed, February 1914

The 1914 parliamentary session was crucial, but the three Cabinet meetings in the week before the session opened were reminiscent of those held before the Bill's introduction in April 1912. The Cabinet lacked an overall strategy and advance planning was non-existent. Problems were dealt with in a piece-meal manner at the very last conceivable moment. On 5 February the Cabinet discussed Redmond's letter of the previous day and generally considered his arguments 'unanswerable'. Further consideration was postponed until the Cabinet of 9 February – the very day the session opened. After prolonged debate, ministers agreed that Asquith should not make any proposal about Ulster the following day. However, Redmond only just won his point and Birrell warned him that the Cabinet 'won't be willing to wait *very long* before making up their minds as to what *ought* to be offered publicly to Ulster'.[36]

Since this decision was only reached the day before the session opened, the Opposition was taken by surprise. The Unionists had decided to dramatise the opening of this vital session by moving an amendment to the Address in both Houses, demanding an election on the Home Rule Bill before it was considered further. They assumed that Asquith would immediately follow their amendment with an offer based on his December *Suggestions*.[37] The Unionist amendment was debated on 10 and 11 February, after the King's speech, but Asquith's speech disconcerted the Opposition. Instead of making the anticipated proposals, he spoke in general terms, repeating the well-worn arguments against a dissolution. Towards the end, however, he made a fundamental concession with the admission that it was the Government's obligation to take the 'initiative in the way of suggestion'. The Prime Minister promised to submit suggestions to the House, as the price of a peaceful settlement, when the necessary financial business had been transacted. He also felt obliged to deny charges that the Government was 'trifling with this matter or seeking to gain time'.[38]

Bonar Law was 'entirely taken aback by Asquith's line and decided not to follow him'. Chamberlain privately felt this was a great mistake, since it was their leader's responsibility to destroy the false impression created by Asquith's obscure comments. These had caused speculation among Unionist backbenchers that the Government was ready to adopt exclusion and even that Asquith had already made acceptable proposals to Bonar Law in secret. Chamberlain believed the Prime Minister was deliberately lulling 'our men and the country into a sense of security whilst he was gaining time and waiting for something to turn up'.[39] The King was equally concerned, since he was also aware that Asquith's private suggestions were unacceptable to the Unionists. George V informed his Prime Minister that:

Your not unfavourable attitude towards the exclusion of Ulster, which policy I have always maintained is the only means of averting civil war, seems to have given an impression that the Government may adopt such a course. If this is not the case, may not harm be done by raising false hopes and delaying the announcement of what is the precise limit of your concessions. [40]

The contributions of Carson, Bonar Law and Redmond introduced a conciliatory note into the debate. Carson promised that 'it will be my duty to go to Ulster at once and take counsel with the people there', if the exclusion of Ulster was proposed to avoid civil war. His final plea to his 'Nationalist fellow countrymen', to try to win over Ulster by sympathetic understanding rather than force, had a powerful impact on the House. Bonar Law supported Carson's conciliatory line, though he made it absolutely clear that the exclusion of Ulster was the only possible means of reconciling the Unionists to Home Rule. He also warned that limited plans such as Home Rule within Home Rule would do great damage; they were created only to be rejected, merely to allow the Government to improve its tactical position. These public statements constituted a significant advance, for the Unionists now appeared ready to end their resistance to Home Rule for the rest of Ireland, if Ulster was excluded. This admission was no surprise to those familiar with the private views of the Unionist leaders, but equally they recognised the enormous difficulties involved in reaching agreement over 'Ulster exclusion'. Redmond maintained a conciliatory tone despite his misgivings. Since Asquith had created a new situation by agreeing to initiate proposals, the Nationalists would consider them in the friendliest spirit, provided that the Unionists in return accepted them as the price of peace. [41]

7 Lloyd George's Exclusion Scheme Revived February to March 1914

The general belief that the Government was about to propose some form of Ulster exclusion was justified. After the Cabinet on 9 February, the Prime Minister made no further attempt to press for the formal proposal of his December *Suggestions* for Home Rule within Home Rule. The debate convinced

THE MISSING WORD.

THE "PREMIER" PARROT (*emerging from profound thought*). "EX——EX——EX——EX——"

JOHN BULL. "LOOK HERE, HERBERT, IF YOU 'RE *GOING* TO SAY 'EXCLUSION,' FOR HEAVEN'S SAKE SAY IT AND GET IT OVER!" [*Parrot relapses into profound thought.*

195

Asquith that the *Suggestions* could no longer yield tactical advantage and even the Nationalists recognised that Home Rule within Home Rule must be ruled out as too limited. The Prime Minister must at last put forward a definite scheme, which he seriously intended to be considered as a genuine basis for an agreed settlement. During the Address debate he had finally assumed responsibility for making a proposal and on 16 February he repeated his promise to make a statement very soon.

It had been clear since November 1913 that some form of Ulster exclusion was almost certainly the only way to gain the agreement of the Unionists to Home Rule. Asquith had known all along that Bonar Law and Carson refused to consider any variant on Home Rule within Home Rule, but the *Suggestions* had served a purpose. It seems likely that the Lloyd George exclusion scheme of November 1913 had never been forgotten, either by its author or the Prime Minister. It was merely placed in cold storage, while Asquith used his *Suggestions* to gain further time and keep the situation under control. By mid-February 1914, the moment had arrived for Lloyd George to step onto the centre of the stage once more with his ready-made proposals for Ulster exclusion. Asquith had allowed the Unionists and Nationalists to believe that he disapproved of the Lloyd George plan, turning attention instead to the far more limited *Suggestions*. An unexpected reversion to the Chancellor's exclusion plan in March 1914 was intended to surprise the Opposition by its generosity. This was probably Asquith's general strategy if no more congenial alternative presented itself. No doubt he would have welcomed an Opposition acceptance of his *Suggestions*, but he can scarcely have expected it. Meanwhile, he probably kept the November exclusion plan in the back of his mind.

On 16 February the Chancellor sent the Prime Minister a lengthy memorandum, presenting the case for his exclusion scheme as strongly as possible. Lloyd George may have decided independently that this was the right moment to resurrect his scheme. More likely, this was decided in collaboration with the Prime Minister. The plan had altered little since the original proposal was made on 12 and 13 November 1913, but a few more details were provided. Any county in Ulster was to be allowed to contract out of the Home Rule Act, provided that at least one-tenth of the registered voters signed a requisition demanding a plebiscite, which in turn had to be passed by a simple majority. At the end of an unspecified term of years the excluded counties would be automatically incorporated with the rest of Ireland, 'unless the Imperial Parliament in the meantime provided otherwise'. The November proposal had suggested five or six years as the exclusion period and omitted the details concerning the plebiscite. Lloyd George tried to minimise the effects of his plan, arguing that a supposedly limited alteration would remove the Ulster Unionist justification for resistance, since they could scarcely rebel in anticipation of future oppression. The Unionist demand for an election was answered by the plebiscites in the affected Ulster counties and also by the intervention of at least one general election before the termination of the exclusion period. [42]

Lord Blake has argued that Lloyd George's scheme was purely tactical and was never seriously intended as the basis for an agreed settlement. [43] This was certainly true of Asquith's December *Suggestions*, but not of the Chancellor's exclusion plan. Obviously any scheme for Ulster exclusion was partially tactical; neither side sought exclusion from choice, but rather as a *pis aller*. Therefore the chosen plan needed superior tactical advantages and Lloyd George tended to over-emphasise these in his memorandum. But the scheme was almost certainly intended by Asquith and Lloyd George as their basis for negotiating an agreed settlement. They had no alternative except to coerce Ulster into accepting the original Bill and few ministers were prepared to contemplate coercion.

Asquith and Lloyd George proceeded to re-open negotiations with the Irish leaders, to secure Nationalist acquiescence in the Lloyd George scheme, with a reluctant Chief Secretary in attendance. Two interviews took place, on 27 February and 2 March, though the Cabinet were not informed until 4 March. Both meetings were dominated by Lloyd George, who confided to Riddell that Asquith was worried, but did not say much:

The P.M.'s trouble is that he hates anything unpleasant or in the nature of a

000000,00000,0000,0000,0000,0000,000,000,000,000,0,0,0,0,0,0,0,0,0,0,0,0,0,0,0,0,0,0,0,0,0,0,0,0,0,0,0,0,0,0,0,0,0,0

---

row. He hates an unpleasant interview. He said to me, 'I think you had better have a preliminary conversation with the Irish'. He thought it would be an unpleasant and troublesome task !

Even Lloyd George complained afterwards that he had '. . . a tough job. The Irish are rare negotiators. They bluff so well that you really cannot tell whether they are bluffing or not'.[44] This was high praise from Lloyd George. At the first interview, Lloyd George and Birrell met Redmond, Dillon and Devlin at the Treasury for a preliminary discussion of the Chancellor's exclusion scheme. Lloyd George agreed to Redmond's two conditions, that the Nationalists could only support a plan approved by the Unionists and that 'the scheme in substance would be the last word of the Government'. Redmond was reassured that if the plan was rejected the Government was determined to proceed with the Bill as it stood and to face any consequences in Ulster. The scheme was discussed more fully at the second meeting on 2 March, when Asquith and T.P. O'Connor increased the numbers to seven, and Asquith confirmed that the proposed concession would be the Government's last word.[45] Redmond submitted a memorandum that evening, defining the limits of concession acceptable to the Nationalists. The three year exclusion period must be the Government's last word which could not be extended under any circumstances. He emphasised that the Nationalists could only acquiesce in this solution 'as the price of peace', at the enormous risk of alienating their Irish friends.[46]

At the Cabinet on 4 March, Lloyd George again assumed the initiative in describing the two interviews with the Irish leaders, while Asquith read aloud Redmond's memorandum. Charles Masterman, the most recent recruit to the Cabinet, illustrated the Chancellor's predominance at this point, when he told Riddell a couple of days later that Lloyd George was 'the only man in the Cabinet who had initiative, and that his superiority in that respect is marked'. Most ministers had been kept in the dark about the resurrection of the Lloyd George scheme and they were by no means unanimous in their support. The critics pointed out that if the Tories really objected, they could find 'plenty of excuses for a wrecking malevolent policy'. Asquith informed the King of the efforts to win round the critics:

Many difficulties, financial and administrative, were dwelt upon by Mr. McKenna, Mr. Samuel and others as necessarily involved in the adoption of any such scheme. But it was pointed out that these were difficulties incident to 'exclusion' in any form, and that if the principle were agreed upon, there were not likely to be any insurmountable differences in the adjustment of the machinery.[47]

The advocates of the Lloyd George scheme argued that if the Unionists accepted the principle, accommodation might be reached by extending the exclusion period from three to six years. This point was highly significant. Redmond's letter stipulated a three year exclusion period, as the 'last word', and this was presumably the time-limit mentioned by Lloyd George and Asquith at the two interviews. Since the Chancellor had suggested a five or six year limit even in November 1913, and clearly the Unionists would accept no less, the three year limit was no more than a bait for the Nationalists and was never intended to be the 'last word' for very long. Despite opposition from such ministers as McKenna, Samuel and Runciman, it was agreed that Asquith should recommend a settlement based on the Lloyd George plan in the Commons on 9 March. Redmond was informed that the Cabinet accepted his conditions, without binding themselves regarding 'matters of detail', which might require further negotiation if the Opposition accepted the proposals.[48]

The Prime Minister had evidently intended to propose the three year time limit on 9 March, using it as a starting-point for bargaining. He was obliged, however, to renegotiate 'matters of detail' with the Nationalists earlier than anticipated. His plans were frustrated because the Cabinet decision of 4 March was 'leaked' to the lobby correspondent of the *Daily News*, who published his scoop the following morning. Asquith's angry enquiries among his colleagues failed to uncover the culprit and the advantage of surprise was lost. The Opposition were suspicious that the published scheme was yet another subterfuge like Home Rule within Home Rule. Even the more moderate Unionists shared Lord Charles Beresford's view that the Prime Minister was 'frivolling, humbugging, and using the most dishonest methods'. Carson and Lansdowne believed Asquith's offer would be 'plausible and sticky' but it would not be acceptable to the Ulster Unionists.[49] A royal appeal that the Opposition should consider Asquith's proposals carefully brought a stiff reply from Bonar Law. He pointed out that these proposals had not been communicated to the Unionists but the rumours indicated that the exclusion option was to be offered for a very limited time only. Carson must refuse such a condition and Bonar Law insisted that he would lose the confidence of his party if he accepted. This reply did not surprise the King, who had already written to Asquith expressing grave fears that the three year limit would make Carson's position almost impossible.[50]

Asquith's hopes that the Unionists would accept his scheme cannot have been high in the first place. After the reactions to the press revelations, he had no option but to seek a further concession from Redmond on the time-limit immediately, rather than reserving it as a bargaining counter. The long-suffering Chief Secretary was given the thankless task of explaining to Redmond that, within four days, the three year limit had ceased to be the Government's last word. After this interview on 6 March, Redmond informed the Prime Minister that Birrell '. . . put it to us in such a way that we feel we cannot refuse to consent to an extension to five years', despite their 'deepest disappointment'.[51] The Prime Minister's reply was not a letter of thanks but a demand for a further extension. The generosity of the concession was ignored and Asquith argued that only a six year exclusion period would allow for a second general election before the term expired. The Nationalists acquiesced, though Devlin had only obtained the agreement of the Ulster Nationalists to the original three year limit after sustained efforts. The discovery that this 'last word' was actually doubled after only four days must have seemed like betrayal. Two people, at least, were pleased at the outcome. Churchill sent Lloyd George a note of congratulation on the success of the negotiations for a six year limit: 'This is a great triumph for your diplomacy'.[52]

8 The Second Reading: Lloyd George's Scheme Offered and Rejected, March 1914

The Government had to decide on the procedure for the presentation of their proposals. Only two methods existed for passing their scheme into law simultaneously with the Home Rule Bill. It could be incorporated into the basic structure of the original Bill by using the 'suggestion' stage, which had not been employed in the 1913 session. This involved the risk that the Opposition would seize the opportunity to try to wreck the whole Bill, or at least interfere with other aspects of its provisions. It also required the cooperation of the Lords, which was hardly likely to be forthcoming. The Cabinet recognised these problems when the Lloyd George scheme was first discussed on 13 November 1913. They decided instead to adopt an alternative method proposed by the ingenious Samuel, which was more favourable to the Government. Samuel suggested that a separate Amending Bill should be introduced, embodying the agreed alterations while leaving the Home Rule Bill intact. If the Amending Bill was rejected, the Government still retained the option of carrying the existing Home Rule Bill under the Parliament Act, with or without 'suggestions'.[53]

The preliminary procedure for presenting the Lloyd George plan to the Commons also had to be settled. Redmond had insisted that it should be put forward in general terms only, on Second Reading, preferably in the form of a White Paper. A secret Cabinet committee, consisting of Asquith, Crewe, Lloyd George, Grey and Haldane, met on 3 March to discuss the question.[54] A White Paper was then drafted by 6 March, outlining the procedure governing optional county exclusion, and was published four days later. Lloyd George's memorandum of 16 February was faithfully followed, providing that any Ulster county might be excluded from Home Rule for six years, if a majority voted for exclusion in a county poll. The White Paper was exceptionally brief, adding that certain unspecified modifications would be needed in the operation of the Home Rule Bill if any counties decided in favour of exclusion.[55]

The necessary financial and administrative adjustments were in the process of being drafted, though Asquith refused to reveal them to the Commons until the principle of the scheme was agreed. Before 6 March Lloyd George had already organised the preparation of a lengthy memorandum commenting on the practical implications of the White Paper. It was proposed that the excluded counties would retain the existing administrative system as far as possible and could be governed by the British department responsible for the Irish reserved services. The financial reorganisation would create the chief problems, since the excluded area would remain within the British taxation system, and it would be difficult to estimate how far the Irish transferred sum must be reduced to take this into account. Problems would be fewer if the Irish Parliament's taxation powers were postponed until exclusion terminated, thus preventing the erection of customs barriers within Ireland. Lloyd George's memorandum concluded that if the exclusion scheme could be agreed in principle 'no doubt these difficulties, formidable as they are, and involving practically a complete re-arrangement of figures, might be got over'.[56]

The Prime Minister presented his proposals to the Commons when he moved the Second Reading of the Home Rule Bill on 9 March. Only the bare essentials of the scheme, as set out in the White Paper, were mentioned. Asquith concentrated on defending the general principle, refusing to discuss the practical difficulties of operating the plan. He made a significant public admission of the acute gravity of the situation, acknowledging that if the Bill passed in its present form, they had to face 'the prospect of acute dissension and even of civil strife'. He attempted to refute the logical corollary that his original policy had been inadequate or defective and cleverly underlined the need to compromise between the surrender of principle and the application of force. Asquith did not expect his proposals to be received with enthusiasm in any quarter, since they were not supported on their own merits, but as the price of peace.[57]

The Prime Minister admitted that the two crucial points of difficulty were exclusion area and time. But he was obviously relying upon the ambiguities in the scheme to gain the acquiescence of the Unionists and Nationalists. The provision for inclusion after six years was intended to appease the

Nationalists, whereas the Unionists were supposed to concentrate their hopes on the possibilities of reprieve provided by the intervening elections. The question of the exclusion area was deliberately left undefined, but the Cabinet had estimated that the four north-east Ulster counties of Antrim, Armagh, Down and Londonderry would opt for exclusion, together with the cities of Belfast and London-derry.[58] In effect, then, the provisions of the scheme implied the temporary exclusion of the four north-east counties, with a strong possibility that exclusion would become permanent, if the Unionists won either of the next two general elections.

Carson was also capable of calculating that county option meant the exclusion of only four counties, whereas he had always demanded at least six and preferably all nine. For the moment he ignored this deficiency, and concentrated all his energies on attacking the six year time limit, which was a more vulnerable target. He argued that the problems were merely being postponed and aggravated by the next two elections and Ulster would remain a pawn in the British political game for the next six years: 'Ulster wants this question settled now and for ever. We do not want sentence of death with a stay of execution for six years . . .'. Carson made an astute alternative offer, that those Ulster counties which opted for exclusion should remain in the United Kingdom Parliament until that assembly decided otherwise. If the six year time limit was thus removed, Carson would feel obliged to call a convention in Ulster to consider the scheme. However, he dropped a broad hint that further demands would later be made on the issue of geographical area; in his opinion, the proposed scheme for dividing the counties according to referendum decisions would raise all manner of impracticable anomalies. Carson confirmed this suspicion in a private letter to St. Loe Strachey three days later: 'I fear if the Government give way on the time-limit it would be impossible to carry out their scheme of a ballot or referendum . . . really the only way out is by a clean cut'.[59] Carson's alternative offer appeared deceptively similar to the Prime Minister's proposal, confusing and disarming the uninitiated. T.P. O'Connor saw the trap only too clearly:

From the House of Commons point of view, it may seem a small thing whether the excluded counties have to come in automatically or by an express Act of Parliament. To Irish opinion it means whether exclusion is temporary or perpetual . . . she would regard herself as asked to surrender the unity of her Nationhood . . .

Redmond also recognised the danger, and insisted that the exclusion period must end automatically after a fixed term of six years.[60]

Bonar Law was aware that many British voters would consider Asquith's offer reasonable, but if he reacted favourably to the proposal he ran the danger of splitting the Unionists. Law was obviously under pressure from within his own party to reject the proposal, especially from the southern Unionists and their spokesmen. Even if the Unionist leader had been prepared to consider Asquith's scheme on its merits, the Prime Minister's behaviour since September 1913 left Bonar Law feeling resentful and suspicious that this was another tactical manoeuvre. Yet Bonar Law did not want to fall into the trap of rejecting an apparently reasonable suggestion outright and so put his party in the wrong with the British public. His immediate reply to the Prime Minister on 9 March was cautious, stating that Carson must speak for Ulster, but leaving no doubt that he considered the time-limit unacceptable. Bonar Law indicated the two directions which his counter-attack would follow. Firstly, he demanded that Asquith's proposals should be presented in the precise, detailed form in which they would be enacted, so that the Opposition could examine a specific text instead of vague intentions. At question time on 16 March the Unionists put down twenty-six questions, challenging Asquith to explain in detail the implications of his proposals. The Prime Minister refused to be drawn and Carson declared that the offer of the previous Monday had evidently been a 'hypocritical sham'. The Opposition underlined their displeasure by moving a vote of censure on 19 March, regretting the Government's refusal to formulate their detailed proposals before the resumption of the Second Reading.[61]

The vote of censure debate provided the opportunity for Bonar Law to develop the second line of counter-attack, following Carson's example in presenting the Government with an alternative offer. On 9 March the Unionist leader had demanded that the Prime Minister should submit his proposals to a referendum of the whole United Kingdom, rather that just the Ulster counties. During the intervening week, he decided to extend this into a positive offer so that the public would see that the Opposition met Asquith's proposal with an equally reasonable offer. The demand for a referendum on Asquith's Ulster proposals was simply an extension of the well-worn Unionist cry for a dissolution and had been forcefully advocated for some time by Selborne, Curzon and Lord Robert Cecil. When he moved the vote of censure, Bonar Law emphasised that his party had not closed the door hastily upon any genuine Government offer; the ministry's refusal to present their plan in precise legislative form cast doubt on their sincerity. He tried to convince the House of his own party's sincerity, by making a formal offer to abide by the country's verdict on the principle of Ulster exclusion. Bonar Law's tone was considerably more moderate than at question time on 17 March. The change was dictated partly by tactical considerations and partly by a real desire to find a way to avoid bloodshed. [62]

Carson congratulated Law on a masterly speech: 'I do *not* know what answer the P.M. can give to the referendum proposal but I imagine he is in a hopeless condition as I see Dillon refused it'. Carson underestimated Asquith's stoicism and resilience. The Prime Minister informed the King that nothing would induce him to agree to a referendum. [63] Asquith then resumed private negotiations by letter with Bonar Law, within three days of the referendum offer of 19 March. The Prime Minister proposed that an immediate referendum should be abandoned, in return for the definite exclusion of six counties, with a plebiscite at the end of the six year exclusion period as to whether those counties would remain outside Home Rule. This was an attempt to retain the six year time limit, in exchange for concessions over the area, since an initial poll would only exclude four counties. This change of tactics allowed Asquith to argue that a British referendum should then be jettisoned along with the Ulster county poll. [64] The offer came too late. By then the Curragh incident had intervened.

Bonar Law's referendum offer effectively counteracted any public indignation which might have resulted from a direct rejection of Asquith's proposals. At the same time it increased the resentment and depression of many Liberals. The Prime Minister's offer had been a serious attempt to reach a settlement on this occasion, but the Opposition could hardly be blamed for suspecting otherwise, in view of Asquith's record over the preceding months. Nor was it surprising that Bonar Law should at this stage adopt the kind of tactical manoeuvre so cleverly used by Asquith throughout the winter negotiations. Unionist rejection of the Lloyd George exclusion scheme had grave repercussions. The result was stalemate and deadlock. The tension was far more acute than it had been during the deadlock of January to September 1913. It was aggravated by the false hopes generated by the 'conversations' of the previous winter, and by the increased level of unrest in Ireland.

The Prime Minister evidently attempted to treat the rejection of his proposals as a minor setback — as one more move in a highly complicated chess game. It was merely a question of time and patience before move and counter-move finally achieved a compromise result which both sides could reluctantly accept as a *pis aller*. Asquith's attitude and assumptions depended on the continued control of Home Rule policy by politicians at Westminster.

But by 20 March 1914, Asquith's time had run out, and events in Ireland overtook a rapidly deteriorating political situation at Westminster. Certain members of the Government, notably Lloyd George and Churchill, were more realistic about this situation. They were also more bitter about the rejection of the exclusion scheme, which they had regarded all along as the best possible final solution, and not merely as one possible negotiating counter among many. They felt the ministry now had no alternative but to force through the Home Rule Bill as it stood and prepare for the coercion of Ulster.

VII
THE CURRAGH CRISIS AND FINAL RECKONING, MARCH – APRIL 1914

'. . . if the story told here is not correct, then I can only say it is the most wonderful combination of circumstances and coincidences that has ever been told, even in fiction.' (Walter Long's Memorandum on 'The Plot', 27 March 1914, B.L.P. 39/2/22.)

1 The Political and Military Background to the Curragh Incident

The Curragh affair has been the subject of several detailed studies.[1] These have concentrated on developments in the army and have largely accepted the Unionist charges that the Liberal Government was engaged in a plot to coerce Ulster. The source material now available suggests that there was no sinister conspiracy. This conclusion, however, opens up new questions about the responsibility of the Government to take long-term military precautions to deal with Ulster's resistance. In refuting the 'plot' charges, the Government tended to lose sight of its right and obligation to make military preparations of any kind in Ulster. This chapter examines the Liberal Cabinet's aims and motives in March 1914 and assesses the overall significance of the Curragh crisis from a new perspective.

The Prime Minister's Ulster policy involved a massive gamble. In the first eighteen months after the policy decision of February 1912, Asquith's approach was based on the assumption that the Unionists were bluffing and the dangers of civil war vastly exaggerated. By the late autumn of 1913 the Cabinet belatedly recognised the gravity of the situation, faced with overwhelming evidence that the Ulster movement had grown dramatically from June 1913 onwards. From then on, the Prime Minister took the risk that violence or civil strife in Ulster would not erupt before his last minute political compromise with the Opposition was finally achieved. By 19 March 1914 the Cabinet's political options had become very dangerously limited. It was vital that the ministry should be in a position to argue that they would press on with their original Home Rule Bill if the Opposition failed to agree to reasonable terms for a compromise.

Once ministers acknowledged that Ulster's resistance had to be taken seriously, and that a political compromise might conceivably prove unattainable, they should have examined the military implications. To deal with the situation effectively, the Government had to be able to show that it was willing and able to use the army to deal with Ulster's resistance, in the event of the breakdown of negotiations. The Unionists frequently expressed the belief that the Government would not dare to use military force against the Ulster Volunteers. Up to the summer of 1913 ministers made little effort to refute this assumption, generally evading questions about the use of the army in Ulster. In the course of 1913, however, the Cabinet became more aware of the need to assert the principle that the army would be used to impose Home Rule on Ulster, if necessary. The Chief Secretary wrote anxiously to Asquith on 30 August 1913:

. . . believing as I do in the *serious* character of Ulster resistance, involving as I am certain it does, *military operation*, which must either be on such a scale as to *overawe* the rebels, or to dispose of a considerable number of them . . .

the Government had to be ready to use the army since the Irish police were unreliable. By October Birrell thought the Government might have to face up to the possibility of interfering in advance, to prevent the threatened 'anarchy, disorder and bloodshed', and they must prepare for such an eventuality. Asquith informed the King that illegal resistance to the Home Rule Act would have to be crushed, though the army would only be used in the last resort, when 'more indirect means had been tried and proved to be ineffectual'.[2]

In some quarters it was felt that something more was required than these general statements of intention. The views of Lord Haldane, Seely's predecessor at the War Office, were particularly significant. As early as September 1913 Lord Esher reported to the King, after a talk with the Lord Chancellor:

[Haldane] is urging upon the Prime Minister and the Cabinet that precisely similar precautions to those taken to guard against the strike in Wales, and the coal strike, should be taken in Ulster. He suggests sending at once for Sir Arthur Paget, and discussing with him the necessary measures: giving him General Macready (who exhibited useful qualities of judgement and tact in Wales) as a special Staff Officer, and forming a 'Composite Force', comprising battalions of southern regiments and free from Irish influences, to be sent immediately into Ulster. The Lord Chancellor obviously thinks that by a display of firmness, both as regards policy and maintenance of order, the situation can be met . . . with good management, and firm military handling, not a drop of blood need or would be shed.

In January 1914, Haldane was still convinced that serious trouble could be averted by sending 'an overwhelming force' into Ulster to maintain order well in advance.[3] Sir David Harrel, who had been Irish Under-Secretary in the 1890s, shared Haldane's view about the urgency of firm preparations. Harrel advised his former chief, Lord Morley, in January 1914, that the Government should: '. . . prepare for the worst by the same elaborate police and military plans and precautions as he and I had made ready in 1893, – only more elaborate, because then everybody knew that Home Rule would not become law, and everybody knows today that it will.' Even the normally pacific Morley reminded Asquith on 17 March that in 1893 General Wolseley 'had counselled a swift descent on and coercion of Ulster'.[4]

The Government had a very strong case for making contingency plans to deal with Ulster's resistance if the Ulster Unionists refused either to accept Home Rule or to agree to a compromise settlement. The precautions recommended by Haldane and Harrel were not only defensible, they were eminently sensible. Judged by Haldane's standards, however, the Government's long range military planning was singularly deficient, though with two notable exceptions. The decision to send Major-General Sir Nevil Macready to Ireland in November 1913 was a wise step. Macready was Director of Personal Services at the War Office, with responsibilities which included the use of troops in aid of the civil power. His previous experience in controlling labour disputes in South Wales and Lancashire proved his abilities in that delicate area, so that he was well qualified for a distasteful task in Ireland. Seely briefed Macready to report on the situation facing the civil and military administration in Ireland in the event of a disturbance — 'to watch the North', as Sir Henry Wilson put it. When General Macready was sent to Ulster in March 1914, he commented:

I was convinced that through a policy of drift the Government had lost all control of the situation, which was entirely in the hands of Carson and his followers. Every Government service was either effete or unreliable, results due on the one hand to the policy of Dublin Castle, and on the other to sympathy with the Orangemen . . . [The Royal Irish Constabulary] had undoubtedly deteriorated into what was almost a state of supine lethargy, and had lost even the semblance of energy or initiative when a crisis demanded vigorous and resolute action.[5]

The attempt to limit the accumulation of arms and ammunition in Ireland was also sensible and necessary, though the timing and effectiveness of the move were more questionable. Birrell had been concerned about the sharp rise in the estimated number of arms at the disposal of the Ulster Volunteer Force, since the summer of 1913. The Cabinet discussed the question on 24 and 25 November, in the light of Birrell's reports and Simon's legal advice. Simon explained that no special statutory power existed in Ireland to prohibit the importation and use of arms, after the Irish coercion Acts were allowed to lapse in 1906. But certain provisions of the customs legislation could be invoked to authorise the forfeiture of arms and ammunition *en route* from Great Britain to Ireland, and also from abroad, though the legality of the latter was more doubtful. On 1st December, the Cabinet decided to issue the necessary Royal Proclamations for these purposes, in view of the evidence that two armies were being organised.[6]

By February 1914, Simon concluded that the Proclamations had been fairly effective in preventing the importation of arms into Ireland. Sir Almeric Fitzroy welcomed the Proclamations as 'the first challenge to recalcitrant Ulster', which might test the strength of the spirit behind the preparations for revolt. Lord Esher, on the other hand, feared they might do 'incalculable harm' in precipitating matters and he understood that several ministers, including Morley, shared his anxiety.[7] These misgivings were justified. The Proclamations aroused

FORE-ARMED.

Sir Edward Carson (*in course of promenade on the quay, to Customs Officer Birrell*). "CAPITAL IDEA THIS OF STOPPING IMPORTATION OF ARMS. NOW THERE'S A DANGEROUS CHARACTER; YOU SHOULD SEARCH HIM. THAT'S JUST THE SORT OF BAG HE'D HAVE A COUPLE OF HOWITZERS CONCEALED IN."

intense resentment amongst the Nationalists. They interpreted the move as blatantly unfair discrimination against the infant National Volunteer movement, almost immediately after its inauguration. The timing was unfortunate, to say the least, since the U.V.F. had been allowed to arm for the past year with no legal intervention. Though it did not reduce the Nationalists' sense of grievance, the Proclamations actually involved a severe setback to the plans of the U.V.F., since they were still far from being effectively armed. The result was a reappraisal of the U.V.F. arms policy, culminating in the major gun-running coup at Larne in April 1914.

The only other action contemplated by the Cabinet before March 1914 was the possibility of arresting Carson and the ringleaders of the Ulster movement. After the imprisonment of James Larkin, leader of the Dublin industrial agitation, the clamour for Carson's arrest from left-wing Liberal and Labour supporters reached its height. Charles Trevelyan's comments were typical: 'Larkin's methods may be intolerable. But most progressives think his main objects right and Carson's wrong. Yet he is imprisoned and Carson romps about free'. When the Cabinet discussed the Larkin affair in November 1913, Pease remarked that it was hard to justify to the voters the Government's restraint in neglecting to prosecute a man in Carson's position who preached sedition and drilled forces to resist the law. [8]

From August 1913 the Chief Secretary recognised that Carson was openly challenging the Government to prosecute him, but Birrell hesitated. His letter to Asquith of 3 October suggests that, for a while, Birrell moved towards the view that Carson should be prosecuted:

. . . whilst most completely convinced that to interfere with this wicked enterprise of Carson's *up to the present time* would have been folly (I think everybody who knows anything agrees as to this) it *may* at any moment become a grave question *how much longer* we can stand on one side and allow rebellion to be preached and prepared for . . . the question is – can he be allowed to preach and practise *sedition* and *mutiny right up* to the passage of the Bill . . . [9]

The Cabinet finally answered Birrell's question in the affirmative. A few days after receiving Birrell's letter, the

Prime Minister informed the King that the Government did not intend to arrest Carson for sedition, because it would 'throw a lighted match into a powder barrel'. Sir John Simon advised his colleagues late in November that the leaders of the Ulster movement could justifiably be prosecuted for many breaches of the law, including treason–felony and illegal drilling, but conviction on the main charges could only be obtained through the verdict of a jury. The Government decided that, however conclusive the evidence, no Irish jury would convict, and popular passions in Ulster would be inflamed with no certain deterrent effect. Moreover, the Nationalist leaders insisted that prosecution would 'inevitably secure for the victims an invaluable and much-coveted place in the annals of Irish martyrology'.[10]

Despite considerable justification for this policy of non-intervention, its risks increased enormously as the time for the threatened civil war drew nearer. Once the Cabinet reached the decision against prosecutions, a public announcement might have been advisable to prevent rumours to the contrary precipitating trouble. The most serious rumours that warrants were about to be issued for the arrest of the Ulster leaders were widely circulated during the week preceding the Curragh affair. No evidence exists that the Government had any such intention and the rumours may have arisen from faulty interpretation of information about the ministry's military plans. Bonar Law commented on 20 March that he never believed in the rumour 'for it is contrary to Asquith's whole nature to precipitate anything', and Carson maintained a degree of scepticism about the existence of the warrants.[11] But many Ulster Unionists took the rumours seriously enough for Captain Craig to order the Ulster Volunteer Force to prepare to mobilise at a moment's notice, on 19 March. The Prime Minister did not see fit to issue a public statement dispelling the rumours until 23 March, when he announced in *The Times* that the Government had no intention of arresting the Ulster leaders. This was too late. By then the rumours had already contributed to the alarm and confusion which culminated in the Curragh incident on 20 March.

Thus few special steps were taken before March 1914 to prepare to deal with Ulster's potential resistance to the Home

Rule Bill. The ministry made the minimum number of moves and vacillated about the wisdom of others. This failure can be explained in several ways. The Cabinet's attitude still contained a strong element of wishful thinking and the hope that Ulster was bluffing sprang eternal. Even on the day of the Curragh incident the King gained the impression that 'Asquith seemed to be still convinced that there could be nothing to fight about and that even if there were, there were no people in Ulster who would fight'. The Cabinet was also still ambivalent about the use of military force to deal with Ulster's opposition. Morley alternated between expressions of acute dismay at the prospect of armed conflict and the use of menacing language against the 'rebels'. Lord Esher thought this uncertainty typical of the whole Cabinet.[12]

This ambivalence was compounded by the fact that nobody was at all sure what form the anticipated trouble in Ulster would take; the nature and extent of the threatened resistance were alike ill-defined. Liberals and Nationalists tended to emphasise the practical difficulties of maintaining a rebel provisional government in opposition to the British Government. J.J. Clancy, a Nationalist M.P., wrote a lengthy memorandum arguing that Ulster's trade would be destroyed, her social system shattered, and bankruptcy universal. The Unionist leaders were fully aware of the grave practical difficulties involved in the establishment of an Ulster provisional government, aiming to resist a Home Rule Act passed by the British Government. They also realised that the British Government could not afford to wait until these problems ultimately undermined the rebellion; an Ulster Unionist revolt was likely to be suppressed by the British army long before Clancy's predictions could be fulfilled. There was little doubt that the British army could overwhelm the Ulster Volunteers, though Captain Wilfrid Spender, Quarter-Master General of the rebel army, described some of the military problems to his cousin, Harold Spender:

Your side can of course beat us if you are prepared to keep 4 divisions (⅔rds of our army) stationed in Ulster for some months but even if this did not lead to very great military difficulties, foreign complications would be a fearful risk. To use lesser force will certainly mean the most terrible loss of life, and if your side settle on force I hope you will use your influence to make it overwhelming from the first . . .

Other questions were raised, such as how long this military suppression would take, how much blood would be shed in the process, and the effects it would have on the army, the British Government, and British public opinion. Carson obviously hoped such a situation would not arise. He admitted that Ulster could be coerced into submission, but protested that it would then have to be governed as a conquered community, which would hardly produce a peaceful or permanent settlement.[13] There is little evidence that the Government examined these questions very carefully.

The situation was still further complicated by fears that some army officers might refuse to fight against the Ulster Protestants, who merely asked to remain under the British Crown. Bonar Law warned Churchill in September 1913 that the Unionists might even urge officers to ignore Government orders to use force against Ulster. There is no doubt that many British army officers did dislike the prospect of being sent to deal with resistance in Ulster. The army was theoretically non-political, but many officers were conservative by instinct and their sympathies were often with the Ulster Protestants. Soldiers were trained to obey orders, but Asquith evidently believed there was a possibility that they might not do so in this case. He warned Redmond in November that War Office information pointed to the 'probability of very numerous resignations of commissions of officers in the event of the troops being used to put down an Ulster insurrection'. But Asquith was clearly uncertain about this and may have exaggerated the dangers to put pressure on Redmond, since he previously told the King that there was insufficient basis for such fears.[14]

The military problem was aggravated early in 1914 by the possibility that the Unionists might amend the Army (Annual) Act. This measure had to be renewed each year to legalise the existence of a standing army and the Opposition considered amending it to prevent the Government using troops in Ulster at all. Selborne, Carson, Chamberlain and the three Cecils were enthusiastic about the plan, but criticism from the Unionist rank and file led to its abandonment by 20 March. There was profound uneasiness about the implications of taking steps which appeared to justify mutiny and rebellion, and which could turn the electorate against the Lords and the Unionist Party once again. Asquith had contemplated immediate dissolution if the Unionists proceeded with their foolhardy plan, but was no doubt relieved to learn that wiser counsels had prevailed.[15]

The ministry's failure to make long-range military plans to deal with Ulster can also be explained by the deficiencies of J.E.B. Seely at the War Office. It was more common for the Secretary of State for War to be a civilian, but Seely was a soldier with a reputation for gallantry in the Boer War. The qualities which distinguished him as a soldier were less helpful at the War Office, where his courage turned into arrogance, and his impetuosity became lack of forethought. Seely had previously been Under-Secretary at the War Office and the Colonial Office, but few of his colleagues were enthusiastic when he replaced Haldane in 1912. He was generally regarded as one of the weaker members of the ministry, but he was evidently the only available candidate at the time. Munro-Ferguson considered Seely 'a very poor creature indeed', and Herbert Gladstone thought him 'too self-centred and having an exaggerated estimate of his own sagacity and insight'.[16] Seely's unhappy appointment in itself suggests that the Liberal Cabinet had given little thought to the long-term military implications of their Ulster policy.

Seely's unsuitability for the position became quickly apparent and he failed to gain the confidence, respect or affection of the officers as Haldane had done. Colonel Repington, *The Times*' military correspondent, believed the general efficiency of the War Office had fallen by fifty per cent in the six months after Seely took over, and added that the new War Minister 'does nothing and carries no guns'. Lord Roberts commented after a visit to Seely on 21 March that 'Seely appeared to me to be drunk with power, and quite unable to realise the result of the high-handed manner in which he was treating the Army'.[17] One important result of this misguided appointment was that Churchill at the

Admiralty was able to exert considerable influence over his weaker colleague at the War Office.

There was a strong case for the argument of Haldane and Harrel in 1913 that elaborate military precautions should be taken well in advance to prepare for the anticipated trouble in Ulster. The Army crisis of March 1914 could well have been averted if Haldane had remained at the War Office. Instead, the precautions which Haldane considered so urgent in September 1913 were delayed for six critical months. Seely's preparations for dealing with Ulster were almost non-existent up to March 1914 and extremely deficient when measured against the policy favoured by his predecessor at the War Office. Sir Almeric Fitzroy later charged the Government with 'slackness and want of forethought in dealing with the elements of Ulster discontent, of not having measured its force or prepared themselves for the solution of an inevitable problem'.[18] Decisions were taken far too rapidly, in March 1914, with little or no preliminary planning, where a more competent War Minister would have made comprehensive preparations months beforehand.

The justification for the Government's decisions of March 1914 has been obscured by the inept execution of their plans and by the Unionists' emotive use of the term 'plot'. This 'plot' rhetoric has left the impression that the Government's activities were totally reprehensible, whereas their intentions can be defended as prudent and belated precautions against an illegal Opposition enterprise. The British Unionist leaders considered themselves justified in condoning resistance in Ulster against an Act of Parliament. The Government had far greater cause for planning to use force to impose a legal measure which was actively resisted.

2 Military Moves Precipitated, March 1914

One problem which has provided ammunition for Unionist critics, and which has puzzled subsequent historians, is the Government's timing. Critics have asked why the Government moved so suddenly to deal with Ulster in March 1914, when active resistance was not expected until the Home Rule Bill passed, several months later. Lord Blake has argued that 'neither then, nor later, have any really convincing reasons been given for the Government's sudden alarm about Ulster'.[19] This, of course, ignores the glaring fact that substantial cause for alarm had existed for many months before March 1914.

The ministry's sudden activity in March 1914 certainly contrasted sharply with the previous prevarication, but it was not caused by a sinister plot. Two developments coincided early in March to force the Government's hands. The first was the Unionist rejection of the Lloyd George exclusion plan on 9 March. This came as a severe shock to several ministers, Lloyd George and Churchill especially. They regarded this proposal as eminently reasonable and as their last word. Its rejection caused alarm and despair, as Churchill told the Commons three weeks later: 'I was wounded and grieved deeply to find that this offer, on which so many of us had pinned our hopes, was so unceremoniously rejected and repulsed'.[20] Churchill had been the strongest advocate of Ulster exclusion from the very beginning and was all the more frustrated and disappointed when the proposal was dismissed.

The implications seemed clear to ministers like Lloyd George and Churchill. The Unionist rejection apparently left the Government with no option but to press on with their original Bill and make belated preparations to deal with unpleasant consequences in Ulster. On 14 March Churchill expressed this view emphatically in a controversial speech at Bradford, which has been interpreted as the first move in the 'plot' against Ulster. Lloyd George encouraged Churchill to make a speech that would 'ring down the corridors of history', for he shared the conviction that the time had come to make a stand. They had both sympathised with Ulster's cause all along, but 'we stand for law and order, and must see that the nation is not held up by a few malcontents'. Lloyd George assured the First Lord:

You are the only member of the Cabinet who could make such a speech. You are known to have been in favour of conciliation for Ulster. Now you can say that, having secured a compromise, the Ulstermen will either have to accept it or take the consequences.

Churchill's rhetoric at Bradford was provocative and

unrestrained. He declared that the Unionists had rejected the Prime Minister's final and reasonable offer to provide special treatment for Ulster. But the Government would not surrender to threats of force and there were 'worse things than bloodshed, even on an extended scale'. If every concession was dismissed, and the Government exposed to 'menace and brutality', then 'let us go forward together and put these grave matters to the proof!'[21]

The Bradford speech was not part of a secret plot hatched by Churchill, Lloyd George and Seely. The Prime Minister had agreed beforehand that Churchill should make the speech. Admittedly, Asquith had been rather alarmed when he learnt about it from Lloyd George, protesting that 'my game is more the olive branch', but he acquiesced. Moreover, two days afterwards, the Prime Minister nodded assent when challenged in the House by Lord Evelyn Cecil to say whether he endorsed Churchill's speech. On that occasion, Churchill was loudly cheered by the Liberals. At a Downing Street lunch afterwards Asquith argued that this enthusiasm proved that the Bradford speech expressed the feelings of the party.[22]

The second development which helped to precipitate the Cabinet's military plans coincided almost exactly with the rejection of the Government's exclusion offer. Early in March, the Chief Secretary prepared a synopsis of police reports reaching Dublin Castle from December 1913 onwards. Under the title *Further Notes on the Movement in Ulster*, these were circulated to the Cabinet for discussion at the meeting on 11 March. Some ministers became fully aware for the first time of the acute gravity of the Ulster situation, precisely two days after Asquith made his parliamentary offer to the Unionists.

These police reports were undoubtedly alarming, revealing a dramatic growth in the Ulster movement in the months following December 1913. The strength of the Ulster Volunteer Force was estimated at over 80,000 at the end of January 1914. Reports on the quantity of arms available varied widely from estimates of about 17,000 rifles to claims that the whole U.V.F. could be armed. Arms had been distributed from Belfast to various country districts, drilling was carried out in all the Ulster counties, and 'secret mobilization' was practised in some areas. All this was serious enough, but information received from county Tyrone and county Down appears to have caused the Cabinet most concern. Reports from county Down between December and January stated that a 'confidential circular' had been issued to the U.V.F., calling for information about the strength of the forces at police barracks, coastguard stations, post-offices and railways, in case these places had to be seized. This was independently substantiated by more detailed reports from Omagh in county Tyrone, on 7 February:

> . . . the following orders have been drawn up for the Ulster Volunteer Force in a typewritten document:-
> 1. Police are to be disarmed without bloodshed.
> 2. All arms at military barracks in Ulster are to be seized, and it is said that wax impressions of keys of military stores and magazines are in the possession of the Volunteers.
> 3. The number of soldiers at each military depot willing to assist the Volunteers are given.[23]

These reports were first seen by Birrell's colleagues between 6 and 11 March. This information, combined with the Opposition rejection of the Ulster exclusion proposal, undoubtedly explains the crucial Cabinet decisions taken during the week that followed. The police reports were serious enough to cause grave anxiety. Unfortunately, the ministry's credibility was subsequently weakened because Asquith persistently refused to publish these reports, in response to questions in the House. The Prime Minister's claim that they were confidential merely increased doubts about their existence. It is hard to understand why the Government did not try to defend themselves by publishing these reports later. The Cabinet's caution may be explained by the comment in Dublin Castle's *Intelligence Notes* that no corroboration was received to prove that the significant information from Omagh was reliable.[24] The Cabinet lacked confidence in the reliability of the R.I.C. and the spy system was rudimentary. Even if the information was entirely correct, the Ulster leaders might have denied its authenticity and diverted attention with a counter-attack on the ministry's use of police spies.

Other sources have recently proved that the alarming information in the police reports was indeed reliable, but the Cabinet could not have been sure of this. A.T.Q. Stewart has shown that the U.V.F. had developed a plan of action for assuming military control of Ulster, known as 'The No.1 Scheme'. An important section headed 'The Coup' recommended that a sudden paralysing blow should be struck simultaneously, to sever all railway communications whereby troops could be sent to Ulster, to cut all telegraph and telephone lines and to close all approaches to Ulster by road. In addition, 'all depots of arms, ammunition and military equipment should be captured', careful enquiries were to be made as to the strength of such depots and plans made to seize them by overwhelming force, or by secret arrangement with the troops.[25] The 'confidential circular' and 'typewritten document' described in the police reports circulated by Birrell clearly refer to 'The No.1 Scheme'.

Further corroboration is provided by a memorandum sent to Seely on 14 March by Brigadier-General Count Gleichen, who commanded the infantry brigade stationed in Belfast. Gleichen stated that the U.V.F. had over 110,000 men, more than 80,000 rifles, plenty of ammunition and some machine guns. He also confirmed that they had made arrangements to stop troops coming into Ulster. Colonel Repington, *The Times'* military correspondent, spent ten days in Ulster and described the U.V.F. organisation in two articles published on 18 and 19 March. He maintained that the U.V.F. would fight if they were not left alone, they would resist desperately, and very rapid mobilization of a large force was possible. Sir Henry Wilson, General Paget and General Macready were all aware, from November 1913 onwards, that the Cabinet had reason to fear 'a Jameson raid on some depot'. Sufficient evidence survives to show that the Government's concern regarding the safety of various arms depots, and the intentions of the U.V.F., was not fabricated to provide the excuse for a 'plot'.[26]

On 11 March the Cabinet discussed the implications of the Unionist rejection of the Lloyd George exclusion plan. The police reports contained in Birrell's Cabinet paper were examined at the same meeting, and the connection between the two items was all too obvious. The Prime Minister reported to the King:

Some considerable time was given to a discussion of the military situation in Ulster, suggested by the latest series of police reports, which indicate the possibility of attempts on the part of the 'Volunteers' to seize by coups de main, police and military barracks, and depots of arms and ammunition.[27]

Ministers could not know whether the police reports indicated that the U.V.F. were contemplating an immediate coup, or making careful plans to come into operation when the Home Rule Act passed. Either way, the Cabinet would have been foolish to ignore the information. The rejection of Asquith's exclusion offer, coming at precisely the same time, was quite enough to provoke a strong reaction.

3 The Cabinet Committee on Ulster: Conspiracy or Incompetence?

The accusations that the Government was engaged in a sinister 'plot' sprang entirely from Unionist sources. The charges were published in full in the *Daily Mail* on 18 April and in *The Times* on 27 April. They claimed that a section of the Cabinet, led by Churchill and Seely, but excluding Asquith, planned a large-scale military and naval coup against Ulster. This was intended to provoke the U.V.F. into premature, reckless action, which would justify intervention by the army to smash the Volunteers, on the grounds of restoring law and order. The Unionists believed in this story, though they were forced to fabricate some of the details in the absence of solid evidence. Most historians have accepted the 'plot' theory. A.T.Q Stewart concluded 'that an operation was planned for the coercion of Ulster, and that it was badly planned'. Sir James Fergusson argued that it was 'designed for the sudden and complete paralysing of the Ulster Volunteer Force'.[28]

On 11 March the Cabinet appointed a special committee on Ulster, consisting of Crewe, Birrell, Churchill, Seely and Simon, 'to look into the matter in all its aspects'. More than enough justification existed for establishing this committee. Indeed, this step was taken months, if not years, too late. The role played by Churchill and Seely, the aims and decisions of the committee, and the nature of the instructions given to General Paget have been the subject of considerable controversy. The moderating influence of Lord Crewe, as chairman of the committee, was removed because of his sudden illness on 12 March. The Chief Secretary seems to have played little part and nothing is known of Simon's contribution. With good reason, then, Churchill and Seely were widely assumed to control the committee, with the weaker man very much under Churchill's influence. Esher commented: 'Winston is running the whole show!! Marvellous that his colleagues allow him so much rope'.[29]

If any records of the committee's deliberations ever existed, only a brief memorandum written by Seely on 16 March has survived. The only written evidence of the instructions given to Lieutenant-General Sir Arthur Paget, Commander-in-Chief of the troops in Ireland, is a letter from the War Office dated 14 March. This advised Paget to take special precautions to safeguard arms depots, especially Armagh, Omagh, Carrickfergus, and Enniskillen, in view of reports that they might be seized by 'evil disposed persons'. Seely was evidently worried by the lack of response; he wired Paget two days later asking for an immediate reply and requesting that Paget meet him at the War Office on 18 March, equipped with detailed plans. On 17 March, Paget sent a telegram refusing to move troops north to protect the four places mentioned. A letter followed, explaining that '. . . in the present state of the country, I am of opinion that any such moves of troops would create intense excitement in Ulster and possibly precipitate a crisis'.[30] Paget's response was scarcely an auspicious beginning.

That same day, 17 March, the sub-committee reported to the full Cabinet at a meeting described by Lloyd George as 'the bloody Assize'. The committee outlined the instructions given to Paget. They also made the important decision that whatever additional force might eventually be needed 'in the case of disturbance' in Ireland should be supplied by moving regular troops from Great Britain. Seely's figures indicated that about 23,000 regular troops were already in Ireland, including about 9,000 quartered in the province of Ulster.

13,000 more men would be ready at Aldershot to move over 'as precautionary steps for their support in the event of the Ulster Volunteers opposing the movement' of troops. As a further precautionary measure, the Royal Irish Constabulary in Ulster, currently scattered in small detachments all over the countryside, were to be placed under General Macready, as single commanding officer at Belfast. The Cabinet also learnt that Churchill was planning simultaneous naval movements, whereby the third battle squadron would engage in man-oeuvres at Lamlash, off the Scottish coast seventy miles from Belfast.[31]

The nature of the instructions given to General Paget at the various meetings held at the War Office, the Admiralty and 10 Downing Street, on 18 and 19 March, has also been questioned. Paget received no written instructions. The only written records of the conferences consisted of two exceed-ingly brief memoranda by Seely, noting the main decisions. This looked highly suspicious after the event and constitutes one of the many blunders associated with the ministry's management of the operation. The limited sources available indicate that Seely, Paget, French, and Ewart attended all the conferences and Churchill most of them. The remaining members of the Cabinet committee, Crewe, Birrell and Simon, were present part of the time, as also were Lloyd George, Asquith and Macready. The Prime Minister's participation in at least one of the crucial conferences is especially important, in view of subsequent Unionist allegations that Asquith was kept in ignorance of his colleagues' secret conspiracy.

According to the brief memoranda by Seely, the discussions at the two conferences on 18 March essentially involved detailed approval of the decisions reached by the full Cabinet the previous day. Three 'precautionary moves' were to be carried out on the night of Friday 20 March. Troops would be sent to reinforce the four arms depots mentioned to Paget on 14 March, and also to Newry and Dundalk. The battalion quartered at Victoria barracks in Belfast would be moved out to Holywood, four miles outside the city, and ships would be sent to Carrickfergus, Dundalk and Derry. Seely marked in his memorandum, against these points: 'Prime Minister decided "yes" to move Friday night'.[32]

Sir John French's account of the discussions on 18 March states that, after the precautionary measures were sanctioned, 'the question was discussed as to what further and larger operations might be necessary'. An informal lunch followed, between Paget and Seely, when the conversation turned 'almost entirely on the question of large operations'. At the War Office next day, Paget again talked of:

. . . the bigger operations which might become necessary and said in a wild kind of way 'I shall lead my army to the Boyne.' Whereupon French told him not to be a 'bloody fool'.

These 'larger operations' were the cause of much of the subsequent controversy. Seely's brief memoranda merely noted the possibility of some 'overt hostile act', in which case Macready was to become Military Governor of Belfast. This caused Simon to protest to Seely, in a manner which did not suggest a sinister conspiracy: 'I GREATLY DEPRECATE the expression "Military Governorship" – nothing could be more unfortunate, as it seems to me, than to use the *language* of civil war when you are only making a special command to *obviate* Civil War . . . .'[33]

The most convincing explanation of these 'larger operations' was subsequently provided by Churchill in his speech to the Commons on 30 March. The First Lord stated that Paget took a far more serious view of the potential consequences of the troop movements than the Government. Paget feared they would be provocative, but had been over-ruled when he had earlier advised against them. Churchill emphasised that the Government did not share Paget's misgivings, but felt that Paget was quite justified in making preparations to deal with the hypothetical consequences he envisaged:

Sir Arthur Paget had full discretionary power if new and totally different circumstances arose; if the depots were attacked or the columns marching to reinforce them were opposed, to make such dispositions of the police force under his command as the emergency might require; and he was told that if necessary as the result of such events, large reinforcements would be sent to him from England.

Churchill enumerated several contingent possibilities which

were 'present in Sir Arthur Paget's mind' but did not 'belong to the precautionary movements alone authorised by the Government'. These included the possibility that the troop movements would precipitate an 'organised warlike movement' of the U.V.F., 'requiring to be met by concentrated Military Force'.[34]

Churchill's explanation is consistent with the other fragmentary evidence, suggesting that the charges of conspiracy were unjustified. The proposed military movements were no more sinister than those suggested by Haldane six months earlier. General Ewart's diary entry for 20 March confirmed Seely's statement that the troop movements were entirely precautionary and '. . . not provocative in any way. They are merely designed to protect barracks, arms and ammunition'.[35] The Cabinet committee envisaged operations at two levels – the immediate plans to reinforce the arms depots and contingency plans to send additional troops if the U.V.F. resisted the initial movement to guard the depots. All the military moves can be explained at these two levels, with the possible exception of Churchill's decision to send the third battle squadron to Lamlash. Two further points deserve to be underlined. The 'larger operations' discussed at the War Office conferences on 18 and 19 March were clearly sanctioned by the full Cabinet on 17 March, in its decisions about additional forces necessary 'in the case of disturbance' in Ireland. Secondly, the Government was proved to be correct in its judgment that the troop movements would not be provocative. All the moves were executed as planned, without disorder, and there was no need for any reinforcements.

The Cabinet would have been totally negligent had they not discussed the possible consequences of the proposed troop movements and the evidence suggests that these were considered. If Paget expressed the fears indicated by Churchill, he should have been given clear instructions regarding the ministry's intentions, rather than a dangerously vague 'discretionary power'. Even if Seely and Churchill were able to distinguish, at the time, between specific immediate orders and hypothetical contingencies, it was hardly wise to expect Paget to make the same distinction. It seems likely that Churchill and Seely were not entirely clear about their own aims, so that they were scarcely able to communicate unambiguous directions to Paget. Confusion was probably compounded by Seely's indiscreet remarks during several conversations with Paget, when no one else was present. As French remarked to Riddell: 'no doubt Paget got a wrong impression when in London, and acted on it'. Lloyd George was more expansive: 'There was no plot, but no doubt Winston and Seely talked to Paget about hypothetical situations, and led him to think active operations were intended'.[36]

The decision to exercise the third battle squadron off the Isle of Arran, so close to Ulster, was the only part of the operation which could not easily be explained in terms of precautionary moves to safeguard arms depots. It was perhaps inevitable that, with Churchill effectively in control of the committee, a somewhat unnecessary emphasis should have been placed on naval movements. His actual intentions are still far from clear. He subsequently claimed that he intended to use the third battle squadron as a reserve support for the army, in case the troop movements precipitated a crisis. There is no evidence, however, that Churchill was using the third battle squadron as an integral part of a sinister conspiracy to subdue Ulster, unknown to the Prime Minister. Asquith himself informed the King on 17 March that the battleships were to be sent from Gibraltar to Lamlash. Moreover, the battle squadron could not have reached Lamlash until at least two days after the precautionary troop movements had been completed. The orders were in fact countermanded on 21 March, by which time the battleships had only reached the Scillies. Unionist suspicions about the naval movements gained strength from the glaring gaps and inconsistencies in the subsequent explanations made in reluctant instalments by Asquith and Churchill. The Government's case would have been far stronger if either minister had stated the perfectly reasonable justification for placing a battle squadron close enough to support the army in dealing with Ulster's threatened resistance to the Home Rule Act.[37]

The Liberals consistently denied the existence of any 'plot', and no evidence has been found in their private papers to disprove their claims. When the second White Paper on the

Curragh affair was published on 22 April, Churchill wrote to his wife: 'We have now published everything and I am confident these wild charges will become gradually discredited'. Haldane assured his mother that 'there never has been any plan for using military force to coerce Ulster'. Percy Illingworth denied the 'grotesque' charges levelled against the Government, in a speech at Bradford early in May: 'It was perfectly true that precautionary measures were taken to prevent disorder, and the only fault which could be found was that those measures were not on a sufficiently large scale'.[38] Lloyd George informed Sir George Riddell that no plot existed and Morley told Fitzroy that 'no conspiracy to precipitate bloodshed was entertained by the Cabinet'. Mildred Buxton wrote to her husband Sydney, after a heated discussion with a friend who believed in the 'plot' theory: 'I think he was really surprised that now you are out of the Government I did not believe it too'. Finally, if there was a plot, then presumably it would have required the cooperation of the generals most closely concerned. Yet General Ewart repudiated 'the legend . . . that there has been a wicked plot to coerce Ulster or to provoke Ulster to take the initiative'. Nor were Generals French or Macready informed of secret orders for a conspiracy against Ulster.[39]

Since there is no firm evidence to substantiate the 'plot' charges, it is all the more essential to explain why so many Unionists believed these accusations to be true, and why the Government had so much difficulty in refuting them. The answer was probably provided in a memorandum written by Walter Long on 27 March. He remarked that if the story of the 'plot' was not correct, '. . . then I can only say it is the most wonderful combination of circumstances and coincidences that has ever been told even in fiction'. Balfour commented that the Government 'seem to have made an extraordinary mess over this Army matter and very unnecessarily to have precipitated a crisis which might otherwise, perhaps, never have occurred'. As Lord Blake has now conceded: 'Perhaps the real charge is bungling amateurish incompetence rather than conspiracy'.[40]

Judgments on the Liberal side were naturally less harsh, but led to the same conclusions. Haldane confessed to his mother that 'there has been much misunderstanding and muddle and who is to blame it is hard to tell'. In a generous letter of condolence after Seely's resignation, Birrell described the crisis as 'an *untoward* incalculable incident . . . the result of a number of accidents the responsibility for which can never be finally determined . . .'. Seely himself admitted that '. . . while the matter was sound the manner was, or appeared to be, faulty'. The *Nation* provided the biggest understatement, describing the incident as a blunder which revealed 'a certain slackness in Cabinet methods'.[41]

What was wrong in March 1914 was not so much the nature of the action contemplated, but the way it was carried out. Their mistakes lay in the belated, over-hasty and uncoordinated nature of their plans and their inept execution, which caused the entire project to misfire catastrophically. The Opposition were so amazed at the degree of confusion, the uncertainty of aims and the appalling mismanagement that they were convinced they could only be explained by a sinister conspiracy.

4 Crisis at the Curragh and Repercussions in London

The crisis at the Curragh army camp arose from the quite separate problem of Paget's treatment of possible disaffection amongst his officers. It was agreed at the War Office conferences on 19 March that officers domiciled in Ulster should be allowed to remain behind, but any other officers threatening to resign or refusing to obey orders should be dismissed without pensions. Churchill subsequently explained that the Army Council gave Paget these principles for his personal guidance, to be used only in the case of 'grave emergencies' arising in the case of individual officers who refused to obey orders. Paget was given no instructions to put these guiding principles as hypothetical questions to the whole body of officers in the Irish Command. Seely undoubtedly did not convey these instructions so clearly to Paget, who gained quite a different impression. Paget seems to have been thoroughly confused by Seely's attempts to distinguish between legal and military obligation, on the one hand, and between hypothetical and actual situations on the other.[42]

The consequences are well known. Paget returned to Ireland in an excited, over-wrought mood, lacking both written instructions and diplomatic finesse. He summoned his seven commanders to a conference in Dublin at 10 a.m. on 20 March. No notes were taken, but several subsequent accounts survive. My account is primarily based on Paget's own report, which naturally presents his foolish behaviour in the most favourable light. He seemed to overlook his specific instructions, which only involved the movement of two battalions and some infantry companies. Instead, he informed his commanders that certain moves were to be carried out which would 'create intense excitement', possibly leading to active operations against the U.V.F. The country 'would be ablaze on the following day'. His rambling and impassioned speech created the impression that 'active operations of an offensive and aggressive character, and on an extensive scale, were to be undertaken at once against Ulster'.[43]

Paget then explained that, apart from officers domiciled in Ulster, those who refused to obey orders to march north would be dismissed. Any officer who 'did not feel that he could obey the orders given him in the eventuality' described, should make this clear and should not attend a second conference that afternoon. Paget subsequently claimed that he had only intended to test the attitude of his senior officers in this way; he had not meant them in turn to put the same hypothetical question to the whole body of officers. He admitted, however, that the expression he used 'undoubtedly might convey the impression that I was putting a pistol to their heads'. Paget did not appear to realise that, by giving his officers any alternatives, he was placing them in a position where choosing to obey the orders implied political approval of them. Four out of the seven commanders understood that they were ordered to give their subordinate officers the alternative between doing their duty in Ulster or saying immediately that they preferred to be dismissed. The two senior officers of the fifth division, Major-General Fergusson and Brigadier-General Hubert Gough, put these alternatives before their officers. Faced with the conflict between conscience and duty, the two commanders themselves reached different conclusions and influenced their men accordingly. Fergusson, in command of the fifth division, based at the Curragh camp in county Kildare, decided that a soldier's first duty was to obey orders. He managed to win round most officers in the division after some painful scenes, but failed to influence Gough's third cavalry brigade.[44]

Gough and the officers of his three regiments did not appear at the second conference on 20 March. Instead, they sent a minute to Paget, requesting further information before they could take such crucial decisions at such short notice. They asked for clarification of their orders, explaining that they were fully prepared to undertake duties to preserve order and property. However, if the duty involved the initiation of active military operations against Ulster the majority would prefer to be dismissed under protest. This attitude was essentially reasonable, in view of the implications of the alternatives. Paget sent a series of telegrams to the War Office on 20 and 21 March, stating that fifty-eight officers in the three regiments of the third cavalry brigade preferred 'to accept dismissal if ordered north'. Gough and the officers commanding the three regiments were ordered to report to the War Office immediately.[45]

The news reached London by Saturday 21 March. The King told Asquith he was 'grieved beyond words at this disastrous and irreparable catastrophe which has befallen my Army'. The Prime Minister, on the Friday evening, initially assumed that Gough had influenced his officers to 'combine for a strike'. By the Saturday Asquith had fuller information and thought it more likely that 'there was a misunderstanding'. Gough and his three officers were interviewed at the War Office on 22 and 23 March, by Ewart, Macready, French and Seely. It was soon clear that Paget's ultimatum had placed his officers in an unfair dilemma and that direct orders to move to Ulster would have been obeyed without question. Ewart concluded that 'Paget must be mad', for putting a pistol to their heads in such an unnecessary manner.[46]

Paget's behaviour in presenting the officers with a hypothetical question was foolish and inexcusable. Therefore, the Army Council felt it was vital to reinstate the cavalry brigade officers, with minimum fuss, before the effect of their resignations injured army discipline any further. Unfortunately, by this time Gough was angry, resentful and suspicious, and quite prepared to leave the army unless he had absolute reassurance that such a situation could never recur. French tried to persuade Gough and his subordinates to return to duty as if nothing had happened, treating the whole incident as a misunderstanding. Gough refused, unless he was given a written pledge that 'they would not be employed to coerce Ulster into acceptance of the Home Rule Bill'. Seely and the Army Council finally gave in, because they feared 'sympathetic action at Aldershot and throughout the Army', unless the officers were persuaded to return to duty. Accordingly, Ewart drafted a memorandum on 23 March on Seely's instructions, and this was shortly afterwards revised and approved by the Cabinet. This merely stated that the Army Council were satisfied that the resignations were due to a misunderstanding, and that Paget's questions were only intended to ensure that lawful orders for the protection of lives and property would be obeyed.[47]

The sequence of subsequent events is still not entirely clear. Seely returned from his royal audience just as ministers were leaving the Cabinet room, and he remained behind talking to Morley. At that moment, Seely received a note from Gough, asking for further reassurance that the army would not be required to enforce the Home Rule Act on Ulster 'under the expression of maintaining law and order'. This note reinforced Seely's fear that the Cabinet's revised version of Ewart's document would not satisfy Gough. On his own initiative, Seely therefore added two sentences, which became known as the 'peccant paragraphs', and Morley agreed to the addition, 'only half understanding what it was all about'. The controversial sentences stated that the Government retained the right to use the army to maintain law and order, 'but they have no intention whatever of taking advantage of this right to crush political opposition to the policy or principles of the Home Rule Bill'. The amended memorandum was returned to Ewart, with instructions from Seely that he and French should sign it on behalf of the Army Council. French and Ewart complied, assuming that the document was sanctioned by the Cabinet. When this was shown to Gough and the three colonels, they were still not satisfied. They demanded a further pledge that the last paragraph meant that under no circumstances would their troops 'be called upon to enforce the present Home Rule Bill on Ulster and that we can so assure our Officers'. French agreed to this in writing. Armed with these written assurances, the four officers returned that night in triumph to Dublin.[48] This was an extraordinary admission that the army would not be used to coerce Ulster in order to enforce Home Rule.

By 24 March, the Prime Minister recognised the full extent of the crisis but it was too late to recall the document. Asquith was obliged to repudiate Seely's additions in the Commons on 25 March. This course inevitably involved the resignations of Seely, French and Ewart, who were responsible for the fatal document. 'In a state of great excitement and disturbance', Seely admitted his mistake in the Cabinet on 25 March. He justified his failure to see the significance of the 'peccant paragraphs' on grounds of his 'anxiety to keep the officers and army from wholesale rebellion and resignation'. The Prime Minister criticised Seely's conduct 'in strong but necessary terms' and the War Minister offered his resignation.[49]

One Liberal member subsequently described this incident as 'an extraordinary jumble at a Cabinet meeting – the story of which is scarcely credible and if believed indicates grotesque slackness of management . . .'.[50] Seely's foolishness rivalled that of Paget. He had given Gough a document which completely eliminated the Government's option to impose Home Rule on Ulster by force. French and Ewart believed they were obeying Cabinet orders and Morley's advanced age helps to explain his part in the affair. Under the circumstances, Gough's behaviour had been entirely reasonable up to the point where he resigned and protested about Paget's ultimatum. The Curragh officers did not 'mutiny' or refuse to obey orders. However, their own behaviour also became questionable once they took advantage of the situation to demand pledges limiting the Government's policy.

5 Inquest on the Curragh: from Total Retreat to Partial Recovery

The Curragh incident provoked intermittent uproar in the Commons for the next four weeks. The Unionists quickly accumulated an abundance of ammunition to use against the Government. The main charge was that a section of the Cabinet deliberately plotted to use the army to provoke Ulster loyalists to violence, thus providing an excuse for crushing their movement. The Government's attempt to refute this charge, by dismissing the whole affair as a 'misunderstanding', was unconvincing. This was partly because the ministry was too much on the defensive in the first week of the parliamentary battle. Ministers were over-anxious to explain away the whole episode in terms of the mismanagement of precautionary moves to guard arms depots. In the first few days of their defence, the Government entirely failed to justify their legitimate right to make far-reaching preparations to deal with illegal resistance to an Act of Parliament. More important, the appalling blunders and unhappy coincidences which haunted the whole affair seemed too incredible for simple belief. It made far better sense to interpret them as a sinister plot. Even the Prime Minister's wife believed that, if Asquith's colleagues had not deceived him, then 'there is something behind all this of which I know nothing'.[51]

The Government's inept attempts to minimise the gravity of the crisis and explain away some of the worst blunders only increased Opposition suspicions. Confusion was compounded because many ministers knew little, and understood less, about the activities of the Ulster sub-committee. The situation was aggravated further by the long-standing divisions within the Cabinet over Ulster policy, which were highlighted now they were obliged to face the issue of Ulster coercion. Confusion, ignorance and divided counsels provoked a series of stupid mistakes and inconsistent statements, which convinced the Unionists that the Government was trying to conceal a wicked conspiracy.

Paget's foolish behaviour might have been accepted as such, if it had not been compounded by Seely's inept activities at the War Office. The Liberals could believe that 'Seely made a series of the most appalling blunders', and lament with

Margot Asquith that 'keeping Seely ruined us'. It was harder for the Unionists to accept that Seely's original instructions to Paget were perfectly innocent, when nothing was stated in writing and the Government was so reluctant to yield information. The 'peccant paragraphs' were interpreted as Seely's desperate attempt to cover up after the plot had failed, 'Seely admitting an error of judgment and Winston using swear words to cover their retreat'.[52]

Opposition suspicions were magnified by the Cabinet's technique of saying as little as possible, as reluctantly as possible. On 23 March, Asquith optimistically informed Bonar Law that 'the incident at the Curragh (which was due to a misunderstanding) is at an end'. Haldane and Morley tried to explain the affair in the Lords on the same day, in ignorance of much relevant information, including Seely's 'peccant paragraphs'. Morley admitted that the Government had no intention of using the army, 'as things stand', to crush political opposition to the Home Rule Bill. Haldane committed himself even further: 'No orders were issued, no orders are likely to be issued, and no orders will be issued for the [immediate] coercion of Ulster'. Two days later Haldane feared that he had misinformed Parliament in this speech, in ignorance of what had really happened. Seely was convinced that Haldane's statement was even more conciliatory than his own 'peccant paragraphs'. Certainly its admissions were almost equally damaging, especially if read out of context, but at least they were not produced at the dictation of army officers. Haldane's foolish attempt to soften the impact of his statement, by inserting the word 'immediate' in the *Hansard* version of his speech, provoked a further uproar. Morley escaped fairly lightly from his share in drafting the 'peccant paragraphs', probably because of his advanced years. Unfortunately, Churchill's attempt to gloss over this episode contradicted Morley's more honest account, and earned a sharp rebuke from Chamberlain in the *Morning Post*, condemning the 'severe economy of truth practised by Ministers'.[53]

The Government worked hard to avoid giving a detailed account of the War Office discussions and the events leading to the Curragh incident. The thin White Paper published on 25

March contained only eight items. It was justly criticised by Sir Almeric Fitzroy as '. . . a miserable document of shifts and gaps; an explanation that will have to be much explained. It is obviously an essay, and a clumsy one, in apologetics'. The Prime Minister claimed that the first White Paper would give the House 'all the facts so far as they are contained in writing'. Intense Opposition pressure led to the publication of a much enlarged second White Paper a month later, which cast doubts on Asquith's veracity. Lewis Harcourt's wife was probably not alone in her reaction:

I am at sixes and sevens over all this fuss and 'revised' White Paper – Wouldn't it have been better to give the whole thing at once. It does look so much better than when it appears like hiding things and contradiction. The papers mangle things so one cannot quite understand.[54]

It was not difficult for the Opposition to believe that the Cabinet had spent the long interval between the two White Papers attempting to concoct a credible story.

Fitzroy remarked on 28 March that 'the subsequent proceedings of Ministers have given to the whole transaction the character of a shuffling imbecility'. Part of the explanation is revealed by Pease's note on a Cabinet held on 31 March: 'The discussion recalled incidents, and the small discrepancies of statements made by different ministers – all anxious to be accurate'; they agreed that twenty men observing the same incidents would always produce inconsistencies in their statements.[55] The rest can only be explained by a mixture of confusion, ignorance, and an understandable, if misguided, attempt to conceal the more inept behaviour of those involved.

An appalling parliamentary position was improved slightly because the Unionists did not make the most effective use of their opportunities. As Pease remarked, Bonar Law came to the Government's aid 'by filling up holes we had made for burying ourselves'. The Unionists were particularly sensitive to ministerial charges that they had encouraged army officers to allow their political views to interfere with army discipline. Herbert Samuel commented that 'the outburst of passion in the country over the idea that the army could intervene in politics has frightened the Tories', and put new spirit into

Liberals throughout the country. John Burns remarked on the change in the temper in the Commons on 24 March, when a Labour member launched a powerful attack on the Unionists 'for fostering discontent in army and mutiny amongst officers'.[56] The Oppositions' vulnerability on this score made them over-cautious and more liable to make mistakes. The business of the 'peccant paragraphs', however, allowed the Unionists to recover the initiative.

A week passed before ministers regained sufficient confidence to fight back strongly. It was not until 30 and 31 March that Churchill and Grey delivered the powerful statements which should have been made many days earlier. Churchill forcefully denied that the military movements were 'the first step in an insidious but deeply laid strategic scheme for grasping the vital key positions for a general advance on Ulster'. He provided the first detailed explanation of the whole affair, emphasising that if the Ulster Volunteers had attacked the troops making the precautionary moves, then the wider contingency preparations would indeed have been absolutely necessary. Most important, Churchill at last declared that the Government had the right to coerce Ulster under certain circumstances:

So extraordinary is the position we have reached that the doctrine is seriously put forward that the only force which it is legitimate to use is rebellious force. . . . But against armed rebellion, if it occurs, force is certainly justified.

Burns commented that Churchill replied to F.E. Smith '. . . in first rate fighting style. He crumpled up the "Plot" story and turned the tables against Carson Law and Lansdowne with great effect'.[57] Churchill's intervention helped to retrieve a situation which looked almost past hope. He issued a long-overdue reminder to both sides of the House that the Government had every right to plan the military operations in question.

It has been argued that Asquith's unexpected assumption of the War Office on Seely's resignation had a similarly bracing effect on the party, and also on the army.[58] While the Prime Minister's casual behaviour since 20 March had exasperated Churchill and Lloyd George, other ministers praised

237

Asquith's ability to remain calm in a crisis. The Prime Minister's announcement on 30 March that he felt it his duty to become Secretary of State for War was enthusiastically received on the Liberal benches. Pease noted that the House was 'taken by surprise by this masterly and plucky stroke of our great leader'. Herbert Samuel believed that, by stepping into the breach, Asquith had made the party 'not only respect him as they have always done, but love him, as they never did before'. A Liberal backbencher commented that Asquith's unexpected announcement 'made a wonderful impression in the House and left us feeling that the tables had been effectively turned'.[59] The Prime Minister was obliged to vacate his seat in the House immediately, in order to seek re-election in East Fife – a procedure which was still mandatory on acceptance of any Cabinet office. A wildly enthusiastic crowd of Liberals cheered Asquith when he departed from King's Cross station on 3 April.

By taking the War Office from Seely, the Prime Minister undoubtedly went some way to restore the army's morale and to revive its shattered confidence in the Government. The officers respected Asquith and were relieved by his public announcement at Ladybank that 'the Army will hear nothing of politics from me, and in return I expect to hear nothing of politics from the Army'. As the *Yorkshire Observer* commented on 15 April: '. . . one does not exactly see Curragh brigadier-generals coming to dictate terms to the Prime Minister'.

Even so, the emotional reaction to Asquith's announcement was perhaps a little excessive. The wisdom of the move was questionable in some respects. Asquith had made himself War Minister, as well as Premier, at a time of acute crisis, and was consequently absent from the Commons from 30 March until 14 April. Bonar Law declared that it was absolutely wrong that the Second Reading of the Home Rule Bill should take place in the Prime Minister's absence at such a critical time. Leopold Amery later derided the move as '. . . a climax to the comedy of errors . . . There was, indeed, nothing in the circumstances, in Asquith's temperament or in the subsequent course of events, to warrant this enthusiasm'. Few of Asquith's colleagues expressed similar reservations, though

Haldane was more critical because he knew how much work was required at the War Office. He admitted that Asquith's move was very dramatic, but warned that the new War Minister would find his task a heavy one. Not many people, apparently, shared Sir Almeric Fitzroy's view that Asquith's decision to become his own War Minister was quite extraordinary: 'what, then, will befall the functions of the Premier ?'[60]

The rather short-sighted ministerial reaction can probably be explained partly in terms of sheer relief. Morley shared Fitzroy's belief that 'most of the mischief arose from the reluctance of Asquith to be master in his own house'. The Prime Minister appeared to be taking control in a firm manner that was rare in his management of Irish affairs. Most ministers were also more familiar with other aspects of government, where their high praise of Asquith's talents was often better deserved.

6 Consequences of the Curragh

The Government's partial retrieval of the situation was purely parliamentary in nature. Up to 20 March, the ministry's declarations that the army would be used to impose Home Rule on Ulster, if a political compromise was rejected, held a high degree of credibility. This was lost after the Curragh fiasco. When the crisis was at its height on 22 March, even the Prime Minister admitted the gravity of the military consequences:

The military situation has developed . . . and there is no doubt if we were to order a march upon Ulster that about half the officers in the Army – the Navy is more uncertain – would strike. The immediate difficulty in the Curragh can, I think, be arranged, but that is the permanent situation, and it is not a pleasant one.[61]

Asquith's fears were confirmed a month later by reports from the commanders of the two divisions of the British army in Ireland. Major-General Pulteney stated that his troops would not enforce Home Rule on an actively reluctant Ulster. Major-General Fergusson agreed that the great majority of officers would refuse to act aggressively against the Ulster

Volunteers. He believed that the weak treatment of Gough, combined with the subsequent repudiation of the guarantees he was given, had increased the bitterness, resentment and mistrust of the troops in Ireland. Consequently:

. . . the troops can only be depended on to do their duty up to a certain point — if the situation develops into civil war they will in the end disintegrate. This is tantamount to saying that they are not to be depended on to coerce Ulster into accepting the Home Rule Bill.

Birrell confirmed these reports that army morale was very low and informed Asquith that even the optimistic General Paget was by no means confident that all the troops would move north if ordered.[62] Asquith's assumption of the War Office had evidently by no means counter-acted the damage already done.

Before the Curragh affair, troops would almost certainly have obeyed direct orders to march to Ulster, so long as they were presented with no alternatives. But afterwards it could no longer even be assumed that they would simply obey orders. General Macready was more optimistic than the other commanders that troops would continue to obey orders, but he fully recognised that the Cabinet had no confidence that this was so:

The nerves of the Government had been rudely shaken by the Curragh incident . . . I have always been devoutly thankful that the question was never put to the test because, with the absurdly inadequate number of troops, any attempts of the U.V.F. to gain their objective by force of arms would have resulted in very serious bloodshed . . .

Macready's opinion was important, since he was given command of the troops in Ulster 'for all purposes connected with the rendering of support to civil power'. He found the whole situation 'so impossible, in view of the numerical weakness of the troops and the nervous excitement in Belfast', that he went to London on 29 April to explain the situation personally to the Prime Minister. He discovered that the Government was unwilling to assert its authority over the Ulstermen, and was informed that there was no intention of reinforcing the garrison in Ulster. By 19 May Macready was

"THERE'S MANY A SLIP . . ."

far more anxious, but when he again saw Asquith he was given the 'heroic instructions' that if Carson proclaimed his provisional government, 'the only course was to remain on the defensive and do nothing'. Even as late as 24 July, when Macready received further instructions from the Prime Minister:

There was to be no change from the former policy, troops were to 'sit tight' and make no moves of any kind. If a Provisional Government was proclaimed the consequential proclamation by Carson would be awaited to enable the Cabinet to determine their next move. A more thoroughly unsatisfactory position for any soldier it is hard to imagine.[63]

The important point then, is that whether or not Macready's estimate of the army's loyalty was correct, the Government believed that it could not trust the army. The Cabinet assumed that it had lost the military power required either to enforce its original Home Rule policy or to impose a compromise settlement on its own terms on an unwilling Ulster. The fiasco of 20 March had effectively deprived them of the power to meet force with force. Lord Esher had recognised this two days afterwards:

Of course, the net result of the whole business is that the two instruments the Government possess have broken in their hands. The Home Rule Bill, even if they get it through, is useless against the resistance of Ulster. The army is smashed.[64]

Fitzroy shared Esher's gloomy view of the Government's position:

Their cardinal error throughout has been that they never made up their minds, first, whether in the last resort they would coerce Ulster, and secondly, whether they were able to do so. Owing to maladroit manipulation, the instrument has now broken in their hands before they were ready to use it.

Evidently Asquith appreciated these realities at the height of the crisis, though he subsequently regained his customary composure and his myopic complacency. On 25 March Fitzroy noted that the shock to the Prime Minister had been terrible: 'George Murray was with him on Sunday, and never saw him so overcome. The folly of having created such a situation, without the power to handle it successfully, is incalculable'. A month later Asquith told Pease that 'we must settle somehow', since they could not rely on the army if they tried to force the Home Rule Bill through Parliament and precipitated riots. Early in May, Morley revealed to Lord Esher that 'Asquith had stated at the Cabinet that the army could not be used in or against Ulster'.[65]

The Curragh crisis highlighted the Cabinet's inability to confront the issue of coercion squarely, and to face the military situation realistically. The existing Cabinet divisions were aggravated by the crisis. A few ministers, including Simon, Burns and Charles Hobhouse, wanted to stand by Redmond and 'damn the consequences'. Simon deplored the ministry's weakness, which inevitably gave Carson the upper hand: 'whereas if we *said* we were going on and *got our own people to believe us*, C[arson], would regard a Provisional Government as a false step'. John Burns also claimed that Ireland would be 'permanently tranquillised' if the Government pressed their policy 'very forcibly'.[66] These ministers had clearly not learned the lessons of the previous two months. They still overestimated their military capacity to enforce their original policy, and miscalculated the likely consequences if they made such an attempt. But this kind of attitude was more common among the rank and file than in the Cabinet. Lloyd George told the King on 15 May that the Liberal Party as a whole were against any concessions since they did not realise the danger of the situation, whereas he was convinced that civil war was inevitable without a speedy political compromise.[67]

The Curragh fiasco effectively strengthened the influence of that section of the Cabinet which opposed the use of force against Ulster. Morley regularly threatened to resign 'if a drop of blood is shed in Ulster'. He believed that the Curragh incident gave 'an immense momentum to the pacifists in the Cabinet and on both sides of the House of Commons'. The crisis convinced him that 'the Carsonites will get everything they ask for'. After a Cabinet on 13 May Morley confided in Fitzroy that the majority of ministers favoured 'purchasing peace in the last resort on Carson's terms'. Six weeks later Dillon was dismayed to learn Morley's opinion that 'Carson has won and the sooner the public know it the better'. Pease also concluded that 'the Irish Nationalists must see they must exclude Ulster till it was ready to come in without coercion'.[68]

Sir Edward Grey's previous misgivings about the coercion of Ulster were powerfully reinforced by the Curragh incident. Grey wrote to Asquith at the height of the crisis on 23 March, insisting that 'we cannot and ought not to use force to bring the Home Rule Bill into operation till the opinion of the country has been taken'. He appeared undaunted by the prospect of introducing the coercion of Ulster as an electoral issue. Two months later, on 20 May, Grey warned the Prime Minister that the Cabinet's position regarding the coercion of Ulster should be made absolutely explicit in a public statement. The Foreign Minister's view of the Government's position was quite extraordinary: 'The Cabinet has not and has never had, I believe, the intention of using armed force to impose upon the Protestant Counties of Ulster summary submission to Nationalist Home Rule'. Churchill and Lloyd George would have been unlikely to agree with this interpretation and Seely might well have wondered how this statement essentially differed from the 'peccant paragraphs' given to Gough. Grey believed that a more emphatic explanation of their intentions would diminish the risk of outbreaks in Ulster, by showing the Ulster Protestants that there was no need to 'make preparations to resist force by force'.[69]

The views of Grey and Morley illustrated the weakness of the Liberal philosophy in confronting an issue involving the use of coercion. A public statement of Grey's policy of appeasement, coming after the Curragh crisis, was likely rather to strengthen the resolve of the Ulster Volunteer Force and to reinforce their assumption of the Government's weakness. It would seem to be a futile gesture at this stage, unless accompanied by a foolproof formula for political compromise. The advocates of appeasement were rather less concerned with the massive problems of reaching an acceptable political solution when bargaining from a position of weakness. They were also surprisingly unconcerned, even now, about what the Government would do if appeasement and political compromise failed. Charles Hobhouse noted in his diary in mid–May: 'I tried to induce the Cabinet to consider what actual steps should be taken if the Ulster Provisional Government was actually set up. But no one felt inclined to move until the trouble actually arrived'.[70] This attitude was also demonstrated by General Macready's account of the Government's feeble, defensive instructions for conducting military policy in Ulster.

The gun-running coup organised by the Ulster Volunteer Force on the night of 24–25 April dramatically underlined the consequences of the Curragh. About 35,000 rifles were landed at Larne and distributed throughout north-east Ulster in a brilliantly organised operation. The secret was remarkably well kept, the Volunteers encountered no effective resistance, and the news did not reach Dublin Castle until the following morning. Viewed from a strictly limited parliamentary perspective, this coup could be interpreted as giving the Government a tactical advantage. Churchill commented that the Ulstermen 'have put themselves entirely in the wrong, and justified to the full the modest precautions which were taken' in March. It was perfectly true that the Larne gun-running coup was a far more comprehensive exercise in illegality than anything contemplated by the Government. Birrell remarked that 'as Plotters, they beat us hollow'.[71] But the Government might have shown more anxiety about the practical long-term consequences than about scoring a debating point.

The gun-running exploit at Larne left the U.V.F. more effectively armed at precisely the time when the Government's military confidence had been shattered. Leopold Amery commented:

The challenge to the Government was direct and unmistakable. For a night all Government services had been suspended and the Government's servants forcibly coerced, while measures of the most effective character were being carried out to provide Ulster with the means of wrecking the Government's policy. No self-respecting Government could afford to be treated with such contumely.

General Macready was not in the least surprised at the news of the coup. He believed that 'the continued policy of drift had enfeebled the resources at the disposal of the Government in the North of Ireland to an extent which gave the Orangemen practically a free hand'. [72]

Moreover, the Cabinet's weak and vacillating reactions to the coup only encouraged Ulster Unionist recalcitrance. The Lord Lieutenant felt strongly that a definite announcement should be made that the Government intended to arrest all the Larne ringleaders. Lord Aberdeen argued that: '. . . any appearance of doubt or hesitation at this juncture will not only bring disaster to the Government, but will leave a stigma which would afterwards be felt to be almost intolerable'. Macready shared the view that strong action might have led to bloodshed, but might have allowed the Government to regain its prestige and recover some measure of control. [73]

Instead, the Government wavered for five days while Asquith sought legal opinions. Initially the Cabinet agreed that such an unprecedented provocation required 'instant and effective action'. But, after three more Cabinet meetings, Asquith decided on 30 April against prosecuting the gun-runners, or even moving extra troops into Ulster. Pease noted that the party was anxious that a strong line should be taken, but the Cabinet felt 'tact and patience' were required. The Chief Secretary advised against criminal proceedings, pointing out the practical difficulties involved in prosecuting such large numbers of the 'representative Ulster "rabble" '. Birrell was influenced by the views of the Nationalist leaders, and by police reports from Belfast indicating that '. . . any attempt to arrest leaders or to seize the arms of the Ulster Volunteers would without doubt lead to bloodshed and precipitate what would practically amount to war all over Ulster'. A carefully timed conciliatory statement by Carson in the Commons on 29 April made certain that the Cabinet would once again retreat. No action was taken to prosecute the gun-runners, or to strengthen the armed forces in Ireland. Yet Birrell knew as well as Macready that the Irish police were outnumbered throughout Ulster and that a substantial increase in military strength was necessary to protect and support them against the U.V.F. [74]

The Curragh crisis left the Government demoralised, divided and bereft of the means to enforce its policy. The two armies continued to organise in Ireland, and the Larne coup increased the amount of force required to impose a settlement, just when Asquith's ability to command a force was called into question. The Curragh crisis compounded the confusion within the Cabinet over the coercion of Ulster. The optimists continued to hope for the best, with no idea how this might be achieved. The realists accepted the implications of the Curragh, but saw absolutely no solution. Most ministers believed the Curragh crisis had effectively removed their option to proceed with the original Bill and coerce Ulster into submission if necessary. Churchill defined the dilemma: 'It was no longer a question of our coercing Ulster; it was a question of our preventing Ulster from coercing us'. The Curragh crisis undermined the Government's credibility to the point where the military sanction was rendered ineffective. Instead, the Cabinet had little choice but to seek a political settlement on Unionist terms. They had no clear idea what they would do if the pressures acting on the Opposition prevented such a settlement. The Liberal Government's Home Rule policy was undermined far more effectively by the Curragh crisis than by the intervention of the First World War.

VIII
THE LAST MONTHS OF THE LIBERAL IRISH QUESTION: DEADLOCK AND DESPERATION, APRIL – JULY 1914

'History if it concerns itself with us at all will write us down as either the most patient, wise, foreseeing Government this or any country ever had, or else as the [most] inept, blind and cowardly crew that ever disgraced Downing Street. No middle judgement will be possible' (Hobhouse diary, May 1914, p.171).

Asquith had lost a major political advantage in 1912 when he failed to take the opportunity of excluding Ulster from the Bill during the first parliamentary circuit. After January 1913 the terms of the Parliament Act made the agreement of the Opposition essential to any such arrangement. From then on, the Government had only two alternatives. They either had to reach a compromise over Ulster with the Unionists, or they had to overcome Ulster's resistance to the Home Rule Act by force. The significance of the Curragh affair was that it effectively removed the second option. The Government no longer believed it could use the army to impose its will on Ulster. A political settlement with the Opposition seemed the only way out. Sir Almeric Fitzroy commented that after the Curragh the Government had little alternative but to come 'to terms with the malcontents. Ulster controls the situation, and, it would seem, the fate of the Ministry'. Balfour found the situation alarming: 'The Government are in very deep water, and are ready to clutch at anything which will save them from drowning'.[1]

The gun-running coup at Larne had emphasised the Government's impotence, while simultaneously increasing the military power of the Ulster Volunteers. The possibility of a bloody confrontation increased when the Irish National Volunteers followed the U.V.F. lead. By the summer of 1914 they could equal U.V.F. numbers, and they organised their own gun-running operation at Howth on 26 July. Once again, inept management by the Government made matters worse. The police and the army intervened this time, causing direct confrontation with a Dublin crowd and consequent bloodshed. This led to an outcry from the Nationalists. Dillon complained bitterly that Ireland was now convinced that the Government was deliberately treating the south more harshly than the north. The attempt to disclaim responsibility in the subsequent White Paper did not help. General Macready commented: 'A more disgraceful exhibition of weakness on the part of a Government it would be hard to find'.[2] The Howth tragedy increased the Irish pressure on the Nationalists to reject compromise and it underlined the Government's ineffectiveness yet again. As the two armies faced each other, the preparations for the establishment of Ulster's provisional government were accelerated.

The situation in Ireland was deteriorating so fast that the Government had all the more reason to strive for a political compromise, but far less chance of reaching one. Some ministers, such as Crewe, Buxton, Samuel and Asquith, regained an amazing complacency in the weeks after the Curragh. But their optimism was based on the assumption that the Unionists would eventually agree to a settlement. In fact, the Curragh incident and the two gun-running coups which followed, made this far less likely. After these crises, the Ulster Unionists expected minimal resistance to the establishment of their provisional government. They had little incentive to make concessions, and consequently increased their demands. Bonar Law underlined this point in a desperate last-minute talk with Asquith on 17 July:

. . . the people of Ulster knew that they had a force which would enable them to hold the Province, and with opinion so divided in this country, it was quite impossible that any force could be sent against them which could dislodge them, and that therefore they knew that they could get their own terms, and that it was certain they would rather fight than give way . . .[3]

Consequently, Carson was far more intransigent after the Curragh than he had appeared to be throughout the negotiations of the winter of 1913-14. Lord Stamfordham rightly commented to Crewe on 5 June: 'Every day it seems more apparent that the question is becoming one only to be decided by the Irishmen themselves'.[4] Since January 1913, the Government needed the agreement of the Unionist Opposition to a settlement. But after the Curragh and Larne, the Ulster Unionists were in a powerful bargaining position and far less inclined to allow their British Unionist allies to agree to any compromise.

Desperate attempts to reach a political settlement had, therefore, to be resumed in the worst possible circumstances for the Liberals. The gravity of the deadlock was underlined by the resort to two expedients which had been abandoned in 1913 – United Kingdom devolution, and a conference of the party leaders. The Unionist Round Table group seized the opportunity to launch an intensive campaign for a federal solution, from March to May 1914. Churchill and F.E. Smith returned enthusiastically to the cause. They helped the Round Table group to draft a House of Commons' appeal for the exclusion of six Ulster counties until United Kingdom devolution could be established. This appeal secured the signatures of 78 Liberal members and 56 Unionists,[5] but it had no success with most party leaders. The federal proposals aroused intense hostility and anger among the Nationalists and some sections of the Liberal Party. Robert Harcourt warned Churchill of the extent of the fury among those who felt strongly that 'this was not the moment to parley with the enemy'. The radicals saw the proposal as humiliating surrender, while Redmond protested to Asquith that it was 'impossible and even disastrous'.[6] By mid-May the federal proposals were abandoned yet again.

Any real hopes of a political settlement were concentrated on the negotiations for Ulster exclusion which meandered on from April to July 1914. These negotiations are beyond the scope of this book and have already been given more than due emphasis elsewhere.[7] The sheer futility of these efforts was the inevitable consequence of the ministry's impotence. The last stages of the interminable progress of the Home Rule Bill assumed a farcical character. Asquith's offer of the Lloyd George scheme for six year exclusion by county option, which effectively meant four counties only, had been rejected by Carson on 9 March. Ten days later, Bonar Law had made his counter-offer, that Asquith's proposal be decided by referendum, and Carson suggested permanent exclusion for an unspecified area of Ulster.

The Second Reading of the Bill was resumed on 31 March, after the Curragh crisis, with Grey speaking for the Government, while the Prime Minister was away defending his seat. Grey's speech was conciliatory, but he vetoed the referendum proposal and stated that the six year time limit could not be extended. Agar-Robartes condemned the Government's policy, proposing instead that Ulster should be given a second option at the end of six years.[8] He joined Sir Clifford Cory in voting against the Second and Third Readings, while Captain Pirie supported William O'Brien's Cork Nationalists in abstaining. The Committee and 'suggestion' stages were dispensed with, in the absence of any agreement, and the unamended Bill passed its Third Reading in the Commons on 25 May.

After considerable debate in Cabinet, Asquith decided on 23 May to introduce a separate Amending Bill in the Lords, to receive the royal assent at the same time as the main Bill. He proposed merely to repeat the six year county option scheme of 9 March. The King protested strongly that this would be useless, since those terms were 'repudiated by Ulster'.[9] A minority in the Cabinet, led by Lloyd George and Grey, shared the King's view, and the pressure to abandon the time-limit intensified by the end of May. Lloyd George had discovered early in May that the Nationalists were really far more concerned about the question of area. He therefore tried to persuade the Cabinet that 'limited exclusion is already gone; all the fight will be over area'. Sir Edward Grey gave him firm support, even contemplating resignation unless Ulster was excluded indefinitely. Birrell also agreed, on 15 June, that the proposals in the Amending Bill 'present no solution to the difficulties of the situation'.[19]

Despite these powerful protests, Asquith persisted with his plan to re-introduce the six year county option scheme as the Amending Bill in the Lords on 23 June. It was hopelessly inadequate by then. The Lords allowed it to pass Second Reading, so that they could transform it in Committee to suit the more extreme Ulster Unionist ideas. When the Bill reached the Third Reading on 14 July, the Lords had struck out the six year time limit and the provisions for county option. They substituted an amendment by Lansdowne, permanently excluding all nine counties. Roy Jenkins has argued that: 'for the first time Asquith was brought up against a complete *impasse* . . . The time had clearly arrived to put into practice his theory that negotiations were most likely to succeed when the pressure for settlement had become urgent upon both sides . . .'.[11] But this deadlock had existed since March 1914, and it should have been obvious that the Lords' rejection of a patently inadequate Amending Bill was inevitable. To gamble on such a theory, at this dangerously late stage, verged on the suicidal. Moreover, the Government's evident weakness since the Curragh had substantially reduced the pressure for compromise on the Ulster Unionists.

The pressure on the Government was far more intense. The transformed Amending Bill was scheduled for consideration by the Commons on 20 July, leaving only six days in which to reach an agreement. There was, in any case, very little time left, since the Home Rule Bill and its Amending Bill had to receive the Royal Assent by the end of the 1914 session, to conform with the Parliament Act's provisions. The pressure from Redmond increased Asquith's difficulties. Consequently, he gave his approval to a series of informal negotiations with the Opposition leaders in July, conducted by Lord Murray of Elibank, the former Chief Whip, while Lloyd George, Asquith, Birrell and J.A. Spender talked at various times to Redmond and Dillon. The Government was in a desperate position. They had admitted that the Home Rule Bill and its Amending partner were interdependent, yet they were at the mercy of the Opposition for an agreement on the latter. They could not now return to their original position, even if the King would allow it, because their Amending Bill had publicly acknowledged the glaring deficiency in their measure.

After the informal negotiations in July, Asquith finally agreed to the King's persistent requests that all the party leaders should meet together. A conference was held at Buckingham Palace from 21-24 July. The reasons for this conference are somewhat obscure. Jenkins has suggested that, by mid-July, Asquith thought the time was at last ripe: '. . . both sides seemed likely to acquiesce in the exclusion, without a time limit, of the resultant five or five-and-a-half county *bloc*'. Admittedly the negotiations had shifted attention from the question of time-limit to that of area, since the latter was evidently the more intractable problem. In discussing 'details' on 17 July, Carson insisted that all of Tyrone must be excluded, though the Nationalists would obviously reject this. Asquith urged Bonar Law when they met the same day '. . . that it would be a crime if civil war resulted from so small a difference'. The Prime Minister was still convinced that 'there was so much chance of agreement' that it would be wrong to risk it for the sake of a few days' delay.[12] Asquith might well have persuaded himself that the difference between the two sides was really so small.

But if this was indeed Asquith's reasoning, it had no justification whatever. The informal negotiations had been entirely fruitless. The Prime Minister's report to the Cabinet on 13 July indicated no reason for optimism:

. . . Carsonites not prepared to give up Tyrone as in H.R. area. Nationalists equally strong . . . The issues so far reaching not only civil war, but interests in India, industrial world and throughout empire might be broken up by catastrophe in Ireland.

A few days later, after talking to Bonar Law, Asquith informed the King that 'neither party is prepared to give way, in the sense of partition in regard to the county of Tyrone'.[13] The dispute over the exclusion area symbolised a far wider gulf, which was possibly unbridgeable by July 1914. Morley commented on 20 July that: 'The issue of Tyrone is narrow enough, but then, as history so abundantly shows, when men want to fight, a narrow issue will do just as well as a broad one'. Lansdowne also remarked that the two sides were 'still widely separated, and I fear in some cases upon questions which are fundamental'.[14] The Prime Minister seems never fully to have appreciated the fundamental difference in principle which divided the two Irish parties.

Bonar Law certainly gave Asquith no reason to expect that an agreement would follow from the Buckingham Palace conference. When the Unionist leader learnt of the suggestion, he told Asquith plainly on 17 July that a conference held while the question of Tyrone was undecided would be 'perfectly useless', since it would be 'utterly impossible' for Carson to

give way on that point. Bonar Law informed Lord
Stamfordham that:

. . . there was so little prospect of agreement that we should not have been
prepared to enter into a conference, summoned at the last moment, and
without any definite basis of discussion, except in deference to the wishes of
His Majesty.

Stamfordham passed on to the Prime Minister the gloomy
warning that no basis existed as a preliminary for discussion
between the two sides.[15] It is difficult to accept that the Prime
Minister can really have been hopeful of a successful outcome
in the light of these comments. A more convincing
explanation of his reason for calling the conference is provided
in his own letter to the King on 17 July. He explained that if the
Amending Bill was debated on 20 July, as scheduled, neither
side could offer any acceptable form of compromise, 'in view
of the dominating opinion of their respective followers'. The
significant sentence followed: 'It may be that such a
Conference will be unable at the moment to attain a definite
settlement, but it will certainly postpone, and may avert
dangerous and possibly irreparable action . . .'.[16] Precisely
what Asquith hoped to gain by a further delay is not at all
clear, but at least the dreaded consequences would be
postponed a little longer.

The Buckingham Palace conference only emphasised the
bankruptcy of Asquith's policy and the hopelessness of the
deadlock. From 21–24 July, Asquith, Lloyd George, Lansdowne, Law, Redmond, Dillon, Carson and Craig represented the two Irish and the two British parties. Instead of
the gap between the two sides being narrowed, it seemed to
broaden. Redmond continued to insist on county option,
which meant the exclusion of only four counties, while Bonar
Law wanted six, and Carson demanded the 'clean cut' of the
whole province of Ulster. It was clear by this time that
Asquith was prepared to give way on the time-limit, but his
proposal on area seemed to the Unionists little better than four
county exclusion. He suggested leaving out of the Bill south
Tyrone, north Fermanagh, and the four north-east counties,
except for south Armagh. Neither the Unionists nor the
Nationalists could accept this, or a similar alternative

proposed by the Speaker. Bonar Law's account concluded: 'It was then evident that all hope of settlement was gone'. The Prime Minister reported to the Cabinet that the Unionists 'did not mean to settle and all expedients had failed'.[17] The Nationalists and the Ulster Unionist representatives at least agreed that the division between them was far wider than the question of partitioning Tyrone. Even Asquith admitted to Venetia Stanley that 'nothing could have been more amicable in tone or more desperately fruitless in result . . . I have rarely felt more hopeless in any practical affair: an impasse, with unspeakable consequences . . .'.[18]

How Asquith intended to break this deadlock remains a mystery. The debate on the Amending Bill in the Commons had been postponed from 20 July until 28 July, in the faint hope that the conference might resolve the issue. When that collapsed, Asquith decided to proceed with the original Amending Bill for exclusion by county option, 'but with the omission of automatic inclusion after a term of years, and the substitution of a fresh power of option' at the end of the initial time-limit.[19] This would clearly settle nothing. But once again the parliamentary farce was interrupted. The gun-running coup at Howth on 26 July made a further postponement necessary. The fury of the Nationalists needed time to cool, but it was obvious that they would now be even more reluctant to agree to concessions. Lord Esher commented on 30 July that Asquith 'has now reduced the south of Ireland to such a condition of chaos as to make any concession to Ulster valueless as a method of pacifying Nationalists and Covenanters'.[20]

The pressure on the Prime Minister against surrendering to Unionist demands was increasing. Apart from the Nationalists, he had to contend with a growing volume of criticism from the Liberal rank and file. A section of the party had objected to the Government's policy of drift since 1913, more on account of the weak and uncertain methods, than because they opposed the principle of exclusion. The critics disliked the continual series of delays and retreats, and the possibility of impending surrender. They also sympathised with Redmond's position and felt the Government had broken too many promises. In September 1913, Asquith believed that

Carson's 'antics' were 'stiffening the backs of the most moderate among our supporters' against any concessions to threats and blackmail. Opinion among the rank and file was evidently hardening against compromise, and by December, Morley claimed that fifty Liberals would vote with Redmond if he declined to accept a compromise settlement.[21]

The views of L. T. Hobhouse and C. P. Scott were typical of many Liberal critics. They had been prepared to come to terms with Carson before March 1914, but they interpreted the Government's renewed negotiations after the Curragh and Larne as total surrender. By May, they preferred to lose Home Rule altogether, rather than 'accept a compromise based on the dictation of Carson with the backing of the army . . .'.[22] Two months later, Christopher Addison stated that rank and file Liberals were infuriated more by the inept handling of the Home Rule issue by their own leaders than by the violent conduct of their opponents:

. . . Few of us could understand, and it is impossible to understand now, how the Government could look on at the organised and open preparations for civil war without making an attempt to put them down . . . If concessions with regard to Ulster had to be made – as they clearly had – why had things been allowed to drift so far ? This was the question men were asking, and it was directed more against Asquith than against anyone. Most of us certainly were convinced that if the situation had been more firmly handled before it had become thus desperate, we should have been spared many distresses . . .[23]

Such dissatisfaction was growing among the Liberal voters in the country, as well as in the House of Commons. Seely was informed even in September 1913 that Nottinghamshire Liberals wanted the Government to 'stand firm and deal with Ulster rebellion *if* it comes *when* it comes'. They did not want an 'unworthy compromise' which would be misinterpreted as a sign of weakness. Resentment increased during the next eight months. By the end of May 1914 Lloyd George received a memorandum from the Yorkshire Liberal Association, which revealed the exasperation among Liberal voters: 'If Home Rule is not settled without a general election we are all wasting our time on land and housing'. They demanded that Home Rule must become law as fast as possible. If the

Government failed to prove that the Parliament Act was an effective means of passing their Bills against the will of the Tories, 'the working people will drop us for a long time to come'.[24] Discontent in Yorkshire mounted during the next three weeks, as Charles Trevelyan discovered after attending a meeting there on 25 July:

. . . they say that the whole of the Liberal working-class is on the point of revolt, that the prestige of the government is gone, and that the great mass of working-men think that the government is funking. They have never approved of leaving Carson alone, they were more angry about the gun-running, and they are quite furious about the Conference . . . Any further delay will mean a violent explosion of Liberal feeling which will be immediately reflected in the House . . . You must suppress Carson, if it becomes necessary, *without an election*. . . . The long and the short of it is the government has got to show itself top dog *now*, or the Liberal Party will disintegrate, even in the West Riding.[25]

Pressure on the Prime Minister was further increased because his time was running out so fast. Under the provisions of the Parliament Act, the Home Rule Bill had to pass by the end of the 1914 session. Liberal backbenchers were exhausted after an arduous session and adamantly opposed to prolonging it. As early as 6 May Percy Illingworth, the Chief Whip, warned the Cabinet that they would wreck their prospects of success at the 1915 general election if they kept the House sitting after the end of August: 'There is a point of exhaustion beyond which it is impossible to drive the House of Commons'.[26] This gloomy verdict was confirmed when the Government's majority fell to twenty-three on a guillotine motion on Lloyd George's 1914 budget. This was chiefly a protest against the drastic methods of closure employed to enable the Government to complete its parliamentary business. The next day 'a largely signed memorial' was sent to the Chief Whip, demanding that business be confined to August, with no autumn session, 'unless the exigencies of Ireland imperatively demand one'. Illingworth replied on 13 July with a memorandum to all Liberal members, stating that the current session would end as soon as the Home Rule Amendment Bill was disposed of: 'The time has arrived for a sustained effort, and with everything at stake for which generations of Liberals have laboured, I am relying on your constant attendance and support for the remainder of the Session'.[27]

In mid July Redmond warned Asquith that he would be forced to vote against the Second Reading of the Amending Bill, if the Government's concessions went too far. In that case, he believed 'a very large proportion' of the Liberal and Labour members would support the Nationalists. Christopher Addison reported that the intense bitterness and anger of the Liberal rank and file reached a climax during the week beginning 20 July. They received Asquith's announcement of the Buckingham Palace conference and the postponement of the Amending Bill with profound mistrust: 'Whatever Cabinet Ministers might be disposed to do, there was no doubt that the bulk of the Liberal Party were vehement in their intention to support Redmond and the Irish Members'. The next day, 'a largely attended' meeting of Liberal members determined 'to apply ginger to the Government; to stick to the Nationalists throughout . . .'.[28] W.S. Blunt noted in his diary that 'the Labour members are threatening a revolt from Asquith and a hundred Liberals as well'. Dillon commented that one of the most valuable results of the Buckingham Palace conference was 'the explosion of feeling in the Radical Press and the Liberal Party'.[29] This explosion had some impact on the Cabinet. On 22 July ministers vetoed a suggestion by Churchill and Grey that a 'British decision' should be imposed on the two hostile Irish factions, over their heads if necessary. Apart from the fact that the Unionists could not agree to this, Pease argued that it would be futile to press their own proposals against Nationalist opposition, 'as our people would side with Redmond and against our solution'.[30]

The deadlock was absolute, and Asquith's Irish policy seemed about to end in disaster, but total humiliation was averted by two unexpected events. The first was the outbreak of war in Europe early in August 1914. The second was the Opposition offer of a political truce in the cause of national unity. Cameron Hazlehurst has suggested that domestic calculations were not responsible for the actual decision to enter the war, but 'the looming presence of Ireland' at least made the decision easier to bear. This conclusion is supported by considerable evidence. After discussing the grave European news with the Asquith family on 28 July, Gladstone's daughter noted in her diary:

Could not help saying to [Asquith], 'if ever a war takes place in the world again, I hope it will be now'. He turned on me a look of understanding and mischief. 'Why ?' 'To settle Ireland'. He said 'You're as bad as Winston; who last night seeing there was more hopeful news said, 'I'm afraid we shall have a bloody peace'.[31]

The next day Samuel commented to his wife: 'The only consolatory fact at the moment is that the big storm cloud of Europe makes the Irish sky seem by comparison quite bright'. Charles Trevelyan '. . . ceased to care about Ireland. The bigger question overshadows it utterly'. Asquith's remark to Pease on 3 August that 'the one bright spot in this hateful war . . . was the settlement of Irish civil strife' was, then, a natural and fairly typical reaction.[32] By 29-30 July, the critical situation in Europe diverted political attention from Ulster. The outbreak of the First World War enabled Asquith to extricate himself from a hopeless Irish policy, with some tactical gain, though with little moral or permanent achievement. He was relieved that an apparently insoluble problem could be shelved.

The Prime Minister was also lucky that the British and Irish Unionists gave high priority to the need for national unity in wartime, offering on 30 July to defer controversial domestic quarrels in the interests of a united war effort. Asquith eagerly took advantage of the offer and postponed the debate on the Amending Bill once more. After six weeks' further futile negotiation, the Home Rule Bill was placed on the Statute Book in mid-September, without any agreement having been reached over Ulster. The Amending Bill was replaced by a Suspensory Act, which postponed the operation of the Home Rule Act until after the war. Unionist bitterness was not mitigated by Asquith's promise that an Amending Bill providing for Ulster exclusion would be introduced during the suspensory period. The Opposition felt strongly that Asquith 'took advantage of our patriotism to betray us', by using the political truce to pass Home Rule without the Amending Bill. This would have been impossible before the war, because Asquith admitted then that the two Bills were interdependent. The Prime Minister justified his action by emphasising the need to win Nationalist support for the war, but inoperative Home Rule was only a pyrrhic victory for the Irish and provided no solution to the Irish question.

The outbreak of the First World War thus allowed Asquith to escape the consequences of his Irish policy. There is no evidence to suggest that a political solution would otherwise have been reached, given a little more time. Indeed, the Buckingham Palace conference indicates quite the opposite. General Macready stated subsequently that he did not know what would have happened in Ireland in 1914-15, if European war had not intervened. In May 1914, however, he warned that when the Amending Bill became law, '. . . disturbances, if they occurred, would be more in the nature of civil war than of faction fights'. Only two weeks before the outbreak of war, Bonar Law told Asquith that if he proceeded with his existing Amending Bill, '. . . an independent state would be set up within the United Kingdom and [that] there would be nothing left for us but to support Ulster to the utmost'.[33] Birrell believed in June 1914 that 'a great conflagration cannot be avoided', if the discipline of the U.V.F. broke down. A.T.Q. Stewart has concluded that 'at the very end of July war in Ulster seemed certain, and only the outbreak of the war in Europe averted it'.[34]

CONCLUSION

Lord Wolverhampton predicted in 1910 that the attempt to implement Home Rule would break up the Liberal Party.[1] The Irish question contributed more to the decline of the party than has generally been recognised, though in a more complex manner than Wolverhampton expected.

The passage of the Parliament Act in 1911 placed the Liberal Party under an obligation to fulfil its long-standing commitment to carry Irish Home Rule. Asquith's failure to do so was all the more tragic in that he missed one of the best opportunities history has ever offered for the peaceful solution of the Ulster problem. He had a chance to deal with Ulster after the Parliament Act at last made settlement a practical possibility, and before the bloodshed of 1916-21 irrevocably embittered feelings on all sides.

The Cabinet did not even bother to examine the Ulster question in 1911 and Asquith rejected the appeal of Lloyd George and Churchill that special provision should be made for Ulster in the 1912 Bill. Under the conditions of the Parliament Act it was still possible to incorporate terms for Ulster into the Bill during the 1912 session, without the agreement of the Opposition. Despite the publicity given to the Ulster exclusion proposal by the Agar-Robartes and Carson amendments, Asquith failed to seize the opportunity for dealing with Ulster on his own terms before January 1913. The Liberal Government's myopia over Ulster throughout 1911-12 contrasted strongly with the Unionist Party's fanatical obsession with the issue. Even as late as November 1912, the Liberals were more concerned with their backbench revolt over the financial aspects of the Bill than with the Unionist campaign of 'Ulsteria', which was rapidly gathering momentum. The Cabinet did not treat Ulster's resistance to Home Rule seriously until autumn 1913, when it was far too late to avert the growing crisis.

As was so often and so tragically the case with British policy in Ireland, on each occasion too little was offered too late. If Asquith had made his March 1914 offer before January 1913 compromise might have been possible, before the two sides became so intransigent and while Asquith still controlled the parliamentary situation. Asquith's Ulster policy was finally wrecked by the Curragh fiasco in March 1914. Up to that point, he could still choose between a political compromise making special provision for Ulster and the enforcement of his original Home Rule Bill for the whole of Ireland. The Curragh crisis made the effective execution of this second option almost impossible, since the Government believed that it could not use the army to coerce Ulster. Asquith was forced to face the consequences of his policy in the spring of 1914, when his options had run out. He relied throughout on a high-risk policy of prevarication and delay which had clearly failed by May 1914. Thus total deadlock over Home Rule and Ulster was reached several months before the European war broke out. The conflagration in Europe has partially concealed from later generations the utter hopelessness of Asquith's Irish policy in the months after March 1914. Asquith lacked Gladstone's boldness and generosity in relation to Ireland. Caution and procrastination were not effective substitutes.

It is not certain, of course, that the Irish question would have been solved between 1911 and 1914 if Asquith had provided special terms for Ulster in the 1912 Bill. It is certain, however, that no British government would have conceded more than Home Rule with Ulster exclusion in the period up to 1914. Such a settlement would at least have provided a starting point and offered better prospects for the evolution of a more stable, non-violent relationship between the north and south of Ireland and Great Britain. This might gradually have developed into dominion status and ultimate independence for the south, without the tragedy of 1916 and the bloody events of 1919-21. It might even, perhaps, have led in time to a united Ireland. Redmond's opposition created one of the biggest obstacles to such a settlement. But Redmond agreed to Ulster exclusion in 1914 as the price of peace. It seems possible, as previously argued, that he might have acquiesced in Home Rule within Home Rule, or even Ulster exclusion, as the price of Irish self-government in 1912. Instead, the Nationalists were offered their ultimate goal at the start, only to see it pulled away from them bit by bit, leaving their faith in the Government shattered.

Asquith's actual policy was a total failure, whatever the prospects of hypothetical alternatives. Nor is there any substantial evidence to suggest that it might have succeeded had the First World War not intervened. It was clear to many on both sides by 1914 that Ulster exclusion was the only practicable solution, and it was equally apparent that innumerable obstacles blocked the path to such a settlement. These barriers might have been surmounted by a carefully considered policy in 1911-12, but they were unlikely to be overcome by a brief last-minute conference at Buckingham Palace in July 1914. How Asquith ever expected to settle the complexities of Ulster exclusion and Irish finance in a matter of weeks remains a mystery.

In some respects, the problems presented by Ireland and the problems of war were similar. They both challenged some of the fundamental tenets of the Liberal philosophy, such as the use of coercion. They both demanded precisely those qualities of leadership which Lloyd George could supply more effectively than Asquith. G.P. Gooch expressed the common view that: 'Many people in both parties came to feel that Asquith was an excellent leader in peace but lacked the dynamism and the drive required in a life-and-death struggle'. C.P. Scott made a similar judgment in May 1914: 'Of course Asquith is strong only in words and in a situation needing immediate decision and action would always fail'.[2] These comments apply as much to the Irish crisis as to the war. Asquith's weaknesses as a war-time leader were already foreshadowed in his mismanagement of the Ulster problem.

In fairness to Asquith, it must be stated that many of his colleagues experienced similar difficulties in coping with these problems. Birrell, in particular, must share the responsibility for the Cabinet's Irish policy, though he paid for his undoubted limitations as Irish Secretary when he resigned as the Government's scapegoat for the 1916 Easter Rising. The Cabinet's Ulster policy from 1911 to 1914 provoked remarkably little criticism from any other ministers, except Lloyd George and Churchill. Most of them did not even become aware of its implications until late in 1913, when the Cabinet became increasingly divided on the issue. This can be attributed in some cases to preoccupation with departmental business, or to lack of knowledge or interest in Irish affairs. It may also reflect the Prime Minister's preference for sympathetic, like-minded colleagues. Undoubtedly, it was a tribute to Asquith's prestige and moral authority in so many other areas.

At a deeper level, however, the explanation for the failure of the Liberal ministers to deal effectively with the Irish question must lie with the political tradition which shaped their principles and attitudes. Asquith himself mirrored the weaknesses as well as the strengths of the Liberal heritage. It was no accident that he was a major force in the Liberal Party from the 1890s to 1916. He was able to mobilise the progressive forces of New Liberalism in promoting social reform, but his party bore the burden of Gladstonian Liberalism in Irish and foreign policy. The pacifist views of many Liberals were reflected as much in their reluctance to coerce Ulster as in their opposition to the First World War. The Irish problem also highlighted the difficulty of reconciling conflicting principles within the Liberal tradition. Asquith's Cabinet was unable to decide how to fulfil national aspirations when these conflicted with the rights of a powerful minority, and when they could only be imposed by force. Birrell posed the problem: to leave Ulster permanently out of the settlement 'would have been an outrage upon Irish unity . . . but to bring her in without bloodshed seemed impossible'.[3]

The Irish question was also significant because of the Liberal time and energy it diverted from other important political issues. By 1911, as Peter Clarke has shown, the Liberal Party, in some regions at least, was proving its ability to accommodate and appeal to the growing working class electorate. The party appeared to be in no danger of extinction, though a fourth consecutive victory at the polls in 1915 may have been unlikely. From 1911-14 the Liberal Government had ambitious plans for land, fiscal and educational reform. The provisions of the Parliament Act, combined with the intractable problem of Ulster, meant that the Irish crisis consumed the attention of the Cabinet and parliament for three long years. These turned out to be three crucial and testing years in the history of the Liberal Party, because of the intervention of the First World War. The general election which should have been held in 1915 was postponed until after the war. By then the Labour Party had improved its organization and increased its popular appeal. The Liberal Party, in contrast, was deeply split into two factions led by Asquith and Lloyd George, and its most fundamental principles had been undermined by the demands of war. Those former Liberal and working class voters who had to choose between Liberal and Labour in 1918 looked back on the last years of peace as a time of relative stagnation in social and economic affairs.

After 1911 the Liberal Government was unable to give the necessary attention to the demands of the radical elements within the party for increased state intervention in the interests of the working classes. Churchill had forecast as early as 1907:

No legislation at present in view interests the democracy. All their minds are turning more and more to the social and economic issue. This revolution is irresistible . . . Minimum standards of wages and comfort, insurance in some effective form or other against sickness, unemployment, old age, these are the questions and the only questions by which parties are going to live in the future. Woe to Liberalism, if they slip through its fingers . . . [4]

It was scarcely surprising that the progressive wing of the party resented the preoccupation with Home Rule from 1911 to 1914, since it impeded progress in those areas with most appeal to the radicals and the voters. Arthur Ponsonby expressed his frustration with the delayed negotiations over Home Rule in November 1913, insisting that the radicals were 'impatient to proceed with drastic social and land reforms'. In January 1913, the *Nation* regretted that 'parliament has been engaged upon issues which were ripe twenty years ago', and had consequently been forced to neglect the more urgent and relevant 'schemes of social regeneration'. Exactly a year later, the *Nation* commented that 'all politics are overshadowed, all other issues rendered insignificant, by the question of Ulster', but 'the politics of the future do not turn on this particular issue'.[5] Lloyd George believed that 'for Liberalism stagnation was death'.[6]

Unfortunately for the Liberal Party, its last years of government were dominated by the issues of Home Rule, Welsh Disestablishment, and the entry into war, which so powerfully alienated the radicals. In June 1914, C.P. Scott confessed that he was beginning to share J.A. Hobson's view that 'the existing Liberal party is played out and that if it is to count for anything in the future it must be reconstructed largely on a labour basis'. After the outbreak of war, Scott remarked gloomily to Dillon: 'We have I think no longer a Liberal Government – had we really one before ?'[7] Morley was equally pessimistic: 'however else we may pick up the pieces, there is an end of the Liberal party and all its landmarks'. In 1913 the *Nation* reflected on the future of Liberalism:

With the passage of Home Rule and Welsh Disestablishment, the *rôle* of the old political Liberal Party comes practically to an end . . . What is to emerge as the new moral basis, the intellectual stimulant of the spirit of Liberalism ? . . . Liberalism cannot stand still; another Session like the present one would kill it, and it is therefore the true wisdom of statesmanship to map out new territory, first for exploration, then for action.[8]

The war prevented this search for new directions after 1914 even more effectively than Home Rule had done before. Continued emphasis on the socio-economic aspirations of the radicals during the crucial years 1911-14 might have ensured that the loose coalition of 'progressive' forces could have rallied the support which went instead to the Labour Party after 1918.

Trevor Wilson has demonstrated the inability of the Liberal Party and the Liberal philosophy to deal effectively with the demands of the First World War. He viewed the war as an unforeseen tragedy, a 'rampant omnibus' which wrecked a Liberal Party which might otherwise have survived. Peter Clarke strengthened one aspect of this interpretation with his persuasive analysis of the party's capacity for accommodation in the social and economic sphere up to 1910.[9] In the early twentieth century, a British political party undoubtedly required the ability to respond to the socio-economic demands of a substantial working class electorate. In *The Crisis of Liberalism* in 1909, J.A. Hobson identified a 'positive policy of social reconstruction' as the means 'that may enable British Liberalism to avoid the shipwreck which Continental Liberalism has suffered when it was driven on the submerged reefs of the economic problem in politics'.[10] Certainly, Asquith's Cabinet did not lack ideas in these areas in the immediate pre-war years – merely the opportunity to carry them into effect.

But the question of the decline of the Liberal Party needs to be seen in a broader perspective. The ability to meet the challenge of 'the economic problem in politics' was not enough for long-term survival. There was a further dimension to the crisis of Liberalism. As a party of government it also had to be able to deal effectively with foreign and imperial affairs, and with the continuing problems posed by Ireland and by war. The last Liberal Government's record on Irish affairs, foreign policy and war-time administration reveals its fundamental areas of weakness. Peter Clarke has recently suggested in *Liberals and Social Democrats* that 'the social democratic case for the Liberal party had been seen at its most cogent in 1910'. He rightly concluded that subsequent disaffection arose not so much from disappointment with the Liberal record on social reconstruction, as from disillusionment over 'a range of issues where its competence ought to have been guaranteed by its own historic tradition . . .'.[11]

In short, the Irish problem of 1911-14 demoralised the Liberal Party at a critical time and contributed significantly to the party's decline. The reversion to the traditional constitutional issues of Gladstonian Liberalism left the electorate apathetic, and frustrated the progressive wing of the party. Irish Home Rule monopolised parliamentary time and energies throughout the three vital years before the First World War. It prevented the Government maintaining the momentum of socio-economic reform, which reached a premature climax in the 1911 Insurance Act. Home Rule highlighted Liberalism's difficulty in reconciling the 'progressive' demands of the twentieth century electorate with the traditional commitments of Gladstonian Liberalism. The long-term damage to the Liberal Party might have been less serious if Asquith's Government had been able to resolve the Irish question. The party sacrificed a great deal in the Home Rule cause, but all in vain. There could be no final 'Liberal' solution to the Irish question because of Ulster's challenge. Home Rule for a united Ireland conflicted with Protestant minority rights and raised the issue of coercion. This dilemma bedevilled and wrecked Asquith's Irish policy and left the Liberal Party weak and exhausted before the First World War began. The war gave the *coup de grâce* to the Liberal Party, but the inability to meet the challenge posed by the Ulster problem was itself a symptom of chronic debility. The Liberal Party was already being consumed by the Orange cancer before it was run over by the 'rampant omnibus' of war.

APPENDIX: LIBERALS WHO FAILED TO VOTE ON CRUCIAL HOME RULE DIVISIONS IN 1912

Key:

x	failure to vote (caused either by absence or deliberate abstention)
(x)	some evidence that absence was unavoidable
p	paired. Names known only for First and Second Reading – including only those who were *also* absent unpaired at other times
★	speech hostile to government position *or* qualified support only
⊛	voted with Unionists
	Federalists. Signed May 1914 federal appeal, or gave other evidence of federalist sympathies.

REGION: S = Scotland, N = N. England, W = Wales, C = Cornwall	FEDERALIST	NONCONFORMIST	On Home Rule			On Ulster exclusion	
			1st Reading 16 Apr 1912	2R 9 May 1912	3R 16 Jan 1913	Agar-Robartes Amendment 18 June 1912	Carson's Amendment 1 Jan 1913
Adkins, Sir W.R.D.	N	X					x
Agar-Robartes, T.	C	X	x	★	★ ⊛	★ ⊛	x
Agnew, Sir G.W.	N	X					x
Armitage, R.	N	X					x
Arnold, S.	N						x
Atherley-Jones, L.A.	N				x		x
Barlow, Sir J.E.		X					x
Barran, R.H.	N	X				x	x
Beck, A.C.T.	X						x
Brocklehurst, W.B.	N						x
Buckmaster, S.O.	N						x
Buxton, S.C.						x	
Cameron, R.	N		p	p			(x)
Cawley, Sir F.	N	X				x	x
Churchill, W.S.	S	X				x	x

	REGION	FEDERALIST	NONCONFORMIST	On Home Rule			On Ulster exclusion	
				1st Reading 16 Apr 1912	2R 9 May 1912	3R 16 Jan 1913	Agar-Robartes Amendment 18 June 1912	Carson's Amendment 1 Jan 1913
Collins, G.P.	S							x
Cory, Sir Clifford	C	X	X	⊛	⊛	⊛	⊛	⊛
Cowan, W.H.	S	X	X			x	⊛ ★	x
Craig, H.J.	N							x
Davies, Ellis W.	W		X				x	
Davies, David	W	X	X					x
Davies, M.L.V.	W						x	x
De Forest, Baron M.								x
Dewar, Sir J.A.	S		X					x
Dickinson, W.H.		X	?					x
Edwards, A.C.	W		X	(x)				
Edwards, Sir F.	W							x
Elverston, Sir H.	N	X						x
Esslemont, G.B.	S		X				x	
Fenwick, C.	N	X	X					x
Fiennes, E.E.					p		x	x
France, G.A.	N		X				x	x
Gelder, Sir W.A.		X				x		x
Grey, Sir E.	N	X		(x)				
George, D. Lloyd	W	X	X				x	x
Greenwood, G.G.							x	x
Greenwood, T.H.	N							x
Greig, J.W.	W							x
Guest, F.E.								x
Harcourt, L.	N						x	
Harmsworth, C.B.		X						x
Harmsworth, R.L.	S	X					x	
Harvey, A.G.C.	N							x
Harvey, T.E.	N		X					x
Havelock-Allan, Sir H.	N	X	X				x	
Henderson, J.M.	S			(x)				
Holt, R.D.	N	X	X					x
Hope, J.D.	S							x
Jardine, Sir J.	S						★ x	x
Jones, Sir D.B.	W	X	X					x
Jones, E.R.	W						x	
Kemp, Sir G.	N			x	x ★		x	
Lamb, E.H.			X			x	x	x
Lawson, Sir W.	N							x
Logan, J.W.	W						x	x

270

	REGION	FEDERALIST	NONCONFORMIST	On Home Rule			On Ulster exclusion	
				1st Reading	2R	3R	Agar-Robartes Amendment	Carson's Amendment
				16 Apr 1912	9 May 1912	16 Jan 1913	18 June 1912	1 Jan 1913
McCurdy, C.A.		X	X	p				x
McLaren, W.S.B.	N				(x)		(x)	
McMicking, G.	S	X						x
Manfield, H.		X	X					x
Markham, Sir A.B.						x	x	
Marks, Sir G.C.	C	X	X					x
Martin, J.							x	
Mason, D.M.								x
Menzies, Sir W.	S				(x)			(x)
Middlebrook, W.	N	X	X					x
Molteno, P.A.	S							x
Mond, Sir A.	W						x	
Montagu, E.S.					(x)			(x)
Munro-Ferguson, R.C.	S	X	X				⊛ ★	x
Murray, A.C.	S						x	x
Needham, C.T.	N						x	
Nicholson, Sir C.N.	N	X						x
Norman, Sir H.	N							x
Nuttall, H.	N	X						x
Ogden, F.	N						x	x
Palmer, G.	N							x
Pearce, W.								x
Pearson, W.H.M.							x	x
Philipps, I.							x	x
Pirie, D.V.	S	X		x	★	★	★ ⊛	x ★
Pollard, Sir G.H.	N							x
Ponsonby, A.A.	S	X						x
Price, Sir R.J.		X						x
Priestley, Sir A.		X					x	x
Priestley, Sir W.E.B.	N	X	X				x	
Primrose, N.		X					x	
Pringle, W.M.R.	S	X					x	
Roberts, Sir J.H.	W		X					x
Robinson, S.	W		X	p	x		x	
Rose, Sir C.D.							x	
Rowlands, J.							x	
Russell, T.W.			X				x	
Samuel, Sir S.M.						x	x	(x)
Scott, A. MacCallum	S	X						x
Seely, J.E.B.							x	

	REGION	FEDERALIST	NONCONFORMIST	On Home Rule			On Ulster exclusion	
				1st Reading 16 Apr 1912	2R 9 May 1912	3R 16 Jan 1913	Agar-Robartes Amendment 18 June 1912	Carson's Amendment 1 Jan 1913
Soames, A.W.		X				(x)		
Strauss, E.A.								x
Summers, J.W.	W				p	(x)		(x)
Taylor, T.C.	N	X	X					x
Walters, Sir J.T.	N		X					x
Walton, Sir J.	N	X	X					x
Warner, Sir T.C.T.							x	
Watt, H.A.	S	X	X		x			x
Wiles, T.		X	X					x
Williams, P.	N							x
Williams, W.L.	W		X	(x)				
Williamson, Sir A.	S	X					x	
Wilson, G.G.	N	X		(x)				
Wilson, John	N		X			x	x	x
		41	34					

	REGION
North of England	39
Scotland	20
Wales	15
Cornwall	3
All other areas	32
	109

NOTES

Notes have been reduced to the absolute minimum, and abbreviated where possible, because of limited space. For detailed documentation, with commentary on sources, consult my doctoral thesis: 'The Irish Question in Liberal Politics, 1911-14' (University of Toronto, Ph.D. thesis, 1976) – cited as Jalland, Ph.D. thesis. The place of publication is London, unless otherwise stated.

Abbreviations

Citations for the Redmond Papers in the National Library of Ireland, and the Campbell-Bannerman, H. Gladstone, A.J. Balfour and J.A. Spender Papers in the British Library have been abbreviated as follows:

MS. Redmond 15182	= Redmond Papers, National Library of Ireland, Add. MS. 15182
H. Gladstone MS. 46018	= H. Gladstone Papers, British Library, Add. MS. 46018 [similarly Balfour MS., Campbell-Bannerman MS. etc.]
English Historical Review	= *E.H.R.*
Historical Journal	= *H.J.*
Hansard	= *The Parliamentary Debates (Official Report). Fifth Series. House of Commons.* (Specific reference will be made in the case of a different Series, or the House of Lords' Reports)

Asq	= Asquith
MS Asq	= Asquith Papers
B.L.P.	= Bonar Law Papers
WSC	= Churchill
King	= King George V
LG	= Lloyd George
L.G.P.	= Lloyd George Papers
P.R.O.	= Public Record Office

Introduction

1   Denis Gwynn, *The Life of John Redmond* (1932); F.S.L. Lyons, *John Dillon: A Biography* (1968).
2   George Dangerfield, *The Strange Death of Liberal England* (1935).

273

3   P.F. Clarke, *Lancashire and the New Liberalism* (Cambridge, 1971);
     Trevor Wilson, *The Downfall of the Liberal Party, 1914-35* (1966).
4   See e.g. H. Pelling, *A Short History of the Labour Party* (1961); Ross
     McKibbin, *The Evolution of the Labour Party 1910-24* (Oxford, 1975);
     P. Thompson, *Socialists, Liberals and Labour. The Struggle for London
     1885-1914* (1967).
5   Roy Jenkins, *Asquith: Portrait of a Man and an Era* (1964); Robert Blake,
     *The Unknown Prime Minister: The Life and Times of Andrew Bonar Law
     1858-1923* (1955).
6   C. Hazlehurst, 'Asquith as Prime Minister, 1908-1916', *E.H.R.*,
     LXXXV (July, 1970), 531.
7   Wolverhampton to Crewe, 9 March 1910, Crewe Papers, C/54.
8   D.A. Hamer, 'The Irish Question and Liberal Politics, 1886-1894',
     H.J., XII (1969).

Chapter I

1   See D.A. Hamer, 'The Irish Question and Liberal Politics,
     1886-1894', *H.J.*, XII (1969).
2   Memo by H. Gladstone, 8 Dec. 1899, Campbell–Bannerman MS.
     41215, fos. 162-4.
3   Grey to Gladstone, 11 Oct. 1901, H. Gladstone MS. 45992, fos.
     77-80.
4   *The Times*, 24 Nov. 1905.
5   Asq to Gladstone, 22 Oct. 1905, H. Gladstone MS. 45989, fos. 131-2;
     Crewe to Campbell–Bannerman, 19 Nov. 1905, Crewe Papers, C/5.
6   Morley to Rosebery, 8 May 1905, Rosebery MS. 10047, fos. 169-70.
7   Ripon's memo, 5 Jan. 1900, H. Gladstone MS. 46018, fo. 11; Grey to
     Gladstone, 11 Oct. 1901, *ibid.*, MS. 45992, fos. 77-80.
8   Asq to Gladstone, 8 Jan. 1900, *ibid.*, MS. 45989, fos. 28-9; Crewe to
     Campbell–Bannerman, 19 Nov. 1905, Campbell–Bannerman MS.
     41213, fo. 337; Crewe to Lord Arran, 15 Jan. 1910, Crewe Papers,
     C/1.
9   Birrell to Redmond, 1 Dec. 1909, and Morley to Redmond, 6 Dec.
     1909, MSS. Redmond 15169, 15207.
10   See P.F. Clarke, 'The Electoral Position of the Liberal and Labour
     Parties, 1910-14', *E.H.R.*, XC, No. CCCLVII (Oct. 1975), esp.
     828-9.
11   Runciman to Emmott, 25 Jan. 1910, Emmott Papers.
12   See analysis in *Home Rule and the General Elections of 1910*, N.D.,
     B.L.P. 40/1/52; *Hansard*, XXIX, 826-7.
13   Asq to King, 1 Oct. 1913, MS. Asq 38, fos. 216-7; Smith to Law, 9
     Oct. 1912, and Long to Law, 2 May 1913, B.L.P. 27/3/26, 29/4/3.
14   Emmott to Runciman, 18 Dec. 1910, Runciman Papers.
15   Ilbert to Bryce, 20 Feb. 1912, MS. Bryce 14, fos. 46-9; *Nation*, 30 Dec.
     1911, 18 Jan. 1913.
16   For a detailed analysis, see Jalland, 'A Liberal Chief Secretary and the
     Irish Question: Augustine Birrell, 1907-14', *H.J.*, XIX (no.2, 1976),

421-51.

17   *Ibid.*

18   *Ibid.* See also Birrell, *Things Past Redress* (1937), p. 193; Birrell to Redmond, May and Dec. 1915, Gwynn, *Redmond*, pp. 427, 463.

19   WSC to Asq, 5 Feb. 1910, R.S. Churchill, *Winston S. Churchill*, II, *Young Statesman 1901-1914* (Boston, Mass., 1967), 351; (cited as R.S.C., *Churchill*, II).

20   Birrell, *Things Past Redress*, pp. 246-254; Emmott diary, I, fos. 62-3, 1 March 1908; Chamberlain, *Politics from Inside* (1936), p.576. See Stephen Koss, *Asquith* (1976) for a stimulating revisionist analysis of Asquith's character and career.

21   See e.g. Burns diary, 16 March 1912, B.L. Add. MS. 46334, fo. 67; Pease diary, 15 Jan. 1913, 31 March and 7 Aug. 1914; Illingworth to S. Buxton, 12 Dec. 1913, Buxton Papers.

22   Sir Almeric Fitzroy, *Memoirs* (2 vols, 6th ed., 1925), II, 475; Ilbert to Bryce 20 Feb. and 5 Sept. 1912, MS. Bryce 14, fos. 46-9, 56-8; Burns diary, 26 March 1912, B.L. Add. MS. 46334, fo. 72.

23   Emmott diary, 20 May 1910; see also Max Green to Lord Aberdeen, 26 Feb. 1910, Aberdeen Papers, 1/5.

24   Haldane, 'Notes on letters contained in my boxes, 1926', Haldane MS. 5923.

25   *Nation*, 27 Jan. 1912.

26   *Ibid*; Margot Asquith to J.A. Spender, 29 Aug. 1906, Spender MS. 46388, fo. 149.

27   See e.g. Fitzroy, *Memoirs*, II, 513; Birrell, *Redress*, p. 250.

28   Birrell at the Oxford Union, *The Times*, 4 March 1911.

29   For a detailed analysis of the devolution debate 1910-14, see Jalland, 'United Kingdom Devolution 1910-14: Political Panacea or Tactical Diversion ?', *E.H.R.*, XCIV (Oct. 1979), 757-85.

30   Printed Cabinet memos, *Devolution*, 24 Feb. and 1 March 1911, P.R.O. Cab. 37/105/16, 18.

31   Pencilled note by LG, headed *Home Rule. Suggestion*, 27 Feb. 1911, L.G.P. C/12/2.

32   C.P. Scott diary, 20 July 1911, B.L. Add. MS. 50901, fos. 21-2; Birrell, *Redress*, p. 212.

33   Pease diary, II, fo. 28, 16 Aug. 1911; Birrell to WSC, 26 Aug. 1911, Verney Papers.

34   Samuel to Gladstone, Sept. 1911, H. Gladstone MS. 45992, fos. 259-66; *Memorandum on Clauses of the Home Rule Bill*, 29 Jan. 1912, P.R.O. Cab. 37/109/8.

35   Pencilled note by Harcourt re. Cabinet, 6 March 1912, Harcourt Papers; Pease diary, II, fo. 33, 6 March 1912.

36   Birrell to Redmond, 6 and 10 April 1912, MS. Redmond 15169; Samuel to wife, 9 and 10 April, Samuel Papers, A/157/609.

37   *Government of Ireland Bill*, 15 April 1912, and *Notes to Clauses*, 7 May 1912, MS. Asq 106, fos. 199-222, and 107, fos. 22-47. See Jalland, Ph.D. thesis for a detailed analysis of the provisions of all drafts of the 1912 Bill, and a comparison with the Bills of 1886 and 1893.

38   See e.g. Pease diary, I, fo. 137, 20 Jan. 1911; Morley to Carnegie, 25
       Oct. 1911, Bodleian, MS. film 569.
39   See Jalland, Ph.D. thesis for a detailed analysis of the fiscal provisions
       of the 1912 Bill, and a comparison with those of the previous Bills.
40   *Report of the Committee on Irish Finance*, Cd. 6153, H.C. 1912-13,
       XXXIV; evidence, Cd. 6799, H.C. 1913, XXX, esp. pp.29-31, 44.
41   *Irish Finance* [7 memos., late 1911], P.R.O. Cab. 37/108/141, 145-6,
       167; *Government of Ireland Bill*, 15 April 1912, MS. Asq 106, fos.
       199-222; *Outline of Financial Provisions*, Cd. 6154, 1 and 4 April 1912,
       P.R.O. Cab. 37/110/57, 59.
42   *The Times*, 30 April 1912; Ilbert diary, 11 April 1912.
43   *Memorandum on Clauses of the Home Rule Bill*, 29 Jan. 1912, P.R.O.
       Cab. 37/109/8; Dillon to Redmond, 14 Jan. 1912, MS. Redmond
       15182.
44   *Nation*, 9 Nov. 1912; *The Times*, 29 Oct. and 20 Nov. 1912; Birrell to
       Redmond, 21 Nov. 1912, MS. Redmond 15169.
45   Fitzroy, *Memoirs*, II, 518 (15 July 1913).
46   Samuel, *A Suggestion for the Solution of the Ulster Question*, 18 Dec.
       1913, P.R.O. Cab. 37/117/95; *Government of Ireland Bill. Note* [early
       March 1914], L.G.P. C/20/2/8; *Hansard*, XXXIX, 1108 (Newman, 13
       June 1912); J.A.R. Marriott, 'The Third Edition of Home Rule',
       Nineteenth Century, LXXI (May,1912), 841.

Chapter II

1   *Census of Ireland* 1911, Cd. 6663; 4 *Hansard*, CCCV, 970 (Redmond,
       1886).
2   P. Jalland, 'Chamberlain, Home Rule and the Ulster Question,
       1885-6', unpublished M.A. dissertation, University of Toronto,
       1968; D.C. Savage, 'The Origins of the Ulster Unionist Party
       1885-1886,' *Irish Hist. Studies*, XII (March, 1961), 185-208.
3   *Ibid*; 4 *Hansard*, CCCIV, 1231 (W. Johnston), and CCCVI, 1180
       (Parnell).
4   *The Times*, 24 Feb, 14 and 17 May 1886; *Report on Belfast Riots
       Commission*, British Sessional Papers 1801-1900, XVIII (1887), 1-23,
       633 ff.
5   'The Riots in Belfast', *Fortnightly Review*, N.S., XL (Sept. 1886), 287.
6   Morley, *Life of W.E. Gladstone* (3 vols, 1903) III, 306; D.A. Hamer,
       John Morley, Liberal Intellectual in Politics (Oxford, 1968), pp.355-6.
7   James Bryce, 'Alternative Policies in Ireland', *Nineteenth Century*,
       XIX (Feb. 1886), 326; Cabinet paper, 12 March 1886, P.R.O. Cab.
       41/19/29.
8   Memo, 20 March 1886, Gladstone Papers, B.L. Add. MS. 44632; 4
       Hansard, CCCIV, 1053-4.
9   4 *Hansard*, CCCV, 1342 (18 May 1886, Labouchère); *The Times*, 19
       May 1886; 4 *Hansard*, CCCVI, 1220 (7 June 1886, Gladstone).
10   See Buckland, *Irish Unionism: II. Ulster Unionism* (Dublin, 1973),
       pp.16-19; F.S.L. Lyons, 'The Irish Unionist Party and the Devolution

Crisis of 1904–5', *Irish Hist. Studies*, VI (1948–9), 1–22.
11 Jenkins, *Asquith*, p.274; H.M. Hyde, *Carson* (1953), pp. 287–9.
12 Gwynn, *Redmond*, pp. 194–5; Amery to Law, 20 Jan. 1912, B.L.P. 25/1/43.
13 Emmott diary, II, fo. 45, 17 Nov. 1911.
14 J.A. Spender and C. Asquith, *Life of Herbert Henry Asquith* (2 vols. 1932), II, 14; Jenkins, *Asquith*, p.274.
15 *Nation*, 30 Sept. 1911, 6 Jan. 1912; Massingham to Redmond, 4 Feb. 1912, MS. Redmond 15254.
16 Fitzroy, *Memoirs*, II, 492–3; Oliver to Law, 20 Aug. 1912, B.L.P. 27/1/47.
17 Morley also had moments of anxiety (see Fitzroy, *Memoirs*, II, 476, 24 Jan. 1912), but Morley's views on Ulster were not consistent.
18 Birrell to WSC, 26 Aug. 1911, Verney Papers.
19 *Ibid.*
20 Churchill, *The World Crisis* (6 vols, 1923), I, 181.
21 See e.g. *The Times*, 4 March, 20 Oct., 18 Nov. 1911.
22 Richard Holt diary, entry for 5 Feb. 1912 (Holt MSS, Liverpool City Library).
23 See e.g. Haldane to Grey, 2 Oct. 1911, Haldane MS. 5909, fos. 151–3; Pease diary, 29 March 1909.
24 R.S.C., *Churchill*, II, 444–5.
25 Carson to Law, N.D. and 28 Jan. 1912, B.L.P. 25/1/55, 65; Dicey to Law, 21 Jan. 1912, B.L.P. 25/1/44.
26 MacDonnell to Bryce, 6 Jan. 1912, uncatalogued Bryce Papers; Birrell to WSC, 28 Jan. 1912, R.S.C., *Churchill*, II, *Companion*, 1389.
27 *Nation*, 27 Jan. 1912; R.S.C., *Churchill*, II, *Companion*, 1381; Fitzroy, *Memoirs*, II, 475–6.
28 See H. Begbie to R. Donald, 17–18 Feb. 1912, L.G.P. C/4/8/1.
29 Asq to King, 7 Feb. 1912, MS. Asq 6, fos. 95–6.
30 WSC to Asq, 17 Sept. 1913, MS. Asq 38, fo. 194; Riddell, *More Pages from my Diary 1908-14* (1934), p.186, 15 Nov. 1913.
31 Chamberlain's conversation with WSC, 27 Nov. 1913, B.L.P. 31/1/3; Sir J.H. Lewis to LG, 13 April 1914, L.G.P. C/5/9/6.
32 See Gwynn, *Redmond*, p.236; Hobhouse diary, p.111, 11 Feb. 1912.
33 Hobhouse diary, pp. 120, 154, 13 Aug. 1912 and 20 Dec. 1913.
34 Harcourt's pencilled Cabinet notes, 6 March 1912, Harcourt Papers.
35 Jenkins, *Asquith*, pp.278–82.
36 Asq to WSC, 19 Sept. 1913, R.S.C., *Churchill*, II, *Companion*, 1400; Churchill, *World Crisis*, I, 181.
37 Scott diary, 15–16 Jan. 1913, B.L. Add. MS. 50901, fos. 75–6; Asq's memo, 17 Nov. 1913, MS. Asq 39, fos. 23–6.
38 Birrell to WSC, 26 Aug. 1911, Verney Papers; Scott diary, 2 Feb. 1911, B.L. Add. MS. 50901, fos. 1–2; Earl Grey to Bryce, 12 Jan. 1912, Bryce Papers.
39 'The Ulster Covenant', anon., *Quarterly Review*, CCXVII (Oct. 1912), 569; O'Brien to Asq, 4 Nov. 1911, MS. Asq 36, fos. 7–10.
40 Hobhouse diary, p. 111, 11 Feb. 1912.

41 Birrell to WSC, 26 Aug. 1911, Verney Papers.
42 *Reports with regard to Probable Resistance to Home Rule*, 14 Feb. 1912, and *Drilling in Ulster*, 28 Feb. 1912, P.R.O. Cab. 37/109/23, 30.
43 *Reports with regard to Probable Resistance to Home Rule* (esp. pp. 5-6, 10).
44 Harrel's letter, 8 Feb. 1912, Birrell Papers, Bodleian, dep. c. 301, fos. 18-35.
45 Fitzroy, *Memoirs*, II, 475.
46 *The Times*, 10 April 1912.

Chapter III

1 Ilbert to Bryce, 20 Feb. 1912, MS. Bryce 14, fos. 46-9.
2 Mary Drew diary, 11 April 1912, B.L. Add. MS. 46265, fos. 18-19; Sir Henry Lucy, *The Diary of a Journalist* (3 vols, 1920-23), III, 77-8; Lucy Masterman, *C.F.G. Masterman* (1939), pp. 242-3; Burns diary, 16 April 1912, B.L. Add. MS. 46334, fo. 83; Dicey to Law, 12 Feb. 1913, B.L.P. 29/1/15.
3 Burns diary, 11 and 15 April 1912, B.L. Add. MS. 46334, fos. 80-82; Samuel to his mother, 15 April 1912, Samuel Papers, A/156/403; M.T. Earle to H. Verney, 14 May 1912, Verney Papers; *Western Daily Mercury*, 3 May 1912; *British Weekly*, 9 May 1912.
4 *Nation*, 13 April 1912. For convenience, the term 'Ulster' will be used in the loose contemporary sense to mean the Protestant dominated north-east section of the province of Ulster, unless the context indicates otherwise.
5 *Hansard*, XXXVII, 133-4 (Guinness); *ibid*, 1778 (Amery); *ibid.*, XXXVI, 1440 (Carson); XXXVII, 291-2 (Law).
6 *Hansard*, XXXVII, 208 (Long); *ibid.*, 269-73 (O'Neill); 1779 (Amery); 293 (Law); 1882 (Finlay); 127 (Guinness); 120 (Moore).
7 *Hansard*, XXXVII, 293-4 (Law); *ibid*, 262 (Chamberlain).
8 *Hansard*, XXXVI, 1399-1426 (Asq); *ibid.*, XXXVII, 305-10 (Birrell).
9 *The Times*, 11, 12 and 17 April 1912.
10 *The Times*, 12, 15, 17-18 April 1912; *Nation*, 20 April 1912; Ilbert diary, 16 April 1912. For details, see Appendix, pp.269-72.
11 *Hansard*, XXXVIII, 707-12; *The Times*, 10 May 1912; *Nation*, 11 May 1912. See Appendix (only nine Liberals were absent, including five paired).
12 *Hansard*, XXXVII, 1705-12.
13 *Ibid.*, 2057-9.
14 *Ibid.*, 2084-5 (Grey). The other five ministerial speakers were Samuel, Seely, T.W. Russell, Birrell, Asquith.
15 Fitzroy, *Memoirs*, II, 484-5.
16 *Hansard*, XXXVIII, 644-50. On Kemp, see also P.F. Clarke, *Lancashire and the New Liberalism*, pp. 278, 293-5, 303-4; and Jalland, Ph.D. thesis, pp. 103-5, 139-40.
17 *Hansard*, LVIII, 246-50 (Cory, 11 Feb. 1914); *Nation*, 20 April, 11 May 1912.
18 *Hansard*, XXXVII, 2149-53.

19   *The Times*, 22 April 1912; *Western Daily Mercury,* 1 May 1911.
20   34 out of the 109 Liberals who were absent or voted against the main Home Rule divisions of 1912 were nonconformists (107 Liberal nonconformists had been returned in Dec. 1910 – S. Koss, *Nonconformity in Modern British Politics*, 1975, p. 231). Of these 34, 13 represented northern constituencies, including 8 from Yorkshire; 8 were Welsh members, 4 Scottish, 3 from the south-west and 6 from elsewhere. [see Appendix]
21   *The Times*, 2 Oct. 1912, signed 'C.R., a Liberal M.P.'.
22   *The Times*, 8 May 1912; *British Weekly*, 9 May, 13 June 1912; see also *Hansard*, XXXVIII, 650-1 (Spicer).
23   *Hansard*, XXXVIII, 334-6.
24   See e.g. *Nation*, 27 April, 4 and 11 May 1912; *The Times*, 6 May, 1912.
25   *Irish Times*, 12 June 1912; Long to Law, 4 June 1912, B.L.P. 26/4/7.
26   Moreton Frewen to Law, 18 June 1912, B.L.P. 26/4/27; *Hansard*, XXXIX, 789-90 (Long).
27   *Hansard*, XXXIX, 780, 1559.
28   *Hansard*, XXXIX, 1068-74 (Carson); 805-7 (Hayes-Fisher); 1116 (Craig); 1131-2 (Guinness).
29   *Hansard*, XXXIX, 774-7 (Birrell); 785-7 (Asq); *The Times*, 14 June 1912.
30   *Hansard*, XXXIX, 771-4 (Agar-Robartes); 785 (Pirie); 804-5 (Cowan).
31   *Hansard*, XXXIX, 777 (Birrell); 1562 (Craig); 1099 (Lough).
32   *Hansard*, XXXIX, 1080-2, 1085 (Redmond).
33   *Hansard*, XXXIX, 1122-7 (LG); 1554-5 (Birrell).
34   *Hansard*, XXXIX, 1085-7 (Redmond); 1121-7 (LG).
35   *Hansard*, XXXIX, 804-5 (Cowan); *ibid*., 784, and XL, 1078-9 (Pirie).
36   e.g. *Irish Independent*, 8 May 1912.
37   *Hansard*, XXXIX, 1119-28 (LG).
38   *The Times*, 19 June 1912.
39   *Observer*, 23 June 1912; *The Times*, 19 June 1912; *Hansard*, XL, 1082-3 (H. Cecil).
40   See Appendix for details.
41   *Mr. Asquith's visit to Dublin*, MS. Asq 39, fos. 55-62.
42   *Nation*, 3 Aug. 1912; *The Times*, 29 July and 1 Aug. 1912; *Hansard*, XLI, 2129-38.
43   *The Times*, 12 Aug. 1912.
44   WSC to LG, 21 Aug. 1912, R.S.C., *Churchill*, II, *Companion*, 1396; Lockwood to Law, 22 Aug. 1912, B.L.P. 27/1/50.
45   WSC to Redmond, 31 Aug. 1912, Redmond MS. 15175; WSC to Ritchie, 8 Sept. 1912, R.S.C. *Churchill*, II, *Companion*, 1396-7.
46   *The Times*, 13 Sept. and 12 Oct. 1912; Emmott diary, II, fos. 77-8, 22 Sept. 1912. For details, see Jalland, 'United Kingdom Devolution 1910-14: Political Panacea or Tactical Diversion ?', *E.H.R.*, XCIV (Oct. 1979), 773-5.
47   See *The Times*, 23-24, 28-29 Sept. 1912; *Nation*, 17 Aug., 21, 28 Sept. 1912; *Daily News and Leader*, 30 Sept, 1912; *Westminster Gazette*, 22

Aug. 1912; Gwynne to Law, 25 Aug., 2 Oct. 1912, B.L.P. 27/1/55, 27/3/3.

48 For detailed analysis of the crisis over the snap defeat see Jalland, Ph.D. thesis, pp. 159-164. See esp. Ilbert diary, 11 and 14 Nov. 1912; *Nation*, 16 Nov. 1912; Asq to King, 12, 14 Nov. 1912, MS. Asq 6, fos. 177, 180; Baird to Law, 11 Nov. 1912, B.L.P. 27/4/21; Hobhouse diary, p. 124, 18 Nov. 1912.

49 *Nation*, 7 and 14 Dec. 1912.

50 *The Times*, 31 Dec. 1912.

51 *Hansard*, XLVI, 380-3 (Carson); Ulster Unionists' letter to Asquith, *The Times*, 30 Dec. 1912.

52 Pease diary, II fo. 63, 31 Dec. 1912; Burns diary, 31 Dec. 1912, B.L. Add. MS. 46334, fo. 232; Hobhouse diary, pp. 126-7, 31 Dec. 1912.

53 Harrel to Birrell, 30 Dec. 1912, Birrell Papers, Bodleian, dep. c.300, fos. 8-10; Hobhouse diary, p.127, 31 Dec. 1912.

54 *Hansard*, XLVI, 394-5 (Asq); 420 (Cave); 455 (Pirie).

55 See Asq to WSC, 19 Sept. 1913, R.S.C. *Churchill*, II *Companion*, 1400.

56 *Hansard*, XLVI, 388-90 (Carson); 454-5 (Pirie); 461-2 (Law).

57 *Hansard*,XLVI, 392-7 (Asq); 443 (Chamberlain); 456-7 (Pirie).

58 *Hansard*, XLVI, 470-8.

59 See *Hansard*, XLVI, 480-4, for division list, and see Appendix for detailed analysis. These figures represent a considerable overlap.

60 *Hansard*, XLVI, 2321-4 (Smith); 2405-6 (Birrell); 2109, 2118 (Balfour); 2400 (Law).

61 *Hansard*, XLVI, 2164-7.

62 *Hansard*, XLVI, 2347-54.

Chapter IV

1 *Nation*, 21 Dec. 1912; Haldane to mother, 29 Jan. 1913, Haldane MS. 5989, fos. 34-5; Samuel to mother, 2 Feb. 1913, Samuel Papers, A/156/428.

2 Morley to Rosebery, 31 Jan. 1913, Rosebery MS. 10048, fo. 19.

3 Holt diary, 16 Feb. 1913 (Liverpool City Library).

4 Burns diary, 4 June 1913, B.L. Add. MS. 46335, fo. 103; Ilbert to Bryce, 6 June 1913, MS. Bryce 14, fos. 87-90.

5 Ilbert to Bryce, 24 June 1913, MS. Bryce 14, fos. 92-3.

6 A.A. Eagleston to J. Pease, 12 Jan. 1913, Gainford Papers; Masterman to LG, May 1913, L.G.P. C/1/1/7A.

7 *Hansard*, L111, 1288-90 (Asquith); 1464-7 (Carson); 1556 (Law).

8 *Hansard*, L111, 1295-7 (Balfour); LV, 80 (Law); L111, 1291 (Asquith); L111, 1583 (Birrell).

9 *Hansard*, LV, 144-50.

10 For a detailed examination of this campaign, see Jalland, 'United Kingdom Devolution 1910-14: Political Panacea or Tactical Diversion ?', *E.H.R.*, XCIV (Oct. 1979), 775-85.

11 *Ibid*; *The Constitutional Crisis*, by 'a Liberal M.P.' [M. Macdonald],

1913; Ponsonby, 'The Future Government of the United Kingdom', *Contemporary Review*, CIV (Nov. 1913), 624-31.

12   *Ibid*; F. to A. Ponsonby, 23 July, 28 Aug. and 4 Sept. 1913, Ponsonby Papers. H. Nicolson, *King George V* (1952), pp. 222-4; Lansdowne's *Memorandum*, 6 Sept. 1913, B.L.P. 39/1/7.

13   Loreburn to O'Brien, 12 and 19 Aug. 1913, mfm. of N.L.I. MS. 11439; Fitzroy, *Memoirs*, II, 522.

14   Hobhouse diary, p. 147, 17 Oct. 1913; *Irish Times*, 18 Sept. 1913.

15   *Freeman's Journal*, 12 Sept. 1913; Birrell to Asq, 20 Sept. 1913, MS. Asq 38, fos. 196-7.

16   Morley to Carnegie, 27 Sept. 1913, Bodleian, MS. film 569; Lansdowne to Curzon, 11 Sept. 1913, Curzon MSS. Eur. F 112/95.

17   Curzon, *Memorandum*, 16 Sept. 1913, Curzon MSS. Eur. F 112/95.

18   For an analysis of the party leaders' attitudes towards federalism, see Jalland, 'U.K. Devolution 1910-14 . . .', *E.H.R.* XCIV (Oct. 1979), 781-4.

19   See e.g. Strachey's *Memorandum*, 20 Feb. 1913, Strachey Papers, S/21/1/13.

20   Memo by Law and Lansdowne, 31 July 1913, B.L.P. 29/6/33.

21   Fitzroy, *Memoirs*, II, 524; Crewe to Asq, 8 Sept. 1913, MS. Asq 38, fos. 126-7.

22   Royal memos, 11 Aug. and 22 Sept. 1913, MS. Asq 38, fos. 120-1, 202-9 (printed in Nicolson, *King George V*, pp.223-9).

23   Asquith's two memos on the King's constitutional position, Sept. 1913, MS. Asq 38, fos. 158-173 (printed in Jenkins, *Asquith*, appendix B, pp. 543-9); Asq to King, 1 Oct. 1913, MS. Asq 38, fos. 216-9.

24   Birrell to Asq, 3 Oct. 1913, MS. Asq 38, fos. 220-1.

25   Esher to Balfour, 8 Oct. 1913, Balfour MS. 49719, fos. 256-7; Balfour to Law, 23 Sept. 1913, B.L.P. 30/2/20; Law to Lansdowne, 24 Sept. 1913, B.L.P. 33/5/59.

26   Balfour to Law, 23 Sept. 1913, B.L.P. 30/2/20.

27   Carson to Law, 20 Sept. 1913, B.L.P. 30/2/15.

28   *Intelligence Notes, 1913*, pp.16-37.

29   Birrell to Asq. 30 Aug. and 28 Oct. 1913, MS. Asq 38, fos. 122-5, 243-4.

30   Dougherty to a correspondent, 9 April 1913, Birrell Papers, Bodleian, dep. c. 300, fos. 31-2; Notes by Morley of conversation with Harrel, 7 Jan. 1914, MS. Asq 39, fos. 87-92.

31   *Memoranda re. Condition of things in Ulster in view of the Home Rule Bill*, 23 March and 15 April 1913, P.R.O. Cab. 37/115/25. (c.f. Dougherty's draft, Birrell Papers, dep. c. 300, fos. 33-6).

32   Birrell's covering note with *The Movement in Ulster*, 21 Oct. 1913, Birrell Papers, dep. c. 301, fos. 170-195; P.R.O. Cab. 37/116/69.

33   *Further Notes on the Movement in Ulster*, Nov. 1913, and *Further Notes from Ulster*, 4 Dec. 1913, P.R.O. Cab. 37/117/83, 85.

34   King's memo, 11 Aug. 1913, MS. Asq 38, fos. 120-1; Birrell to Asq, 24 July 1913, *ibid.*, fos. 109-13; Curzon's *Memorandum*, 16 Sept. 1913, Curzon MSS. Eur. F 112/95.

35   King's memo, 11 Aug. 1913, MS. Asq 38, fos. 120-1; Nicolson, *King George V*, p.220; Lansdowne's *Memorandum*, 6 Sept. 1913, B.L.P. 39/1/7.
36   Birrell to Asq, 30 Aug. and 8 Sept. 1913, MS. Asq 38, fos. 122-5, 128-9.
37   Report from F. to A. Ponsonby, 28 Aug. 1913, Ponsonby Papers; Asq to Birrell, 2 Sept. 1913, MS. Asq 38, fo. 125.
38   M. Macdonald to A. Ponsonby, 11 Sept. 1913, Ponsonby Papers.
39   Asquith's second Memo for King, c. mid-Sept. 1913, MS. Asq 38, fos. 164-73.

Chapter V

1   See royal memo, 11 Aug. 1913, Nicolson, *George V*, p.223.
2   Birrell to Asq, 3 Oct. 1913, MS. Asq 38, fos. 220-1.
3   Asq to WSC, 12 and 19 Sept. 1913, R.S.C., *Churchill*, II, *Companion*, 1399-1400.
4   WSC to Asq, 17 Sept. 1913, MS. Asq 38, fos. 192-4; Law to Carson, 18 and 24 Sept. 1913, B.L.P. 33/5/57-8.
5   WSC to Asq, 17, 21 Sept. 1913, MS. Asq 38, fos. 192-4, 198-201; Asq to WSC, 19 Sept. 1913, R.S.C., *Churchill*, II, *Companion*, 1400; WSC to Law, 21 Sept. 1913, B.L.P. 30/2/18.
6   Law to Carson, 18 and 24 Sept. 1913, B.L.P. 33/5/57-8; Smith's memo, c. 20 Sept. 1913, B.L.P. 30/2/15; Balfour to Law, 23 Sept. 1913, B.L.P. 30/2/20.
7   Carson to Law, 20 Sept. 1913, B.L.P. 30/2/15; Carson to Lansdowne, 9 Oct. 1913, B.L.P. 30/3/23.
8   Lansdowne to Law, 23, 25, 26 Sept. 1913, B.L.P. 30/2/21, 25, 27; Lansdowne to Balfour, 25 Sept. 1913, Balfour MS. 49730, fos. 258-9.
9   Fritz to Arthur Ponsonby, 6 Oct. 1913, Ponsonby Papers; Selborne to Balfour, c. end Sept. 1913, Balfour MS. 49863, fos. 9-10.
10   Lansdowne to Law, 27, 30 Sept. 1913, B.L.P. 30/2/29, 37; Stamfordham to Law, 26 Sept. 1913, B.L.P. 30/2/28.
11   Smith to LG, 26 Sept., and reply 6 Oct. 1913, L.G.P. C/3/7/1-2.
12   F. Harcourt Kitchin to Law, 30 Sept. 1913, B.L.P. 30/2/35.
13   Law to Lansdowne, 1 and 4 Oct. 1913, B.L.P. 33/5/63, 67; Law to Balfour, 27 Sept. 1913, B.L.P. 33/5/60.
14   Gwynn, *Redmond*, pp. 229-31.
15   O'Connor to WSC, 7 Oct. 1913, R.S.C., *Churchill*, II, *Companion*, 1401-2; Smith to WSC, 5 Oct. 1913, *ibid*, 1401.
16   *Daily Telegraph*, 9 Oct. 1913.
17   Curzon to Law, 10 Oct. 1913, B.L.P. 30/3/13; *Daily Chronicle*, 10 Oct. 1913; *Freeman's Journal*, 13 and 20 Oct. 1913.
18   *Nation*, 11 and 18 Oct. 1913; Fitzroy, *Memoirs*, II, 523-4; Pease diary, II, fos. 77-8.
19   Note by LG, N.D [Oct. 1913], L.G.P. C/12/3; *Manchester Guardian*, 20 Oct. 1913; E. Talbot to Law, 19 Oct. 1913, B.L.P. 30/3/37.
20   Asq to Law, 8 Oct. 1913, B.L.P. 30/3/11; Nicolson, *George V*, p. 232.

21 Law to Balfour, 9 Oct. 1913, Balfour MS. 49693, fos. 57-8; Lansdowne to Law, 13 Oct. 1913, B.L.P. 30/3/29.
22 Lansdowne to Carson, 11 Oct. 1913, B.L.P. 30/3/23; Balfour to Law, 13 Oct. 1913, B.L.P. 30/3/28.
23 Law's *Notes of Conversation with the P.M.*, 14 Oct. 1913, B.L.P. 33/6/80; Asq's notes, MS. Asq 38, fos. 231-4.
24 *Daily Telegraph*, 27 Oct. 1913.
25 Stamfordham to Law, 27 Oct., and reply 28 Oct. 1913, B.L.P. 30/3/57 and 33/6/90; *The Times*, 30 Oct. 1913.
26 Asq's notes, 6 Nov. 1913, MS. Asq 39, fos. 3-6; Law's notes, B.L.P. 33/6/93.
27 *Ibid.*
28 *Ibid*; Law to Long, 7 Nov. 1913, B.L.P. 33/6/94; Law to Balfour, 7 Nov. 1913, B.L.P. 33/6/93.
29 Balfour to Law, 8 Nov. 1913, B.L.P. 30/4/16; Long to Law, 7 and 9 Nov. 1913, B.L.P. 30/4/11, 18.
30 Law to Balfour, 18 Nov. 1913, Balfour MS. 49693, fo. 125; Asq to King, 12 Nov. 1913, MS. Asq 7, fo. 69; Pease diary, II, fo. 79; Hobhouse diary, pp. 148-50, 11 Nov. 1913.
31 Blake, *Bonar Law*, p. 165; Jenkins, *Asquith*, p. 292.
32 Fitzroy, *Memoirs*, II, 524.
33 Riddell, *More Pages*, pp. 189, 186 (13-14 Dec., 16 Nov. 1913); McKenna to Runciman, 12 Oct. 1913, Runciman Papers, R1/39.
34 Emmott diary, II, fos. 77-8, 22 Sept. 1912; *Glasgow Herald*, 18 Oct. 1913; Runciman to Gladstone, 27 Oct. 1913, H. Gladstone MS. 46075, fos. 179-80.
35 Harcourt to Gladstone, 4 Sept. 1913, H. Gladstone MS. 46000, fos. 237-8; *Yorkshire Observer*, 8 Nov. 1913; Pease diary, II, fo. 80, 13 Nov. 1913.
36 Pease diary, II, fo. 80; Burns diary, 26 April 1914, B.L. Add. MS. 46336, fo. 83.
37 Samuel to Asq, 10 Oct. 1913, Samuel Papers, A/41/10.
38 Samuel, *A Suggestion for the Solution of the Ulster Question*, 18 Dec. 1913, P.R.O. Cab. 37/117/95; draft memo, *Ulster*, 13 Nov. 1913, Samuel Papers, A/41/9.
39 Hobhouse diary, p. 111, 11 Feb. 1912; Harcourt to Asq, 4 Oct. 1913, Harcourt Papers; *The Journals and Letters of Reginald, Viscount Esher*, eds. Brett and Esher (4 vols, 1934-8), III, 139-41.
40 Gwynn, *Redmond*, p. 236; Fitzroy, *Memoirs*, II, 513, 522-4, 528.
41 Morley to Carnegie, 14 and 28 Nov. 1913, Bodleian, MS. film 569; Esher, *Journals*, III, 153.
42 Fritz to Arthur Ponsonby, 28 Aug. 1913, Ponsonby Papers; Crewe to Lord Pentland, 30 Oct. 1913, Crewe Papers, C/61; Pease diary, II, fo. 80.
43 Grey to H. Gladstone, 11 Oct. 1901, H. Gladstone MS. 45992, fos. 77-80; *Glasgow Herald*, 28 Oct. 1913.
44 Grey to WSC, 28 Oct. 1913, R.S.C. *Churchill*, II, *Companion*, 1405.
45 Asq to King, 12 Nov. 1913, MS. Asq 7, fo. 69; Pease diary, II, fo. 79.

46 LG's memo, *Points discussed at dinner at 11 Downing Street*, 12 Nov. 1913, L.G.P. C/14/1/10.
47 Asq to King, 14 Nov. 1913, MS. Asq 7, fos. 71-2; Cabinet notes, Nov. 1913, L.G.P. C/12/2; Pease diary, II, fo. 80, 13 Nov. 1913; Gwynn, *Redmond*, p. 236.
48 Samuel, *Ulster*, 13 Nov. 1913, Samuel Papers, A/41/9.
49 Pease diary, II, fo. 80, 13 Nov. 1913; Asq to King, 14 Nov. 1913, MS. Asq 7, fos. 71-2.
50 Birrell to Asq, 13 Nov. 1913, MS. Asq 39, fos. 20-21.
51 Gwynn, *Redmond*, p. 233; Riddell, *More Pages*, p. 186; Talbot to Law, 15 Nov. 1913, B.L.P. 30/4/36.
52 Redmond's final account, Gwynn, *Redmond*, pp. 234-6; Redmond's earlier draft, MS. Redmond 15165; Asquith's account, MS. Asq 39, fos. 23-6.
53 *Ibid.*; Redmond to Asq, 24 Nov. and reply 26 Nov. 1913, MS. Asq 39, fos. 29-35, 36-7; MS. Redmond 15165.
54 Memo: *Interview with Mr. John Dillon,* 17 Nov. 1913, L.G.P. C/20/2/4.
55 Gwynn, *Redmond*, pp. 237-8.
56 *Ibid.*, pp. 238-9.

Chapter VI
1 Blake, *Bonar Law*, p. 166; Steel-Maitland to Law, 16 Nov. 1913, B.L.P. 30/4/37; Law to Lansdowne, 26 Nov. 1913, B.L.P. 33/6/102.
2 Chamberlain, *Politics from Inside*, pp. 572-77.
3 *The Times*, 28 Nov. 1913; *Nation*, 6 Dec. 1913.
4 *The Times*, 29 Nov. 1913; Chamberlain to WSC, 29 Nov. 1913, R.S.C. *Churchill*, II, *Companion*, 1406; *Politics from Inside*, p. 579.
5 Fitzroy, *Memoirs*, II, 529; *The Times*, 5-6 Dec. 1913.
6 Chamberlain, *Politics from Inside*, pp. 579-80, 583, 586-8.
7 Asq to Law, 3 Dec. 1913, B.L.P. 31/1/5; Law to Carson, 3 Dec. 1913, B.L.P. 33/6/106.
8 J. Sandars to Balfour, 10 Dec. 1913, Balfour MS. 49768, fos. 76-9; Crewe to Lord Carmichael, 5 Dec. 1913, Crewe Papers, C/61.
9 Law's *Notes of Conversation with the P.M.*, 10 Dec. 1913, B.L.P. 33/6/111; Asquith's pencilled notes, 13 Dec. 1913, MS. Asq 39, fos. 42-5.
10 *Ibid*; Law to Lansdowne, 10 Dec. 1913, B.L.P. 33/6/111; Law to Curzon, 13 Dec. 1913, Curzon Papers, MSS. Eur. F/112/95.
11 Lansdowne, *Possibility of a Settlement*, 16 Dec. 1913, B.L.P. 31/1/38; Balfour to Law, 18 Dec. 1913, B.L.P. 31/1/41.
12 Long, *Notes on Conversation*, 18 Dec. 1913, B.L.P. 39/1/13; Milner to F.S. Oliver, 30 Dec. 1913, Milner Papers, Box 211.
13 Law to Lansdowne and to Selborne, 22 Dec. 1913, B.L.P. 33/6/115-6.
14 Long, *Notes on Conversation*, 18 Dec. 1913, B.L.P. 39/1/13; Lansdowne to Law, 21 Dec. 1913, B.L.P. 31/1/46.
15 *Politics from Inside*, pp. 589-91.

16   Law to Lansdowne and reply, 22-23 Dec. 1913, B.L.P. 33/6/115, 31/1/51.

17   Asquith's memo on talk with Carson, MS. Asq 39, fos. 42-5.

18   Asq to Carson, 23 Dec. 1913, MS. Asq 39, fos. 64-8; *Suggestions in Regard to the Irish Government Bill*, printed for Cabinet on 29 Jan. 1914, P.R.O. Cab. 37/119/20.

19   Carson to Asq, 27 Dec. 1913, MS. Asq 39, fos. 70-71; Lansdowne to Law, 29 Dec. 1913, B.L.P. 31/1/63; Law to Lansdowne, 27 Dec. 1913, B.L.P. 33/6/119.

20   Memo of meeting with Carson, 2 Jan. 1914, MS. Asq 39, fos. 72-74; Law to Balfour, 7 Jan. 1914, B.L.P. 34/1/8.

21   Carson to Asq, 7 and 10 Jan. 1914, and reply 8 Jan. 1914, MS. Asq 39, fos. 79-84, 95-6.

22   Law to Balfour, 7 Jan, and reply 13 Jan 1914, Balfour MS. 49693, fos. 132-3, 138.

23   *The Times*, 16 Jan. 1914; Stamfordham to Law, 20 Jan. and 2 Feb. 1914, B.L.P. 31/2/51, 31/3/4.

24   Hobhouse diary, p.155, 23 Jan. 1914; Runciman to Trevelyan, 4 Jan. 1914, Trevelyan Papers.

25   Scott diary, 15 Jan. 1914, B.L. Add. MS. 50901, fos. 90-91; Trevelyan to Runciman, 5 Jan. 1914, Runciman Papers, R.1/17.

26   Scott diary, 21 Jan. 1914, B.L. Add. MS. 50901, fo. 99.

27   Esher to Harcourt, 13 Jan. 1914, Harcourt Papers; Esher, *Journals*, III, 151.

28   Simon to Asq, 29 Jan. 1914, MS. Asq 25, fos. 170-7.

29   Pease diary, II, fo. 83, 30 Jan. 1914.

30   Scott diary, 6 Feb. 1914, B.L. Add. MS. 50901, fos. 106-7.

31   Asq to King, 23 Jan. 1914, MS. Asq 7, fos. 90-91; Pease diary, II, fos. 82-3, 23 Jan. 1914.

32   *Ibid*; Cabinet notes, 22 Jan. 1914, L.G.P. C/12/3; Scott diary, 23 Jan. 1914, B.L. Add. MS. 50901, fo. 100.

33   King to Asq, 26 Jan. 1914, MS. Asq 39, fos. 97-8.

34   Redmond's memo, *Interview with Mr. Asquith and Mr. Birrell*, 2 Feb. 1914, MS. Redmond 15165; Jenkins, *Asquith*, p. 301; Pease diary, II, fo. 84, 3 Feb. 1914.

35   Redmond to Asq, 4 Feb. 1914, P.R.O. Cab. 37/119/22; Scott diary, 7 Feb. 1914, B.L. Add. MS. 50901, fos. 108-9.

36   Morley to Crewe, 6 Feb. 1914, Crewe Papers, C/37; Birrell to Redmond and reply, 9 Feb. 1914, MS. Redmond 15169.

37   See e.g. Law to Balfour, 30 Jan. and 5 Feb. 1914, and Lansdowne to Balfour, 5 Feb. 1914, Balfour MS. 49693, fos. 139-40, 158, and MS. 49730, fos. 266-7.

38   *Hansard*, LVIII, 71-83.

39   Chamberlain, *Politics from Inside*, pp. 610-12.

40   King to Asq, 11 Feb. 1914, MS. Asq 39, fos. 117-8.

41   *Hansard*, LVIII, 169-79 (Carson); *ibid.*, 270 ff. (Law); *ibid.*, 179-87 (Redmond).

42   LG Memo, 16 Feb. 1914, L.G.P. C/20/2/7.

43 Blake, *Bonar Law*, p.183.
44 Riddell, *More Pages*, p.202.
45 Redmond's memos re. interviews on 27 Feb. and 2 March 1914, MS. Redmond 15257.
46 Redmond to Asq, 2 March 1914, MS. Asq 39, fos. 134-41.
47 Riddell, *More Pages*, p.202; Pease diary, II, fo. 85, 4 March 1914; Asq to King, 5 March 1914, MS. Asq 7, fos. 101-2.
48 *Ibid.*; Asq to Redmond, 4 March 1914, MS. Redmond 15165.
49 Beresford to Law, 2 March 1914, B.L.P. 31/4/1; Carson to Law, 5 March 1914, B.L.P. 31/4/5.
50 George V to Law, 7 March 1914, B.L.P. 31/4/11; Law to King, 8 March 1914, B.L.P. 34/2/36; King to Asq, 5 March 1914, MS. Asq 39, fos. 143-4.
51 Redmond to Asq, 6 March 1914, MS. Asq 39, fos. 145-6.
52 Asq to Redmond, 7 March 1914, MS. Redmond 15165; L.G.P. C/12/3.
53 Samuel's draft memo, 13 Nov. 1913, Samuel Papers, A/41/9.
54 Haldane to mother, 3 March 1914, Haldane MS. 5991.
55 *White Paper*, 6 March 1914, MS. Asq 110, fo. 216; pub. 9 March 1914, P.P. 1914, 67993.
56 *Government of Ireland Bill. Note,* N.D. [before 6 March], L.G.P. C/20/2/8.
57 *Hansard*, LIX, 906-18.
58 Simon's memo, *Effect of Optional Exclusion by Counties on Irish Representation*, 10 March 1914, P.R.O. Cab. 37/119/40.
59 *Hansard*, LIX, 933-6; Carson to Strachey, 12 March 1914, Strachey Papers, S/4/2/1.
60 O'Connor to Spender, 11 March 1914, Spender MS. 46392, fo. 126; *The Times*, 18 March 1914.
61 *Hansard*, LIX, 919, 1653-1661, 2256-2366.
62 *Hansard*, LIX, 922, 925, 2256-58, 2260-65.
63 Carson to Law, 20 March 1914, B.L.P. 32/1/36; Sir George Murray to Rosebery, 20 March 1914, Rosebery MS. 10049, fos. 282-3.
64 Law to Asq, 22 March 1914, MS. Asq 39, fos. 152-3.

Chapter VII
1 A.T.Q. Stewart, *The Ulster Crisis* (1967); A.P. Ryan, *Mutiny at the Curragh* (1956); Sir James Fergusson, *The Curragh Incident* (1964) – the best account.
2 Birrell to Asq, 30 Aug, 3 Oct. 1913, MS. Asq 38, fos. 122-5, 220-1; Asq to King, 1 Oct. 1913, *ibid.*, fos. 216-7.
3 Esher, *Journals*, III, 139-41, 151-2.
4 Notes by Morley, 7 Jan. 1914, MS. Asq 39, fos. 85, 87-92; Hobhouse diary, p. 168, 17 March 1914.
5 Macready, *Annals of an Active Life* (2 vols, 1924), I, 171, 178-9.
6 Asq to King, 26 Nov., 2 Dec. 1913, MS. Asq 7, fos. 78, 81; Memos by Simon, *Power to Prevent Importation of Arms etc. into Ulster*, 26 Nov.

1913, and *Illegalities in Ulster*, 29 Nov. 1913, P.R.O. Cab. 37/117/81-2.

7   *Threatened Legal Proceedings over Seizure of Arms at Belfast*, 17 Feb. 1914, P.R.O. Cab. 37/119/30; Fitzroy, *Memoirs*, II, 528; Esher, *Journals*, III, 145-6.

8   Trevelyan to Runciman, 3 Nov. 1913, Runciman Papers, R/1/17; Pease diary, II, fo. 79, 11 Nov. 1913.

9   Birrell to Asq, 30 Aug, 3 Oct. 1913, MS. Asq 38, fos. 122-5, 220-1.

10 Nicolson, *George V*, p. 232; *Illegalities in Ulster*, 29 Nov. 1913, P.R.O. Cab. 37/117/82; Asquith, *Fifty Years of Parliament* (2 vols. 1926), II, 139-142.

11 See e.g. *Observer*, 19 March 1914; Stewart, *Ulster Crisis*, pp. 151-3; Colvin, *Carson*, II, 309-11; Carson to Law, 20 March 1914, B.L.P. 32/1/36; Law to Croal, 20 March 1914, B.L.P. 34/2/44.

12 G.H. Murray to Rosebery, 20 March 1914, Rosebery MS. 10049, fos. 282-3; Esher, *Journals*, III, 153 (19 Jan. 1914).

13 Memo by J.J. Clancy, *The Fate of Ulster*, MS. Asq 38, fos. 65-71; Law to Carson, 18 Sept. 1913, B.L.P. 33/5/57; Law's memo, 8 Oct. 1913, B.L.P. 33/5/68; Wilfrid Spender to Harold Spender, [Oct. ?] 1913, L.G.P., C/10/1/50; Carson's speech, *The Times*, 26 Sept. 1913.

14 Law to Carson, 18 Sept. 1913, B.L.P. 33/5/57; Asq to King, 1 Oct. 1913, MS. Asq 38, fos. 216-7; Gwynn, *Redmond*, pp. 235-6.

15 See Jalland, Ph.D. thesis, p. 373; Blake, *Bonar Law*, pp. 173-7, 180-2; Hobhouse diary, p. 168, 17 March 1914.

16 Munro-Ferguson to wife, 15 Aug. 1911, Novar Papers, file 39; Gladstone to Samuel, 6 May 1914, H. Gladstone MS. 45992, fos. 279-82.

17 Repington to Haldane, 27 Nov. 1912, Haldane MS. 5909, fos. 272-3; *Field Marshal Roberts' Memorandum*, N.D., Milner Papers, Box 100.

18 Fitzroy, *Memoirs*, II, 548 (29 April 1914).

19 Blake, *Bonar Law*, p.186; Stewart, *Ulster Crisis*, p. 175.

20 *Hansard*, LX, 895.

21 Riddell, *More Pages*, pp. 203-4 (14 March 1914); *The Times*, 16 March 1914.

22 Riddell, *More Pages*, pp. 203-4; *Hansard*, LIX, 1662; Fitzroy, *Memoirs*, II, 541.

23 *Further Notes on the Movement in Ulster*, 5-6 March 1914, P.R.O. Cab. 37/119/36.

24 *Intelligence Notes*, 1913, p. 36.

25 Stewart, *Ulster Crisis*, pp. 126-8.

26 Gleichen, *The Ulster Volunteer Force*, 14 March 1914, MS. Mottistone 22, fos. 193-4; *The Times*, 18, 19 March 1914; C.E. Callwell, *Field Marshall Sir Henry Wilson: His Life and Diaries* (2 vols, 1927), I, 132.

27 Asq to King, 12 March 1914, MS. Asq 7, fo. 103.

28 Stewart, *Ulster Crisis*, p. 175; Fergusson, *Curragh Incident*, p. 212; see also Blake, *Bonar Law*, p. 205.

29 Esher, *Journals*, III, 159 (22 March 1914).

30 Documents subsequently printed in *Correspondence Relating to Recent Events in the Irish Command*, Cd. 7318, 23 March 1914, and Cd. 7329,

22 April 1914. (cited henceforth as *White Paper*, I, Cd. 7318 and *White Paper*, II, Cd. 7329.)

31 Asq to King, 18 March 1914, MS. Asq 7, fos. 105-6; Seely's memo, 16 March 1914, MS. Asq 40, fo. 5; Runciman's pencilled cabinet note, 17 March 1914, MS. Runciman, R/11/5; Pease diary, II, fo. 85, 17 March 1914.

32 Seely's two memos, 18-19 March 1914, MS. Asq 40, fos. 8-10.

33 H.A. Gwynne's memo of conversation with French, [mid April 1914], B.L.P. 39/2/25; Simon to Seely, 19 March 1914, MS. Asq 40, fos. 13-14.

34 Memo by WSC, [c. 25 March 1914], MS. Asq 40, fos. 88-94; *Hansard*, LX, 898-902.

35 Quoted by J. Gooch. 'The War Office and the Curragh Incident', *B.I.H.R.*, XLVI (Nov. 1973), 203.

36 Riddell, *More Pages*, p. 209 (20 April 1914).

37 For a more detailed analysis, see Jalland, Ph.D. thesis, pp. 397-400; Fergusson, *Curragh Incident*, pp. 190-3; Ryan, *Mutiny at the Curragh*, pp. 183-94; *White Paper*, II, Cd. 7329.

38 WSC to wife, 23 April 1914, R.S.C. *Churchill*, II, *Companion*, 1416; F. Maurice, *Haldane, 1856-1915* (2 vols, 1937), I, 344; *Manchester Guardian*, 4 May 1912.

39 Riddell, *More Pages*, p. 209; Fitzroy, *Memoirs*, II, 547; Mildred to Sydney Buxton, 26 March 1914, Buxton Papers; Gooch, *B.I.H.R.*, XLVI (Nov. 1973), 206; Macready, *Annals of an Active Life*, I, 176; Gwynne's memo, B.L.P. 39/2/25. I am grateful to Dr. Cameron Hazlehurst for showing me an early draft of a paper (1972) examining the Curragh 'plot' theory.

40 Long's memo, 27 March 1914, B.L.P. 39/2/22; Balfour to a correspondent, 24 March 1914, Balfour MS. 49863, fos. 154-5; Blake, 'Curragh Incident', *Listener*, 21 March 1974.

41 Maurice, *Haldane*, I, 344; Birrell to Seely, 2 April 1914, MS. Mottistone 22, fos. 334-5; Seely to Morley, 31 March 1914, early draft, *ibid.*, fos. 327-9; *Nation*, 28 March 1914.

42 Seely's memo, 20 March 1914, MS. Asq 10, fo. 19.; WSC's memo, [c. 25 March 1914], *ibid.*, fos. 88-94.

43 Paget's statement, 2 April 1914, *White Paper*, II, Cd. 7329; WSC's memo, MS. Asq 40, fos. 88-94.

44 Paget's statement, 2 April 1914, *White Paper*, II, Cd. 7329; earlier draft, 28 March 1914, MS. Mottistone 22, fos. 268-74; Fergusson's statement, 27 March 1914, MS. Asq 40, fos. 104-6.

45 Gough to Paget, 20 March 1914, MS. Mottistone 22, fo. 20, and telegrams between Paget and Ewart, 20-21 March 1914, *ibid.*, fos. 208-9.

46 George V to Asq, 21 March 1914, MS. Asq 40, fos. 27-8; Jenkins, *Asquith*, p. 309; Notes by J.S. Ewart, 22 March 1914, MS. Asq 40, fos. 69-72.

47 Ewart diary, 22-23 March, Gooch, *B.I.H.R.*, XLVI (Nov. 1973), 204; *White Paper*, II, Cd. 7329.

48 *White Papers* I and II, Cd. 7318 and 7329; Pease diary, II, fos. 86-7, 23 March 1914; W.S. Blunt, *My Diaries* (2 vols. 1921-3), II, 423; note signed by Gough, 23 March 1914, MS. Mottistone 22, fo. 232; Ewart diary, 23 March 1914, Gooch, *B.I.H.R.*, XLVI, 204-5.

49 Asq to King, 28 March 1914, MS. Asq 7, fo. 109; Pease diary, II, fos. 87-8, 25 March 1914; Hobhouse diary, p. 166, 25 March 1914.

50 Richard Holt diary, 10 April 1914 (Liverpool City Library).

51 Margot Asquith to LG, N.D., L.G.P., C/6/12/8.

52 *Ibid.*; Samuel to Gladstone, 14 April 1914, H. Gladstone MS. 45992, fos. 276-7; W.S. Blunt, *My Diaries*, II, 423.

53 Asq to Law, 23 March 1914, B.L.P. 32/1/51; *Hansard, Lords*, XV, 627 (Morley); XV, 637 (Haldane); Haldane to mother, 26 and 31 March 1914, Haldane MS. 5991, fos. 109-10 and 119; *Morning Post*, 27 March 1914.

54 Fitzroy, *Memoirs*, II, 544; *Hansard*, LX, 205; M.E. Harcourt to L. Harcourt, 24 April 1914, Harcourt Papers.

55 Fitzroy, *Memoirs*, II, 544; Pease diary, II, fo. 88, 31 March 1914.

56 Pease diary, II, fo. 88, 31 March 1914; Samuel to Gladstone, 14 April 1914, H. Gladstone MS. 45992, fos. 276-7; Burns diary, 24 March 1914, B.L. Add. MS. 46336, fo. 66.

57 *Hansard*, LX, 893, 902-5; Burns diary, 30 March 1914, B.L. Add. MS. 46336, fo. 69.

58 See e.g. Jenkins, *Asquith*, pp. 313-5.

59 Pease diary, II, fo. 88, 30-31 March 1914; Samuel to Gladstone, 14 April 1914, H. Gladstone MS. 45992, fos. 276-7; T.E. Harvey to W. Harvey, 4 April 1914, Harvey Papers.

60 *Hansard*, LX, 843-4 (Bonar Law); L.S. Amery, *My Political Life* (3 vols. 1953-5) I, 452; Haldane to mother, 31 March 1914, Haldane MS. 5991, fo. 115; Fitzroy, *Memoirs*, 11, 545.

61 Asquith to Venetia Stanley, 22 March 1914, quoted in Jenkins, *Asquith*, p.310.

62 Reports by Pulteney and Fergusson, c. 19 April 1914, MS. Asq 40, fos. 118-20; Birrell to Asq, N.D. [27 April 1914], MS. Asq 41, fos. 71-2.

63 Macready, *Annals of an Active Life*, I, 181, 187-8, 190-1, 194.

64 Esher, *Journals*, III, 159.

65 Fitzroy, *Memoirs*, II, 543; Pease diary, II, fo. 89; Esher, *Journals*, III, 167.

66 Note by Simon, 25 May 1914, L.G.P., Cabinet notes, C/12/2; Burns diary, 26 April 1914, B.L. Add. MS. 46336, fo. 82.

67 Memo on L.G.'s interview with King, 15 May 1914, Royal Archives, Geo V., K. 2553 (5).

68 Faber to Law, 29 April 1914, B.L.P. 32/2/67; Fitzroy, *Memoirs*, II, 547, 549; C.P. Scott diary, 30 June 1914, B.L. Add. MS. 50901, fos. 140-1; Pease diary, II, fo. 89, 24 April 1914.

69 Grey to Asq, 23 March and 20 May 1914, Grey Papers, P.R.O. F.O. 800/100/307-10.

70 Hobhouse diary, p. 171, [13 ?] May 1914.

71 WSC to wife, 27 April 1914, R.S.C. *Churchill*, II, *Companion*, 1417; Birrell to Asq, 26 April 1914, MS. Asq 41, fos. 25-31.
72 Amery, *My Political Life*, I, 454; Macready, *Annals of an Active Life*, I, 185.
73 Aberdeen to Birrell, 26 April 1914, MS. Asq 41, fos. 18-24; Macready, *Annals*, I, 185.
74 Birrell to Asq, 26 and 28 April 1914 and reply of 30 April, MS. Asq 41, fos. 25-31, 55, 60-2, 83; Asq to King, 27 April and 2 May 1914, MS. Asq 7, fos. 115-7; Pease diary, II, fo. 89, 22 April 1914.

Chapter VIII
1 Fitzroy, *Memoirs*, II, 543; Balfour to a correspondent, 24 March 1914, Balfour MS. 49863, fos. 154-5.
2 Scott diary, 27 July 1914, B.L. Add. MS. 50901, fos. 144-7; *The Landing of Arms at Howth*, P.P. Cd. 7631; Macready, *Annals of an Active Life*, I, 196.
3 Law's memo, 17 July 1914, B.L.P. 39/4/43.
4 Stamfordham to Crewe, 5 June 1914, Crewe Papers, C/58.
5 Printed appeal, N.D., MS. Asq 39, fo. 159; similar memorial to Law, B.L.P. 39/4/33.
6 R. Harcourt to WSC, 28 April 1914, R.S.C. *Churchill*, II, *Companion*, 1418-9; Redmond to Asq, 28 April and 5 May 1914, MS. Asq 36, fos. 47-9, and MS. 39, fos. 167-71.
7 See e.g. Jenkins, *Asquith*, pp. 315-23; Blake, *Bonar Law*, pp. 202-18, 227-30; Stewart, *Ulster Crisis*, pp. 213-36.
8 *Hansard*, LX, 1054-64 (Grey); LX, 1467-72 (Agar-Robartes).
9 Asq to King and reply, 23 May 1914, MS. Asq 7, fo. 129 and MS. 39, fos. 161-2, 180-1.
10 Scott diary, 4 May 1914, B.L. Add. MS. 50901, fos. 119-22; Esher, *Journals*, III, 167-8; Cabinet paper by Birrell, 15 June 1914, Birrell Papers, Bodleian, dep. c. 301, fos. 341-8.
11 Jenkins, *Asquith*, p.318.
12 *Ibid.*, p. 319; Law's memo, 17 July 1914, B.L.P. 39/4/43.
13 Pease diary, II, fo. 92, 15 and 17 July 1914; Asq to King, 17 July 1914, MS. Asq 7, fos. 143-4.
14 Morley to Carnegie, 20 July 1914, Bodleian, MS. film 569; Lansdowne to Stamfordham, 20 July 1914, MS. Asq 39, fos. 233-5.
15 Law's memo, 17 July 1914, B.L.P. 39/4/43; Law to Stamfordham, 20 July 1914, B.L.P. 32/4/85.
16 Asq to King, 17 July 1914, MS. Asq 7, fos. 143-4.
17 Law's memo, *Conference at Buckingham Palace*, B.L.P. 39/4/44; Pease diary, II, fo. 96, 24 July 1914; Redmond's memos, 21-23 July, MS. Redmond 15257; Asq's notes, MS. Asq 39, fos. 211, 216, 222-7, 236-42.
18 Jenkins, *Asquith*, p. 321.
19 Asq to King, 25 July 1914, MS. Asq 7, fo. 147.

20   Esher, *Journals*, III, 173.
21   Asq to Crewe, 23 Sept. 1913, Crewe Papers, C/40; Fitzroy, *Memoirs*, II, 529.
22   *C.P.Scott. Political Diaries* (ed. T. Wilson, 1970), p.84.
23   C. Addison, *Politics from Within, 1911-1918* (2 vols, 1924), I, 33-6.
24   Sir W. Smith to Seely, 25 Sept. 1913, MS. Mottistone 2, fos. 126-7; H. Storey to LG, 29 May 1914, L.G.P. C/2/4/27.
25   Trevelyan to Runciman, 25 July 1914, Runciman Papers, R 1/12.
26   Memo by P. Illingworth, 6 May 1914, Illingworth Papers.
27   *Glasgow Herald*, 8 July 1914; Illingworth's memo, 13 July 1914, Illingworth Papers.
28   Gwynn, *Redmond*, pp.334-5; C. Addison, *Four and a Half Years* (2 vols, 1934), I, 27-8; Addison, *Politics from Within*, I, 35-6.
29   W.S. Blunt, *My Diaries*, II, 429; Scott diary, 25 July 1914, B.L. Add. MS. 50908, fos. 23-4.
30   Pease diary, II, fo. 95, 22 July 1914.
31   C. Hazlehurst, *Politicians at War* (1971), pp. 31-3; Mary [Gladstone] Drew diary, 28 July 1914, B.L. Add. MS. 46265, fo. 70.
32   Samuel to wife, 29 July 1914, Samuel Papers, A/157/691; Trevelyan to wife, 30 July 1914, Trevelyan Papers; Pease diary, II, fo. 105, 3 Aug. 1914.
33   Macready, *Annals of an Active Life*, I, 191-2; Law's memos, 17 and 21 July 1914, B.L.P. 39/4/43-4.
34   Birrell's Cabinet paper, 15 June 1914, Bodleian, dep. c.301, fos. 341-8; Stewart, *Ulster Crisis*, p.231.

Conclusion

1   Wolverhampton to Crewe, 9 March 1910, Crewe Papers, C/54.
2   G.P. Gooch, *Historical Surveys and Portraits* (1966), p. 216; *C.P. Scott. Political Diaries*, (ed. T. Wilson), p. 85.
3   A. Birrell, *Things Past Redress*, p. 212.
4   WSC to Spender, 22 Dec. 1907, Spender MS. 46388, fo. 220.
5   Ponsonby, 'The Future Government of the United Kingdom', *Contemporary Review*, CIV (Nov. 1913), 624-31; *Nation*, 18 Jan. 1913, 3 Jan. 1914.
6   Scott diary, 16 Jan. 1913, B.L. Add. MS. 50901, fo. 79.
7   *C.P. Scott. Political Diaries* (ed. T. Wilson), pp. 87-8, 100.
8   Morley to Rosebery, 18 Aug. 1914, Rosebery MS. 10048, fos. 70-71; *Nation*, 2 Aug. 1913.
9   T. Wilson, *The Downfall of the Liberal Party, 1914-35* (1968), pp. 20-21; P.F. Clarke, *Lancashire and the New Liberalism*.
10   J.A. Hobson, *The Crisis of Liberalism* (ed. P.F. Clarke, Brighton, 1974), pp. xi-xiii.
11   P.F. Clarke, *Liberals and Social Democrats* (Cambridge, 1978), p. 195.

SELECT BIBLIOGRAPHY

This study has been largely based on about fifty collections of private papers, supplemented by official publications, *Hansard*, newspapers and periodicals and contemporary published memoirs. Only a few secondary sources have been particularly valuable, including biographies such as Jenkins' *Asquith*, and Gwynn's *Redmond*, and monographs like A.T.Q. Stewart's *The Ulster Crisis*. Asterisks indicate sources which were especially helpful. The place of publication is London, unless cited otherwise.

I. Private Papers

An excellent account is provided of the location, contents, and accessibility of many of the following collections in *A Guide to the Papers of British Cabinet Ministers 1900-1951*, compiled by Cameron Hazlehurst and Christine Woodland, *Royal Historical Society*, 1974. This was still in the process of compilation while my research was in progress, and I am most grateful to both editors for opening up their files to me and providing so much valuable information. I should also like to thank all those who allowed me to consult the papers cited below, and frequently gave generously of their time and hospitality.

(N.B. Manuscript collections consulted at the Beaverbrook Library have since been deposited at the House of Lords Record Office.)

ABERDEEN MSS.	The papers of the first Marquess of Aberdeen and Temair. Haddo House, Aberdeen. Seen at Haddo by kind permission of the fourth Marquess.
*ASQUITH MSS.	The papers of the first Earl of Oxford and Asquith. Bodleian Library, Oxford. Consulted by courtesy of Mr. Mark Bonham Carter. (Cited as MS. Asq).
*BALFOUR MSS. (British Library)	The papers of the first Earl of Balfour. British Library.
(Whittingehame)	Additional papers of the first and second Earls of Balfour, consulted in the National Register of Archives at Edinburgh, by kind permission of the fourth Earl.
Augustine BIRRELL MSS. (Oxford) (Liverpool)	Bodleian Library, Oxford. Consulted by kind permission of Mr. J.C. Medley. Additional personal papers at Liverpool University Library, presented by Birrell's stepson, Sir Charles Tennyson.

R.D. BLUMEN-FELD MSS.	Beaverbrook Library, London.
BRYCE MSS.	The papers of the first Viscount Bryce. Bodleian Library, Oxford.
John BURNS MSS.	British Library.
BUXTON MSS.	The papers of the first Earl Buxton. Newtimber Place, Hassocks, Sussex. Seen by kind permission of his grand-daughter, Mrs. Elizabeth Clay.
CREWE MSS.	The papers of the first Marquess of Crewe. Cambridge University Library.
CURZON MSS.	The papers of the first Marquess Curzon of Kedleston. India Office Library.
ELIBANK MSS.	The papers of the first Baron Murray of Elibank. National Library of Scotland.
EMMOTT MSS.	The papers of the first Baron Emmott. Nuffield College, Oxford.
ESHER MSS.	The papers of the second Viscount Esher. Churchill College, Cambridge. Consulted by courtesy of the present Viscount Esher.
*GAINFORD MSS.	The papers of J.A. Pease, first Baron Gainford. Nuffield College, Oxford. I am grateful to Dr. Cameron Hazlehurst and Mrs. Christine Woodland for allowing me to consult Pease's diary while they were editing it for publication.
H. GLADSTONE MSS.	The papers of the first Viscount Gladstone. British Library.
Mary [GLADSTONE] DREW diary.	British Library.
GREY MSS.	The papers of the first Viscount Grey of Fallodon. Public Record Office.
HALDANE MSS.	The papers of the first Viscount Haldane. National Library of Scotland.
HARCOURT MSS.	The papers of the first Viscount Harcourt. Seen at Stanton Harcourt, by courtesy of his son, the second Viscount. (Papers since deposited in the Bodleian).
Sir Courtenay ILBERT MSS.	House of Lords Record Office.
P. ILLINGWORTH MSS.	Seen by kind permission of Percy Illingworth's son, Mr. Henry Illingworth, at Carron-on-Spey, Morayshire, Scotland.
*Bonar LAW MSS.	Beaverbrook Library, London. Cited as B.L.P.
*LLOYD GEORGE MSS.	The papers of the first Earl Lloyd-George of Dwyfor. Beaverbrook Library. Cited as L.G.P.
Reginald McKENNA MSS.	Churchill College, Cambridge. Consulted by permission of his son, Mr. D. McKenna.
MILNER MSS.	The papers of the first Viscount Milner. Deposited

at the Bodleian and examined by courtesy of the librarian of New College, Oxford.

MORLEY/ CARNEGIE MFM. Microfilm of letters between John Morley and Andrew Carnegie. Bodleian (MS. film 569).

*MOTTISTONE MSS. The papers of J.E.B. Seely, first Baron Mottistone. Nuffield College, Oxford.

Sir Matthew NATHAN MSS. Bodleian Library, Oxford.

NOVAR MSS. The papers of R. Munro-Ferguson, first Viscount Novar. Scottish Record Office.

William O'BRIEN MSS. National Library of Ireland. I am grateful to Dr. Philip Bull for allowing me to use his microfilm of this collection.

PAGET MSS. The papers of General Sir Arthur Paget. British Library.

PONSONBY MSS. The papers of the first Baron Ponsonby. Bodleian Library, Oxford.

READING MSS. The papers of Rufus Isaacs, first Marquess of Reading. India Office Library.

*John REDMOND MSS. National Library of Ireland. Microfilm deposited in Bodleian Library, Oxford.

ROSEBERY MSS. The papers of the fifth Earl of Rosebery. National Library of Scotland.

RUNCIMAN MSS. The papers of the first Viscount Runciman. University of Newcastle-upon-Tyne.

SAMUEL MSS. The papers of the first Viscount Samuel. House of Lords Record Office.

J. SANDARS MSS. Bodleian Library, Oxford.

*C.P. SCOTT MSS. (British Library) Political memoranda in diary form in the British Library. Very little of the substantial amount of material relating to Ireland was published by T. Wilson in *C.P. Scott. Political Diaries 1911-1928* (1970).

Manchester Guardian MSS I am grateful to Dr. Peter Clarke for allowing me to use his transcripts.

SELBORNE MSS. The papers of the second Earl of Selborne. Bodleian Library, Oxford.

J.A. SPENDER MSS. British Library.

Sir A. STEEL-MAITLAND MSS. Scottish Record Office.

J. ST. LOE STRACHEY MSS. Beaverbrook Library.

Sir Charles TREVELYAN MSS. University of Newcastle-upon-Tyne. Consulted with the permission of Trevelyan's daughter, Mrs. Pauline Dower, who kindly allowed me to see some of the family letters not normally open to researchers. I am also grateful for the help of Mr. A.J.A. Morris, who was then writing a biography

294

Sir Harry VERNEY MSS.	based on the papers. The late Sir Harry Verney allowed me to see the papers at his home in Bucks., shortly before his death. I also taped an interesting conversation in which he described his experiences as P.P.S. to Birrell, 1910–14 (interview, 15 Nov. 1972).
Henry WILSON MSS.	The diary of Field-Marshal Sir Henry Wilson. Imperial War Museum.
T. McKinnon WOOD MSS.	Bodleian Library, Oxford.

I am grateful to Mrs. Lucy Masterman for her reminiscences of the years 1906–14 (taped interview, 3 Feb. 1974). I was unable to examine the papers of Winston Churchill, John Morley or John Dillon, which were closed to scholars, and little of value for this study remains in the Carson Papers.

II. Official Publications

(a) *The Parliamentary Debates (Official Report) House of Commons.*
Cited as *Hansard*, with reference to the Fifth Series, unless stated otherwise.

(b) *Cabinet Papers.*
The P.R.O. references have been cited for those Cabinet Papers on Ireland which have actually been deposited in the Public Record Office. Several Cabinet Papers on Ireland, however, were only available in private collections, as cited.

(c) *Government of Ireland Bills*
Of 1886, 1893 and 1912, together with various early drafts for 1911–12. Also consulted in private collections. (16 April 1912 Bill: H.C. 1912–13 (136), II, 505.)

(d) *Parliamentary Papers*
Report of the Committee on Irish Finance [cited as Primrose Report], Cd. 6153, H.C. 1912–13, XXXIV; evidence, Cd. 6799, H.C. 1913, XXX.
Government of Ireland Bill. Outline of Financial Provisions, 1912, Cd. 6154.
Correspondence Relating to Recent Events in the Irish Command, 1914, Cd. 7318, Cd. 7329.
Royal Commission into the Circumstances Connected with the Landing of Arms at Howth, 1914, Cd. 7631.

(e) *Records of the Irish Office in P.R.O. London*, Colonial Office Papers.
CO 903/17–18: Intelligence Notes, 1912–14. Edited and published for the years 1913–16 by Brendan MacGiolla Choille: *Intelligence Notes 1913-16*, Dublin Stationery Office, 1966.

III. Newspapers, Periodicals and Pamphlets

(a) *Newspapers*
The Times and the *Nation* were consulted regularly for the

whole period, since they provided good news accounts and representative opinion for both main parties, with some inside information. Other papers were used in a more selective manner. The *Westminster Gazette, Daily News, Daily Chronicle* and *Manchester Guardian* were examined at crucial times to supplement information from private papers and *Hansard*.

(b)   *Periodicals*

The following proved the most useful, though others were consulted:

* *Contemporary Review* (vols. XCIX-CVI)
   National Review (vols. LVIII-LXIII)
* *Nineteenth Century* (vols. LXX-LXXVI)
   Quarterly Review (vols. CCXVI-CCXXI)
   Round Table

(c)   *Contemporary pamphlets*

Childers, E.	*The Framework of Home Rule* (1911)
Kettle, T.	*Home Rule Finance: An Experiment in Justice* (1911)
Macdonald, J.A. Murray.	*The Constitutional Crisis. A Review of the Situation and a Plea for Settlement. By a Liberal M.P.* (1913).
Macdonald, J.A.M. and Lord Charnwood.	*The Federal Solution* (1914)
Morgan, J.H., ed.	*The New Irish Constitution* (1912)

IV. Selective Secondary Sources

(a)   **MEMOIRS AND BIOGRAPHIES** (Arranged in alphabetical order of subjects.)

Addison, Christopher.	*Politics from Within, 1911-1918*, 2 vols (1924).
Amery, L.S.	*My Political Life*, 3 vols (1953-5).
* *Asquith*	by Roy Jenkins (1964).
———	by Stephen Koss (1976).
Birrell, Augustine	*Things Past Redress* (1937).
———	*The Chief Secretary: Augustine Birrell in Ireland*, by Leon O'Broin (1969).
Blunt, W.S.	*My Diaries. Being a Personal Narrative of Events 1884-1914*, 2 vols (1921-3).
Carson	by H. Montgomery Hyde (1953)
	The Life of Lord Carson, by E. Marjoribanks and I. Colvin, 3 vols (1932-6).
* Chamberlain, Austen	*Politics from Inside. An Epistolary Chronicle 1906-1914* (1936).
* *Winston S. Churchill, Volume II, 1901-1914.*	by R.S. Churchill (Boston, Mass., 1967); and *Companion* volume, part 3 (cited

Young Statesman.	as R.S.C. *Churchill*, II, *Companion*).
Churchill	by H. Pelling (1974).
★ *John Dillon:*	by F.S. L. Lyons (1968).
A Biography	
[Esher]	*The Journals and Letters of Reginald, Viscount Esher,* eds. M.V. Brett and Oliver, Viscount Esher, 4 vols (1934–8).
★ Fitzroy, Sir Almeric.	*Memoirs*, 2 vols (6th ed., 1925).
★ *King George V,*	by Harold Nicolson (1952).
His Life and Reign	
[C. Hobhouse]	*Inside Asquith's Cabinet. From the Diaries of Charles Hobhouse,* ed. by Edward David (1977) (cited as Hobhouse diary).
★ [Bonar Law]	*The Unknown Prime Minister. The Life and Times of Andrew Bonar Law, 1858-1923,* by Robert Blake (1955) (cited as Blake, *Bonar Law*).
Macready,	*Annals of an Active Life*, 2 vols. (1924).
General Sir Nevil.	
★ [Redmond]	*The Life of John Redmond*, by Denis Gwynn (1932).
Riddell, Lord	*More Pages from my Diary 1908-14* (1934).
[C.P. Scott]	*The Political Diaries of C.P. Scott 1911-1928,* ed. Trevor Wilson (1970).

(b) MONOGRAPHS, ARTICLES, THESES, ETC.

Blewett, Neal	*The Peers, the Parties and the People: The General Elections of 1910* (1972).
Boyce, D.G.	'British Conservative Opinion, the Ulster Question and the Partition of Ireland, 1912-21', *Irish Historical Studies*, XVII, no. 65 (March 1970), 89–112.
Buckland, Patrick J.	*Irish Unionism, I, The Anglo-Irish and the New Ireland, 1885-1922* (Dublin, 1972).
★ ———	*Irish Unionism, II, Ulster Unionism and the Origins of Northern Ireland 1886-1922* (Dublin, 1973).
★ ———	'The Unionists and Ireland: The Influence of the Irish Question on British Politics 1906-14', M.A. thesis, Birmingham University, 3 vols (1965).
★ Clarke, Peter	*Lancashire and the New Liberalism* (Cambridge, 1971).
Dangerfield, George	*The Strange Death of Liberal England* (1935).
★ Fergusson, Sir James.	*The Curragh Incident* (1964).
Gooch, John	'The War Office and the Curragh Incident', *Bulletin of the Institute of Hist. Research*, XLVI (Nov. 1973), 202-7.

Hazlehurst, Cameron. 'Asquith as Prime Minister 1908-16', *Eng. Hist. Rev.*, LXXXV (July 1970), 502-31.

——— *Politicians at War. July 1914 to May 1915* (1971).

Hepburn, A.C. 'Liberal Policies and Nationalist Politics in Ireland, 1905-10', Ph.D. thesis, University of Kent, 2 vols (1968).

★ Jalland, P. 'A Liberal Chief Secretary and the Irish Question: Augustine Birrell, 1907-14', *Hist. Journal*, XIX, no.2 (1976), 421-51.

——— 'United Kingdom Devolution 1910-14: Political Panacea or Tactical Diversion ?', *Eng. Hist. Rev.*, XCIV (Oct. 1979), 757-85.

★ ——— 'The Irish Question in Liberal Politics, 1911-14', Ph.D. thesis, University of Toronto (1976).

Jenkins, Roy *Mr. Balfour's Poodle: An Account of the Struggle between the House of Lords and the Government of Mr. Asquith* (1954).

Kendle, J.E. 'The Round Table Movement and Home-Rule-All-Round 1909-14', *Hist. Journal*, XI, no. 2 (1968), 332-53.

★ Ryan, A.P. *Mutiny at the Curragh* (1956).
★ Stewart, A.T.Q. *The Ulster Crisis* (1967).
Stubbs, John O. 'The Conservative Party and the Politics of War, 1914-16', Oxford D. Phil. thesis (1973).

★ Wilson, Trevor *The Downfall of the Liberal Party, 1914-35* (1968).

INDEX

Note: This is a selective index comprised chiefly of names, and titles are given if they were assumed prior to 1914. Only the most important subjects are listed, as the detailed 'Table of Contents' is intended to be used as a complement to the index, which relates purely to the main body of the text.